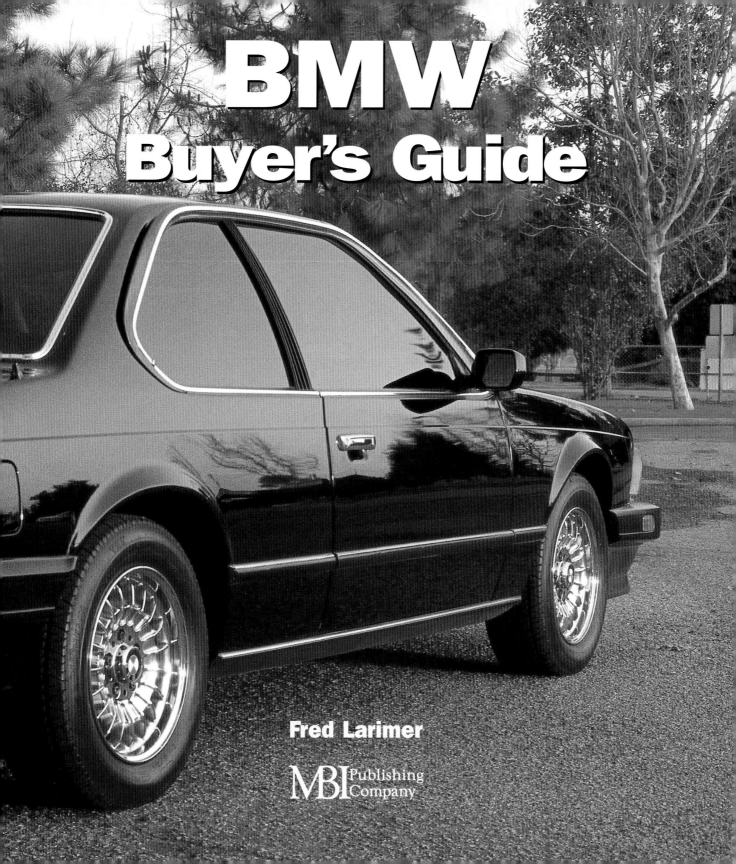

BMW
Buyer's Guide

Fred Larimer

MBI Publishing
Company

To my parents, Fred and Betty Larimer.

———

First published in 2002 by MBI Publishing Company, Galtier Plaza, Suite 200, 380 Jackson Street, St. Paul, MN 55101-3885 USA

MBI Publishing Company books are also available at discounts in bulk quantity for industrial or sales-promotional use. For details write to Special Sales Manager at Motorbooks International Wholesalers & Distributors, Galtier Plaza, Suite 200, 380 Jackson Street, St. Paul, MN 55101-3885 USA.

Library of Congress Cataloging-in-Publication Data Available

ISBN 0-7603-1099-8

Front Cover: The E30 M3 is fast on its way to becoming a collectible and unquestionably embodies the sporting nature that BMW is known for and continues to build upon.

Frontispiece: The spectacular front detail of a 2001 BMW M3 that features 333 brake horsepower and enlarged fender arches to cover its 18-inch wheels.

Title Page: The L6 designation on the right corner of the deck lid identifies this E24 as a 1987 model, the only year for the L6.

Fred Larimer is a longtime BMW owner and enthusiast who has been a member of the BMW Car Club of America for more than twenty years and is a past president of its Los Angeles chapter. Mr. Larimer grew up in Long Beach, California, within earshot of Lions Associated Drag Strip and Ascot Speedway, and his interest in cars began at an early age and has continued unabated. His first exposure to BMW automobiles was in the mid-1960s, when he saw Jerry Titus race a BMW 1800TISA at Riverside International Raceway. Mr. Larimer and his wife, Pamela, live in Garden Grove, California. Their garage houses two E30 BMWs–a 1987 325is and a 1988 M3–and a General Motors Electric Vehicle, an EV-1.

Edited by Chad Caruthers
Designed by Liz Tufte

Printed in China

Contents

Preface

During the course of authoring *BMW Buyer's Guide,* an acquaintance of mine asked me to go with him to look at a 1988 BMW E30 M3 he was considering purchasing. While he had not really been looking for one, he knew the price was on the low side. He also realized that he did not know enough about the M3s to determine whether this one was a good one or not.

It is not the first time I have been asked for advice in buying a BMW, and it is probably not the last time I will look a car over, whether for a friend or for myself. I have owned a variety of BMWs, starting with a 1980 528i, followed by a 1981 633CSi, a 1984 528e, a 1990 M3, a 1994 325 sedan, and I currently own a 1988 M3 and a 1987 325is.

The M3 my friend and I looked at had a few minor mechanical problems, but none serious enough to be major concerns. By having specific knowledge about the good qualities of the E30 M3 as well as knowing the common problem areas, we quickly concluded that the car was a great buy at the advertised price.

The next step was to have an experienced and knowledgeable mechanic check the car out. With the exception of a couple of minor oil leaks and needing a valve adjustment and some new tires, this car checked out fine.

The end result in this instance was that the seller received his asking price and my friend purchased a car he can enjoy. It can work that way for you, too.

Owning a BMW brings with it much pleasure and occasionally some financial pain. I have learned a few lessons, some the hard way, and I hope my lessons can help you avoid a negative experience by providing you with knowledge and information about BMW cars.

FRED LARIMER
GARDEN GROVE, CALIFORNIA

Introduction

As *BMW Buyer's Guide* has evolved and taken shape, I have had the pleasure of meeting and talking to a diverse group of BMW owners. One thing that has impressed me throughout is the genuine enthusiasm the owners have for their cars. It also is apparent that BMWs, in particular the older models as well as the high-performance M cars, are owner-involved cars. If you neglect them, they will come back to haunt you with expensive repair bills. If you maintain the cars regularly and take care of the little things as they arise, the cars will run forever. It is not unusual to find mid-1980s cars with 150,000-plus miles on the odometer that still look good and continue to run well. Several of the older-model cars photographed for this book have more than 100,000 miles on them.

There is a good variety of BMWs available for you to choose from. The goal of this book is to help you determine which are the cars to walk away from and which are the cars to buy. This edition is less of a spotter's guide and more of a tool to help you know where to look, what to look for, and when to expect certain problems to occur.

Researching a BMW: This Book and Beyond
Each chapter of this book contains a brief introduction about the models featured in that chapter. You'll also find detailed specification charts, parts charts, owner testimonials, comments from car experts of that era, rating charts, and garage watches, which provide information on common problems you might encounter with a particular model and what you should examine before purchase.

If you are considering buying a BMW, do your research ahead of time. You have already made a good first step with your purchase of the *BMW Buyer's Guide.* Read all the information you can find on the particular model you are looking for. An abundance of information is available through publications like *Automobile Magazine, Car and Driver, Motor Trend,* and *Road & Track.* There are countless Web sites, message boards, and e-mail digests that contain a wealth of information about BMWs.

Another significant and important source of information is the BMW Car Club of America. With more than 50,000 members nationwide and chapters in most major cities, the membership is a veritable waterfall of information about the cars as well as the repair shops that know where the problems areas may be and how to best repair them. The club's monthly publication, *The Roundel,* is one of the most professionally produced club publications in the world. It is worth every penny of the $35 annual membership fee for the information it contains and the networking opportunities it can provide you in finding answers to your questions. For additional information on the BMW Car Club of America, contact their national office at (864) 250-0022 or visit their Web site at www.bmwcca.org.

Common BMW Problem Areas

Like all auto manufacturers, BMW produces cars that have some common problem areas that buyers should be aware of.

Air Conditioning   BMW's early efforts with air conditioning were not very successful. On a hot day in any model before the E28 5-Series, open the sunroof, roll the windows down, and enjoy the fresh air. The E28 5-Series HVAC systems were a significant improvement over the earlier BMW systems.

Brake Systems   For years, BMW has recommended that the brake system be flushed and the fluid changed annually. If the brake fluid of the car you are looking at is blackish, that would indicate the system has not been flushed for an extended period of time.

Another common brake system problem for cars from the mid-1980s on is warped front rotors. More common in cars that have automatic transmissions or that have been driven hard, you will notice this by a pulsation in the brake pedal when you are braking at low speeds. At higher speeds, the pulsation can be severe enough to shake the steering wheel violently. If not attended to, this problem will place additional stresses on the front suspension bushings and will cause other components to wear out more quickly.

Beginning with the E28 5-Series and used in the 6-Series and 7-Series, BMW replaced the conventional vacuum booster for the brake system with an engine-driven hydraulic pump for the power steering and braking system. This brake accumulator reservoir (also known as the brake "bomb") is a common failure item.

Differential Mounting Point   The Bavarias and Coupes of the 1970s, the E12 5-Series, 6-Series, and to a degree, the E23 7-Series, all have a differential mount that is prone to fatigue and cracking. It is a single-point mount located under the trunk floor, and it is constantly subjected to flexing. Over time, the mount will crack. Reinforcing and rewelding the area can repair it.

Driveshafts, Guibos (Flex Discs), and Center Support Bearings   When you drive the car, do you feel any shake or shimmy in the seat of your pants at low speeds? If you do, this could indicate a problem with the drive shaft or the center support bearing. If not tended to, the ensuing vibrations can cause U-joints to seize.

Another common maintenance item in the driveline is the rubber "biscuit" coupling in the middle of the drive shaft. Called a guibo, this rubber flex disk absorbs some of the driveline stresses. Expect to spend in the range of $150 for a new one and about the same for labor to replace it.

Thrust Rod Bushings   Beginning with the E28 5-Series, BMW revised its front suspension design to use a rubber bushing mounted thrust rod that extends from the front suspension rearward at an angle and attaches to the frame rails with large, hard rubber bushing. Over time, the thrust rod bushing deteriorates and allows unwanted movement of the front suspension.

Engine Cooling Systems   BMWs have a long history of problems with the engine cooling systems. Blown head gaskets and warped heads are pretty commonplace, especially in those cars that use thermal reactors for emissions controls.

With the 1982/1983-year models, the radiators were converted from brass to aluminum core/plastic tanks. While aluminum radiators transfer heat more efficiently, the plastic becomes brittle, and it is not unusual for the tanks to rupture or the hose necks to simply break off.

The mid- to late 1980s E30 3-Series cars experienced problems with the coolant system building up so much pressure that it ruptured the heater core and dumped hot coolant onto the feet of the driver. The factory recalls for this problem were to install a different radiator cap and a pressure-relief valve in the supply line to the heater. Look between the back of the engine block and the firewall; if you see a metallic object spliced into a heater hose, then the recall has been performed.

The M50/2.5-powered E36 3-Series and E34 5-Series cars between 1992 and 1995 had problems with water pumps failing. A redesigned water pump with a one-piece impeller has replaced the trouble-prone unit, and the vast majority of cars have had their water pumps replaced at least once by now. There is no way to visually distinguish the revised water pump just by looking at it. If you are in doubt, probably the best course of action is to have the pump replaced at your earliest opportunity.

The newest BMWs use electronically controlled engine thermostats. There have been reports of these units failing. This may be a long-term problem area to be watched.

In 2001, there were a couple of recalls on the engine auxiliary cooling fans. Problems with the fan malfunctioning and the engine overheating as well as reports of the wiring for the fans overheating and shorting out are common. The majority of cars affected, built between December 2000 and September 2001, have been recalled and the necessary repairs made.

Thermal Reactors   Thermal reactors were used for the 2002s, 320i, 3.0Si, 530i, 630CSi, and 733i. The thermal reactors were dependent on heat to control emissions. This heat also became their enemy. Over time, the constant heating and cooling of the reactors caused cracking, both internally and externally. The thermal reactors were expensive to replace in 1975, and many owners opted to remove them rather than constantly repair them.

If you live in a state that requires all original emissions equipment to be present and functioning, you might want to check your local emissions laws for specific information about the requirements for having these items installed on the car in order to pass smog-certification tests.

Common Engine Problems   By and large, BMW engines will run forever. They do, however, have a couple of weak points to be aware of, and many of these are noted in the appropriate chapters of this book.

Buying a Used BMW

How do you find a good used BMW? The only way to be certain you're buying a solid car is to take it to an authorized dealer or a qualified independent service facility for a prepurchase inspection. Make an appointment and expect to pay between $75 and $105 for this examination. The dealer service technician can provide you with a printed list of problems and estimated repair charges for anything they find. You can take this list back to the seller and use it to adjust the selling price accordingly.

For the following screening process, you'll need no tools other than your eyes, ears, and nose. You will get your hands dirty once. You may want a poultry thermometer for air conditioning and heating temperature tests to stick into the air vent. A tire gauge will be beneficial, too. You might bring a flashlight to shine into the engine compartment and a small mirror to hold in places where you cannot get your eyes. Bring along an

observant friend to serve as a second pair of eyes and, equally importantly, to occupy the seller while you examine their car. Don't be open with the seller. Your color preference or your budget should remain your secret. Don't buy a car at night; what you can't see you'll pay for later.

Drive at least three examples of the model you are seeking. You must build a log of experiences to draw on for that moment when you find the right car at your price.

Inspecting the Car   Look for signs of rust in the lower corners of the wheel wells and doors. Imagine those areas where dirt, debris, and snow can accumulate. Moisture gets trapped in these areas and they will tend to develop rust the quickest.

Run your fingers along body seams, door panels, door jams, and around the roof. There should be no uneven surfaces, gaps, or seams. Where fixed window (and windshield)

The VIN sticker between second and third attaching bolts on the left front fender of this BMW E30 M3.

Note the DOT-R VIN replacement sticker indicating the fender has been replaced on this BMW E30 M3. Also, the Bodyplast filler material is missing where the fender meets the cowl.

seals attach to the body, check for gaps and undulations. This might mean the car has been in a big accident. Look for paint that appears bubbled below the surface. This indicates rust, something that plagued BMWs until the factory began rust-proofing the bodies to protect them.

View the entire car from all angles. The general condition of the exterior, interior, trunk, and engine can tell you volumes about the car.

Look at repair records for the life of the car. Be wary if a private owner has no receipts. Some owners drive BMWs for partial business use and need to keep their receipts; you don't need to keep them, just look them over. Used-car lots seldom have the records. Authorized dealers can check their computers for service histories, but these will not always reveal histories of cosmetic damage.

Everyone consulted for this book agreed that, wherever possible and within reason, you should not buy a car that has been crashed.

Check for VIN stickers in all the right spots. A missing sticker could mean that the part was replaced with a nonoriginal equipment part. BMW placed these VIN labels on the engine, transmission, front and rear bumpers, hood and deck lid, left and right front fenders, front doors, rear doors, and quarter panels. Learn where to look for these VIN stickers—they may be painted over, but look for them anyway as that will tell you useful information about the car.

BMW original equipment replacement parts will have a DOT-R sticker on them. The factory places the sticker in a phys-

A look at the DOT-R VIN sticker placement in left rear corner of the hood on this BMW E28 535is.

ically different location from the original VIN sticker. The presence of a DOT-R sticker indicates that part has been replaced, possibly as the result of accident damage. While that may not be the greatest news, the presence of a DOT-R sticker does mean the shop performing the repair at least used original-equipment BMW parts.

Generally speaking, leased vehicles are adequately maintained. However, be cautious because leasers oftentimes have no long-term interest in the car and therefore have no motivation to spend money on services for a car they will be giving back in a couple of years.

Inspecting the Engine   Shine your flashlight onto every engine surface you can see. The small mirror will show you the back and undersides. Look for gross evidence of leaks, big smears of oil, and obvious trails of gasoline. Some slight seepage is acceptable. If the rest of the car checks out through this screening process, the prepurchase inspection will note any leakages and tell you what they signify.

With the engine compartment open, watch the engine and exhaust pipes. Have the seller start the engine. Does it rock back and forth as the starter engages, suggesting failed motor mounts? Does it take long to start? Is what comes out of the exhaust pipe(s) white, gray, black, or invisible?

On cool or cold mornings, some pale gray steam is normal. As the engine warms, this should stop. A slight puff of white smoke is entirely acceptable. A steady cloud suggests the engine burns oil. Smell the exhaust. If it smells like oil, thank the owner and leave.

Black smoke may come from a vacuum leak, emission system failures, or fuel-injection system malfunctions. Black smoke also may indicate an engine loaded up with carbon because its driving use is short, in-town jaunts. The engine never gets truly warm, so fuel and oil deposits accumulate in the engine.

On the later model cars—1995 and on—equipped with the onboard diagnostics (OBD) systems, make sure the OBD light comes on upon starting. In addition, the amber ABS light should illuminate.

If the seller must pump the gas pedal on a fuel-injected engine, this indicates a massive vacuum/air leak that prevents the engine from getting enough fuel to start on its own. This is an expensive problem to repair. In addition, the engine will not pass smog tests in most states. It may burn exhaust valves and perhaps pistons. Shut off the engine (if it even starts) and be on your way.

Listen for any noise besides a nice exhaust sound, such

This photo shows the VIN sticker in the lower corner of the rear door on this BMW E34 M5. Also note the missing VIN sticker in the lower corner of the front door.

as tapping, thumping, whirring, or hissing. Let the engine run for ten minutes and check temperatures. The needle should remain below the halfway point.

Smell for oil, coolant, or gas. If you small any of these, shut the engine off immediately. Some models develop engine compartment gas line leaks that can start a fire.

If you didn't smell these critical fluids while the engine was running, turn it off, sniff again, and listen. Crackling sounds coming from the engine suggest that the engine is overheating. Water jackets may be clogged, oil may not be circulating properly, the oil cooler may be clogged, or the pump is failing.

Gurgling sounds suggest problems in the cooling system, such as insufficient flow through the radiator, or a failing water pump. The oil cooler or radiator may need cleaning or replacement. The oil or water pump may need replacement.

Check the hoses with the engine off and warm, not before it's started. Don't squeeze with your fingers; they're hot. Use the eraser end of a pencil or the flat end of a common ballpoint pen to press the hoses. If the hoses are firm when they're hot, they are fine. If the hose is too soft, the inner lining has broken down and the hose will fail sometime soon. If the hose has swollen around the clamps or fittings, this also indicates hose failure.

Inspecting the Suspension   Before you move the car, check the air pressure in all four tires. Be sure they have equal tread depth, are the same brand, and are the appropriate size for the car. Mismatched tires suggest the seller dealt cheaply with other service needs as well.

Rub your hand along the tread on all four tires, feeling for ridges or undulations. Ridges on treads indicate poor shock absorber condition. Undulations suggest that the alignment is wrong or suspension is damaged, from hitting a curb, for example.

Examine all four disc brake rotors. Run your finger along the surface of the rotor. You should feel no ridges, just smooth, even surfaces. Feel the outside edge of the rotor. If it has a lip, this suggests the owner has ignored all service warnings that the pads have gone too far and have begun to score the rotors. Depending on the depth of the lip, the rotor may be beyond tolerance. Thank the owner. Leave now.

If there is no lip, reach inside the wheel wells to feel the inside edge of the wheels. If you feel scuffs, bumps, ripples, or cuts on the inside, you may have a bad wheel. Later on, you will be more able to determine what this problem may be during an early portion of the road test.

Now go to the front of the car. Give a quick, sharp push down on the front bumper. Did you feel any binding or hear any noise except a gentle hiss? As the suspension brings the car back up, does the car clunk or gurgle or bounce more than once? Does the car rock? It should do none of these. Repeat this on all four corners of the car, making sure that each corner rebounds (comes back up) at the same rate.

If the suspension does not perform smoothly and quietly, look for another car.

Inspecting the Interior   Does the door bind, squeak, or fall as you move it? It should be even, level, and fluid. Check the doorstop where it is bolted to the leading edge of the door.

Are the door seals cracked, chipped, or split? When rain drips through these onto the carpet, the carpet soaks it up. The top layer of the carpet dries; the under layer holds moisture and rusts out the floorboards. This is especially important for cars from the 1960s and 1970s; if possible, lift the carpets and mats and look for rust. Crawl underneath and look again. Use your mirror to see where you cannot fit your head.

Now climb into the car. Just sit. Do not touch anything.

Close your eyes. Move your body around in the seat and feel whether the seat moves, wiggles, or makes noise. If it does, the floor pan may have been weakened over time because of a crash or rust, which allows play in the seat bolts that should never occur.

Now look at the general condition of the interior. Is the leather cracked or dried out? Are knobs and switches cracked or missing? Is any wooden trim cracked and peeling? Hold the

This is the VIN plate that was attached when this European-specification BMW E30 was imported and federalized.

Here is a California Air Resources Board (CARB) Sticker indicating this European-specification BMW E30 323i 4-door has been smog-approved and can be registered in the state of California.

steering wheel. Try to pull it from side to side and up and down. There should be no play, no movement.

Adjust the seat to fit your comfort and safety level, making certain you can push the clutch pedal to the floor. (You're not driving yet, but you need the leverage.) Put on the seatbelt. Then restart the car yourself without touching the steering wheel.

Inspecting the Brake Pedal and System   Do this section's tests with the engine running. You need engine vacuum boost for the power brake system.

With your hands in your lap, tap on the brake pedal a couple of times to bring the fluid up to pressure. Then press as hard and as far down on the pedal as you can ten times. Use both legs if you need to. Pedal pressure must remain constant. If the pedal pumps up and gets harder as you pump it, you can shut off the engine and leave. A rising brake pedal indicates system problems that may include vacuum leaks, water in the brake fluid, a failed brake booster, or a failed hydraulic brake accumulator.

If the brakes pass this test, keep pumping as hard as possible. What you are doing now is checking for any movement on the dashboard and listening for creaks and moans. If there is any noise or movement around the floorboards or in the dash, turn the car off, thank the seller, and go home. Crash integrity may have been compromised, possibly through an earlier bad crash or through rust damage in the floorboards or firewall.

With the engine running, cycle the automatic transmission through the range of gears. Wait at each selection for a full minute. You should see an rpm drop on the tach and feel

a slight nudge as gears engage. If it takes 30 seconds, for example, for the transmission to catch up to your selection, you don't want that car. In addition, do you notice any excessive vibrations from the engine or transmission with the car in gear at idle? This could indicate failed engine mounts or a failed transmission mount.

If the automatic passes the transmission test, hold your feet on the brake and place the gear selector in second gear, with the engine at idle. Pull up on the hand brake/parking brake/emergency brake. It should be no more than six to eight clicks with increasing pressure. Slowly release pressure on the foot brake pedal and be certain the car does not move. You can do this same test for a manual transmission model by easing in the clutch in first or reverse gear. Look around very carefully before you try this test to make sure you have plenty of open space if the brake fails.

Caution: The ZF 4HP22 4-speed electronic-controlled transmissions of the mid-1980s through the mid-1990s can sustain serious internal damage if placed in neutral with the engine revved up. Do not perform the next test with an automatic transmission-equipped BMW.

If everything passes to this point, then, with the engine still at idle, put the car in neutral, with the parking brake on. When the temperature gauge moves off the bottom stop, and only then, give the gas pedal a couple of good raps.

Testing this before the engine has reached temperature can mask a sticking throttle cable, which you can tell only once engine temperature has begun to rise.

Road Test   During the drive, ask the seller and whoever else may be riding along to remain quiet. You need to be able to hear the car.

Never road test a car in heavy traffic. You cannot possibly get an accurate impression of the vehicle if you are paying close attention to what other drivers are doing.

First drive to a smooth stretch of road with a lot of room to test the brakes. These are not panic stops, just routine braking. At 30 miles per hour, brake with a steady, even pressure. You are looking for any undulation in the steering wheel, shaking, pulling from side to side, pulsing or vibrating through the pedal, the noise of metal-on-metal from failed pads, or a chirping sound that indicates cracked brake rotors. You are also checking for warped front brake rotors.

Now find a potholed road or a broken road surface. You are listening with your ears and feeling with your fingers on the steering wheel as well as the seat of your pants for clunks, rattles, shakes, shimmies, or any unsettling response to potholes or bumps. If doors, side windows, or the back window rattles, it may be only tired weather seals, or it could be a badly repaired body after a crash. If the car sounds like it's falling apart, thank the seller and go home.

In a large, empty parking lot, drive in large circles. With your hands at 10 and 2, turn the steering wheel so one hand or the other (you'll go in both directions) is at 12. Drive safely but fast enough to listen for slight tire squeal. Steering should feel smooth with no chatter in the steering wheel. If it tends to move in the direction of your turn, this is called "falling" and can indicate bent struts.

If you have a bent front wheel, you'll find this now. Turning in one direction, if the car shakes or shimmies, the wheel that is bent will be the one outside the turn. Confirm this by turning in the opposite direction. This unloads the possibly bent wheel, and the car should track and ride smoothly. Reconfirm this by resuming the original turn direction. If the car again begins shaking, you have a bent wheel on the outside. Bent wheels most often are on the curb side, inside the wheel where you cannot see it. BMW wheels are expensive. Negotiate this in your purchase price.

You are also listening for and checking for any problems with a wheel bearing. If you hear a howling noise while circling in one direction and do not hear it going the other direction, you may be experiencing a bad wheel bearing.

During your braking test, if the car has done anything other than stop in a straight line in a very quick manner, you should forget about that car.

If the car does stop amazingly quickly with no muss or fuss, find a quiet alley with walls on both sides to give you the auditory feedback you want here. Drive only at idle speed with both windows open, and listen for any noise other than exhaust and tires. If you hear clunking, whirring, tinking, knocking, squeaking, or any other noise besides exhaust purr and tires rolling, thank the seller and leave.

If the car passes all these tests, go to a freeway for an on-ramp merge test. You want a long freeway entrance ramp where you have great distant vision. You are not seeking record 0–60 times, but only impressions. You do not want a speeding ticket. The acceleration must be impressive and smooth. There should be no bucking or surging.

Note: Exhaust emissions are bigger problems in some states than in others. Check specific requirements in your state before purchasing any automobile. In California, for example, a successful smog test is a condition of purchase; the seller pays for the smog test and the completed certificate accompanies transfer of title.

Inspecting the Good Stuff Perform this last set of evaluations with the engine idling, the transmission in neutral, and the hand brake on.

Check the radio, CD and tape player, speakers, and power antenna. Turn on the air conditioning to maximum cold and wait. If leaves or debris blow out the vents, the drip tray near the windshield has cracked, which allows rain or car wash water to accumulate in the drip tray and back up into the vents. This can flow into the cockpit through these vents.

Turn the fan back through all speed ranges, waiting long enough to be sure they work. Then back to maximum and insert your turkey thermometer into the air vent. It should read between 32 and 38 degrees (factory specs). If it doesn't, the

European-specification E30 323i 4-door. Note location of the CARB sticker in the left rear door jam.

system at least needs an evacuation, oiling, and recharging. When you take it in for this work, insist that the shop do both the evacuation and the oiling. A shortcut here can cost you as much as $1,100 later.

Test the heat and watch the temperature gauge. It should drop slightly. Be alert for radiator coolant or other baking smells inside the car.

Operate the sunroof, test the rear defroster. If either blows a fuse, leave. Listen to the sunroof. Check the weather proofing. If the sunroof fails to operate, get in your own car and drive away.

Inspecting the Electronics   Some owners have after-market-installed theft alarms, stereo systems, cellular telephones, radar detectors, and other add-ons. Improperly installed extras can rapidly run down batteries. Cutting into wires, unless you know exactly what you are doing, is a recipe for disaster. Not all hot leads are the same. Ask the seller if they know who did the work. If it was not a BMW dealer, you may consider having your local dealer remove and reinstall these items. This becomes more important with each newer model year. Incorrectly wired accessories will drain batteries in a matter of days.

Doing the Deal   Pricing is a tough issue. Dealers, resellers, and independent service facilities all agree that you should buy the best car you can afford. BMW resale values remain high. Most of these sources recommend spending perhaps $2,000 less than you can afford because you either will want to or need to put that into the car almost immediately, with tires, wheels, or work you want done.

Don't take a seller's word that something will be fixed or that the problem really is nothing at all. If the problem is to be fixed, get that in writing and add in writing that you will conclude the deal only if the problem is fixed to your satisfaction, pending another complete test drive.

Gray Market Cars

During the late 1970s, 1980s, and early 1990s, a niche market existed for importing European specification cars. Known as gray market cars, these were often high-performance versions of cars that were marketed and sold in the United States. To import Euro-spec cars, license, and insure them, they had to be brought into compliance with the applicable U.S. EPA and DOT regulations. In many cases, this meant installing side-impact beams in the doors, modifying the bumpers to meet U.S. requirements, changing the lights and instruments, replacing the windshields, and installing smog equipment to meet EPA requirements. In some cases, these modifications were made in a complete and professional manner and had minimal negative effect on the cars. In other cases, the modifications were done less professionally and have proved problematic.

Registering and insuring these cars can prove difficult. If the original compliance paperwork is incomplete, you may never be able to register the car for road use. Some insurance companies simply will not insure these cars.

If the BMW you are looking at happens to be a European-specification car, you need to know that parts for these cars are oftentimes different from parts for cars built to U.S. specifications and as a result are not usually stocked by BMW retailers. Parts for the Euro-spec cars may need to be special ordered from Germany. Expect these to be more costly.

Rare and Unusual BMWs

While many of you will have heard of and possibly are familiar with the 3-, 5-, 6-, and 7-Series BMWs, we must not forget that BMW has been producing cars since the beginning of the twentieth century. Certainly there are some very desirable BMW cars produced before World War II as well as afterwards. This book is not intended to address cars built before the 1960s.

Most of the vintage BMWs you will find can be placed into these categories: basket cases, drivers, or restored cars. It is fairly safe to say that when one of these cars comes up for sale, it is quickly sold to a collector and oftentimes at prices that are out of reach for many of us. With recent changes in the laws regarding importing vehicles not previously offered for sale in the United States, more of these vehicles may be imported and, at some point in the future, show up on the market.

A smallish two-door sedan, the 1600-2 (later renamed 1602), first appeared with a 96-brake horsepower inline 4-cylinder engine and modest trimmings. To the uninformed, it just looked like another one of the econo-box cars of the time. Except for the blue and white roundel on the hood and rear panel and a manufacturer with a reputation for delivering sporty performance and handling, it might just have been one of those forgettable shoeboxes-on-wheels.

Weighing in at slightly more than 2,000 pounds and equipped with 4-wheel independent suspension, front disc brakes, a 96-ci inline 4-cylinder (that produced 1 brake horse-power per cubic inch), a 4-speed manual, light and precise steering, the 1600-2 could carry four adults in reasonable comfort.

In September 1967, the 6-volt electrics were upgraded to 12 volts and the front seats featured fold-down backrests. In February 1969, the brakes were upgraded; in April 1971 it became the 1602, bringing the name in line with its "big brother," the 2002, introduced in February 1968.

By the end of 1971, the 1602 had been discontinued and the 2002 was left to carry on the tradition established by the 1602. Between them, these two small BMWs established the benchmark that small, sporting sedans, are measured against, even to this day.

During its production run, the '02, as it is known, received many updates to the cosmetics, mechanicals, trim, and per-formance. Ranging from the Kugelfischer mechanical injection of the "tii" to the 5-miles-per-hour bumpers required to meet U.S. safety standards of the mid-1970s.

The three logical groupings of these cars are the 1967–1971 1600-2/1602s and the 1968–1971 2002s; the 1972–1976 2002s; and the 1972–1974 2002tii's.

The first group can be distinguished by the lack of side-protection strips. Their bumpers were plain appearing, not hav-ing the black rubber trim, and the rear wraparound was shorter. Available as either the 1600-2 or the 2002, the primary dif-ference was the engine: 1990cc compared to the 1573cc.

Other differences were in levels of trim and equipment.

The second group can be distinguished by the presence of side-protection strips and rear bumpers that extended fur-ther forward to the rear wheel wells. The bumpers also had rub-ber protection strips. The 2002 was carbureted, the 2002tii was equipped with the Kugelfischer mechanical fuel injection and wider tires. Emissions controls were added and consisted of lowered compression and the Exhaust Gas Recirculation (EGR) system.

The large aluminum bumpers, additional side marker lights, and larger, square-shaped taillights distinguish the third group. These cars were also equipped with more stringent emissions devices. The last year for a U.S. version of the 2002tii was 1974, and in 1975 the cars were equipped with thermal reactors. California was the only state that received the ther-mal reactors for 1976; the other 49 states reverted back to the EGR system.

The 2002s are simple, no-frills, fun cars to own and drive. They are also wonderful examples of BMW history that will continue to be present in the market for many years to come. If you are looking for a car just to drive or one to work on either for yourself or as a family project, find one that fits your budget and have some fun.

The 1600-02 was a solid little car, economical and roomy for its small size with surprisingly good performance. The 2002 is the same basic body with larger engine. The emissions-era cars suffered drivability problems, the worst being the 1975 model year with the thermal reactor. The tii is the shining star: mechanical fuel injection, factory hot rod. Astounding per-formance for a 2.0-liter.

Parts are still readily available new, reproduced, or used. Rust can be a problem; however, replacement body panels are still available. Enthusiasts have a choice of early, small-bumper round taillights or later, big-bumper square taillight cars to choose from. Many are rescued and restored to better than new condition. Prices for a fully restored car can easily go over $10,000.

Ratings Chart

Type 114

	1600-2/1602	2002	2002tii
Model Comfort/Amenities	**	**	**
Reliability	**	**	**
Collectibility	**	***	****
Parts/Service Availability	***	***½	***½
Est. Annual Repair Costs	***	***	***½

This rear view of the 1968 1600-2 displays the round taillight version. Should a round taillight model interest you, be sure to look over the car closely for accident repairs. Those small lights are difficult to see, and many of these cars have been rear-ended.

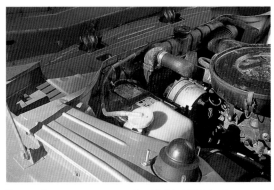

The engine compartment of a 1968 1600-2. Be sure to look for oil and fluid leaks. Broken engine mounts occur in this model and allow the engine to rock under acceleration, and the distributor cap can make contact with firewall. A change in color is evident here.

This engine compartment view of this 1972 BMW 2002 reveals an aftermarket air cleaner.

The front view of a pristine 1972 BMW 2002.

Replacement Costs for Common Parts
1600-2/1602/2002/2002tii

1600-2/1602

Oil Filter	$5
Fuel Filter	$2
Fuel Pump	$75
Starter	$120
Alternator	$120
Clutch	$280
Flex Couplings (each, 3 required)	$44
Front Bumper	$520
Hood	$250 (used)
Left Front Fender New	$150
Used	$75
Right Rear Quarter Panel	$185
Rear Bumper	$520
Windshield	$230
Tail Light Lens	$80
Center Silencer	$100
Rear Silencer	$100
Brake Master	$100
Front Rotor	$30
Front Pads (set)	$35
Front Shocks	$120
Rear Shocks	$100
Tie Rod	$50
Lower Control Arm/Ball Joint	$30

2002tii

Oil Filter	$5
Fuel Filter	$10
Fuel Pump	$450
Starter	$120
Alternator	$120
Clutch	$225
Flex Couplings	$38
Front Bumper	$520
Hood	$250 (used)
Left Front Fender New	$150
Used	$75
Right Rear Quarter Panel	$185
Rear Bumper	$520
Windshield	$230
Tail Light Lens	$80
Center Silencer	$100
Rear Silencer	$150
Brake Master	$175
Front Rotor	$44
Front Pads (set)	$38
Front Shocks	$120
Rear Shocks	$100
Tie Rod	$50
Lower Control Arm/Ball Joint	$30

2002

Oil Filter		$5
Fuel Filter		$2
Fuel Pump		$75
Starter		$120
Alternator		$120
Clutch		$175
Flex Couplings		$36
Front Bumper		$520
Hood (used)		$250
Left Front Fender	New	$150
	Used	$75
Right Rear Quarter Panel		$185
Rear Bumper		$520
Windshield		$230
Tail Light Lens		$80
Center Silencer		$100
Rear Silencer		$100
EGR Valve		$300
Thermal Reactor	New	$2,050
NLA		
	Used	$400
Brake Master		$100
Front Rotor		$30
Front Pads (set)		$35
Front Shocks		$120
Rear Shocks		$100
Tie Rod		$50
Lower Control Arm/Ball Joint		$30

This right-side dashboard view of a 1968 1600-2 shows the heater control to the right of the steering wheel and a more modern radio unit. Air conditioning is a rare option on these cars and was installed by dealer at time of purchase.

The 1967 1600-2 had a mechanical clutch (no hydraulic assist), which needs to be adjusted as it wears. Parts are difficult to find. Later cars had hydraulic-actuated clutches that shared fluid with the brake system. Pump the clutch pedal several times, confirming that the pedal returns each time. The pedal sticking in mid-travel could indicate a collapsing flex hose.

The rear-axle half-shafts on the very early cars had their outboard CV joints encased in a "wet" oil-bath environment. The boots do fail, allowing the CV joint to run dry and quickly fail. The later-model cars (with the short-neck differentials) had their CV joints packed in grease.

Check for rust damage that would render the car unsafe to drive as well as unfit for a restoration. Look for signs of body repairs where you would expect to find rust. Look under the carpeting, in the door jams, and in any other hidden, hard-to-get-to areas for signs of a repaint.

Manual transmissions are pretty reliable. The rubber mountings for the linkage tend to deteriorate, resulting in a sloppy feel to the shifter. Some early transmissions had problems with the output flanges loosening. In automatic transmissions, look for signs of leakage and confirm that the transmission shifts up and down smoothly.

Brake systems are reasonably trouble free. Problems often are traced to owner neglect, such as not flushing the system regularly. Check for signs of leaks and the condition of the reservoir fluid. Brake fluid is a very effective paint stripper. Check below the reservoir for signs of spilled brake fluid.

A one-barrel Solex was the original carburetor. If it has been replaced by another brand, watch for air leaks at the base plate where it is bolted to the intake manifold. Also watch and listen for vacuum leaks on the intake side and exhaust leaks from warped or ill-fitting exhaust headers.

Check motor mounts closely. Very early cars had a C-shaped motor mount on the right side that has a reputation for collapsing. Many have been replaced with a reinforced mount with a welded-in gusset. The left-side mount has a reputation for cracking where it is welded to the subframe.

Look for signs of oil leakage. Excessive noise from the valve-train could be an indication of worn rocker shafts. Dipstick oil that looks like a chocolate milkshake is contaminated with coolant, indicating a blown head gasket. Also take off the oil filter cap and look inside for dirt and sludge.

Check for the presence or absence of emissions-control equipment. Starting in 1968, an air-injection pump was fitted to the cars. Don't be surprised if this pump has been removed. Check your local emissions laws, as the pump may or may not be required to register and insure the car.

Check for the presence of emissions-control equipment. Starting in 1968, an air-injection pump was fitted to the cars. Beginning in 1975, BMW used a thermal reactor in place of a catalytic converter. The cycle of high heat and cooling can cause cracking of the reactor and engine problems.

Watch for air leaks at the base plate where the carburetor is bolted to the intake manifold. Also watch and listen for vacuum leaks on the intake side as well as exhaust leaks from warped or ill-fitting exhaust headers.

Automatic transmissions were available only on the carbureted cars. While reasonably reliable, they are not very popular. Look for leakage at the seals, slippage, and smooth gear changes.

A 1-barrel Solex was used up to 1972, then a 2-barrel Solex. Over the years, many of these have been replaced by the smog-legal Weber 32/36 DGV. Check your local emissions laws to confirm whether this change is legal. If it is not, you may need to locate an original-spec Solex.

Manual transmissions are fairly robust. The weak link is second-gear syncros. Check for leaks from the shift seal and output flange seal and also for bearing noise. Loose

With time, age, and neglect, it is not uncommon for brake systems to have a variety of problems. Watch for seized calipers, spongy pedals, erratic braking, and flex lines that have deteriorated.

Check for rust damage that would render the car unsafe or unfit for restoration. Look for signs of body repairs. Look under the carpeting, in the door jams, and in any other hidden, hard-to-get-to areas for signs of a repaint.

The 2002tii uses a Kugelfischer mechanical fuel-injection system. While these have had a bad reputation, when they are correctly set up they are a pretty good system. The real problem lies in finding a mechanic who understands the system and knows how to adjust it correctly.

The fuel-injection mechanical pump uses engine oil for lubrication, and it is very important to make sure the engine oil is kept clean. In addition, the linkage adjustments are critical. Being out of adjustment by just a few millimeters is enough to cause major headaches.

Check that the fan belt isn't too tight, or it will cause water pump bearing failures. An over-tight fan belts can also cause alternator bushings to fail and the alternator pulley to make contact

Check for the presence of the correct BMW fuel filter—an aluminum canister–type filter—next to the left-hand side of the radiator. The clear plastic in-line filters are intended for use on carbureted cars and are not appropriate for pressurized systems like the Kugelfischer system. They may also be a fire hazard.

Suspension remained much the same throughout production. The semi-trailing arms for the tii's (and the non-U.S. ti and turbos) were boxed for additional strength, and these arms have shown a tendency to trap moisture and rust from the inside out.

Early models had intake runners made from molded plastic, later models from aluminum. The plastic runners are reported to flow better and make a bit more power, but have a history of cracking and splitting. BMW Mobile Tradition reproduces the plastic runners to OE specifications. They, too, crack and split.

If the car you are looking at has been modified with aftermarket suspension items, be sure to confirm that they are the correct items and are installed properly. Also check the brake systems for proper operation as well as the cooling systems. 2002s have a tendency to blow head gaskets.

Specifications
1600-2/1602
2002 1968–1971

1600-2/1602

Engine Type		SOHC Inline 4-Cylinder
Displacement cc/ci		1573/96
Compression Ratio		8.61
BHP @ rpm		96 @ 5800
Torque lbs-ft @ rpm		105.6 @ 3000
Carburetion		Solex 38 PDSI
Fuel Requirement		Premium
Transmission		4-Speed Manual
Steering		Worm and Roller
Front Suspension		MacPherson Strut, Coil Springs, Tube Shocks
Rear Suspension		Semi-Trailing Arms, Coil Springs, Tube Shocks
Wheelbase (in.)		98.5
Weight (lbs.)		2270
Wheels		13 x 4 Steel Wheels
Tires		13 x 6 Bias Ply
		165SR x 13 from 1970
Brake System	Front	9.4-in. Discs
	Rear	7.9-in. Drums
0–60 mph, sec		11.4
Maximum Speed mph		102 (est.) (*Car and Driver, 2/67*)
EPA Estimated mpg		22–28 (*Car and Driver, 2/67*)

2002 1968–1971

Engine Type		SOHC Inline 4-Cylinder
Displacement cc/ci		1990/121.5
Compression Ratio		8.51
BHP @ rpm		113 @ 5800
Torque lbs-ft @ rpm		116 @ 3000
Carburetion		Solex 1bbl
Fuel Requirement		Premium
Transmission	Manual	4-Speed Manual
	Automatic	ZF 3-Speed
Steering		Worm and Roller
Front Suspension		MacPherson Strut, Lower A-Arms, Coil Springs, Tube Shocks
Rear Suspension		Semi-Trailing Arms, Coil Springs, Tube Shocks
Wheelbase (in.)		98.4
Weight (lbs.)		2565
Wheels		13 x 4.5 Steel Wheels
Tires		165SR-13 Steel Radials
Brake System	Front	9.4-in. Discs
	Rear	7.9-in. Drums
0–60 mph, sec	Manual	11.3 (*Road & Track, 4/68*)
	Automatic	13.3 (*Road & Track, 11/69*)
Maximum Speed mph	Manual	108 (*Road & Track, 4/68*)
	Automatic	102 (*Road & Track, 11/69*)
EPA Estimated mpg	Manual	22–27 (*Road & Track, 4/68*)
	Automatic	19.5 (*Road & Track, 11/69*)

Specifications
2002 1972–1976
2002tii

2002 1972–1976

Engine Type		SOHC Inline 4-Cylinder
Displacement cc/ci		1990/121.5
Compression Ratio		8.51
BHP @ rpm	1972–1973	113 @ 5800
	1974–1976	98 @ 5800
Torque lbs-ft @ rpm	1972–1973	116 @ 3000
	1974–1976	106 @ 3500
Carburetion		Solex 2bbl
Fuel Requirement		Premium
Transmission	Manual	4-Speed Manual
	Automatic	ZF 3-Speed
Steering		Worm and Roller
Front Suspension		MacPherson Strut, Lower A-Arms, Coil Springs, Tube Shocks
Rear Suspension		Semi-Trailing Arms, Coil Springs, Tube Shocks
Wheelbase (in.)		98.4
Weight (lbs.)		2565
Wheels		13 x 5.0 Steel Wheels
Tires		165SR-13 Steel Radials
Brake System	Front	9.4-in. Discs
	Rear	7.9-in. Drums
0–60 mph, sec	Manual	10.3
	Automatic	NA
Maximum Speed mph	Manual	104 (est.)
	Automatic	NA
EPA Estimated mpg	Manual	24.5 (est.)
	Automatic	NA

2002tii

Engine Type			SOHC Inline 4-Cylinder
Displacement cc/ci			1990/121.5
Compression Ratio			9.01
BHP @ rpm	1971–1973		140 @ 5800
	1974		125 @ 5500
Torque lbs-ft @ rpm	1971–1973		145 @ 3000
	1974		127 @ 4000
Fuel Injection			Kugelfischer Mechanical
Fuel Requirement			Regular, 91 Octane
Transmission			4-Speed Manual
Steering			Worm and Roller
Front Suspension			MacPherson Strut, Lower A-Arms, Coil Springs, Tube Shocks
Rear Suspension			Semi-Trailing Arms, Coil Springs, Tube Shocks
Wheelbase (in.)			98.4
Weight (lbs.)	1971–1973		2310
	1974		2420
Wheels			13 x 5.0 Steel Wheels
Tires			165HR-13 Steel Radials
Brake System	Front		9.4-in. Discs
	Rear		7.9-in. Drums
0–60 mph, sec	Manual	1971–1973	9.8
		1974	9.5
Maximum Speed mph	Manual	1971–1973	115 (est.)
		1974	116 (est.)
EPA Estimated mpg	Manual	1971–1973	22.7
		1974	23.5

I Bought a . . .

1973 BMW 2002tii

I have owned numerous cars including several BMW 1600/2002 variants (I believe the last count places this as my fourteenth personally owned 1600/2002). Prior to purchasing this particular car I looked at six others – including flying out to see three of them. I love the basic, sporting handling and feel of this car. The engine is incredibly smooth and strong and the car does everything right. There is a Zen-like experience driving this 1973 2002tii.

Three out of my first eight 2002's blew head gaskets. You have to be aware that this is possible on the early 2002 cars or the 1975-1976 cars. I find it is more common in any 2002 that has sat dormant for a long time.

Overall, I do not consider 2002's expensive to own. Some parts are No Longer Available (NLA). However, BMW Mobile Tradition is doing an excellent job of addressing the needs of many owners. Items such as the nose, the early grills, door panels, rubber items, and trim are becoming available after a long absence. Also, I recommend people make sure they have a knowledgeable mechanic interested and excited to work on your 2002 because they are getting harder to find.

Let's be honest, these cars are very basic. The ventilation is archaic. Even the air conditioning systems offered by dealers at the time were woefully inadequate. Since I live in Southern California, this can be a problem. *—Brian Foster, Irvine, California*

1972 BMW 2002

The first thing that attracted me to this car was the classy style. It had the aura of a beautiful car frozen in time. My parents agreed to purchase the car because it would be a great car to drive and easy for my father to make any necessary repairs. I was sixteen; it was my first car and also the first BMW to be parked in our driveway. The '02 was a great car to take to and from high school. My father taught me how to do simple mechanics such as changing a tire and changing the oil.

There have not been many repairs that were needed but an old car always needs some. My family and I have replaced the front brakes (rotors, calipers and pads); front wheel bearings; and also the rear brake cylinders were replaced. Other parts that have been replaced were: strut inserts, rear shocks (Bilstein HD), and a remanufactured alternator. This car has never been down for a long period of time.

I would consider maintenance to be moderately priced and so far the parts needed have been easily found. There has also been no restoring of this car; it was simply taken care of by the previous owners. *—Sarah Woerner, San Diego, California*

The 1973 BMW 2002tii featured mechanical fuel injection and higher performance. Early cars used plastic intake runners, while later cars used these cast aluminum intake runners. Watch for cracking where the front support joins inner fenders.

Small bumpers and round taillights—the classic look of a 1973 BMW 2002tii.

What They Said About the . . .

1600-2

Floor the throttle and it takes off like a scalded dog. Point it into a corner—any corner—and unless you've simply lost your mind it'll track around like it was locked into a slot. *—Car and Driver,* **February 1967**

2002

To my way of thinking, the 2002 is one of modern civilization's all-time best ways to get somewhere sitting down. It grabs you. *—Car and Driver,* **April 1968**

2002tii

The BMW 2002tii is a keen sports sedan—a real blast to drive fast and yet practical enough for a small family to use for daily transportation and extended trips. *—Road & Track,* **October 1971**

2500
2800
Bavaria
3.0S/3.0Si

E3
1968-1977
Chapter 2

BMW introduced the E3-chassis 2500 and 2800 sedans in late 1968 as replacements for the New Class 1500 and 1800 sedans. The E3 sedans are based on a 106-inch wheelbase featuring 4-wheel independent suspension; MacPherson struts; a lower A-arm, coil springs, and tube shocks in front; semi-trailing arms, coil springs, and tube shocks in the rear. The more upscale 2.8-liter used Nivomat self-leveling rear shocks. The 2800 sedan featured a leather interior and higher trim levels throughout.

The new design 6-cylinder was the beginning point for an engine design that was used well into the 1990s. Apart from the longer stroke of the 2.8-liter, the two engines are identical. The 2494-cc and 2788-cc produced 170 and 192 brake horsepower, respectively. A chain-driven single overhead cam (SOHC) operated inclined valves through rockers, and the crankshaft rides in seven main bearings. Two dual-throat Solex/Zenith carburetors feed fuel to the triple-hemispherical combustion chambers, a design so efficient in its original form that it met U.S. emissions standards without additional emissions controls. However, these carburetors have a reputation for being difficult to maintain. A new thermostat design regulated the flow of coolant from both the block and the radiator, allowing more precise control of the engine operating temperature. The Bosch fuel-injection system is relatively trouble free, but the fuel lines tend to become brittle and can leak.

In both sedans, a ZF 4-speed manual transmission was standard and a ZF 3-speed automatic transmission was optional. Four-wheel disc brakes were standard equipment and incorporated dual-circuit redundancy for safely stopping should one circuit fail.

The interior of these spacious sedans offers enough room to carry five adults in relative comfort. The trunks are well finished and surprisingly large. Air conditioning was available as an option, but it was relatively ineffective. Also available as options were power steering (standard equipment on the 2800), a 3-speed automatic transmission, limited slip, air conditioning, metallic paint, and a variety of stereo radio/tape player options. In later years, electric windows, sunroof, and alloy wheels were also available.

High prices and lackluster sales inspired the introduction of the Bavaria, a combination of the two models, minus the Nivomat rear suspension and the leather seating but powered by the 2.8-liter engine. Available as options were the heated rear window and a tool kit that mounted under the trunk lid. At a list price just under $5,000, the Bavaria was a bargain, and sales took a swing upwards.

In 1972, the 2.8-liter engine was upgraded to 3.0 liters. However, the Bavaria nameplate remained. Borg-Warner 3-speed automatics replaced the trouble-prone ZF automatic and the compression ratio was lowered, allowing the cars to be run on regular fuel.

Beginning in 1973, BMW complemented the Bavaria with the 3.0S, which had all the options available for the Bavaria included as standard equipment. In 1974, the cars received the ungainly big-bumpers that were to stay with the E3 sedans until they were discontinued. In 1975, the Bavaria nameplate disappeared and the 3.0Si was introduced, incorporating Bosch L-Jetronic fuel injection and dual thermal reactors to control emissions. After 1976, the 3.0Si was discontinued as BMW had introduced the E12 530i, and the E23 7-Series was soon to be introduced.

The large bumpers added to the 3.0S in 1974 are poorly integrated and awkward looking and spoil an otherwise clean design. The "big six" engine family also has a history of high oil consumption even when new. While these engines are basically reliable and long-lived, do not be overly alarmed at high oil consumption; a quart per 1,000 miles is not unusual.

The E3-chassis 2500s, 2800s, Bavarias, 3.0S, and 3.0Si offer a roomy interior, classic BMW looks and handling, as well as reasonably good performance—even by today's standards. The smooth-running, sophisticated inline 6-cylinder, standard 4-wheel disc brakes, and manual transmission offer good value for the money.

Ratings Chart

E3 Sedans

	2500	2800	Bavaria	3.0S	3.0Si
Model Comfort/Amenities	**½	**½	**½	**½	***
Reliability	**	**	**	**	**
Collectibility	½	½	½	½	½
Parts/Service Availability	**½	***	***	**	**
Est. Annual Repair Costs	***½	***½	***½	***½	***½

This 1974 Bavaria still has the original engine compartment stickers in place and had just received a factory-rebuilt engine. Note the new radiator overflow tank and fresh antifreeze.

The rear seat room of the 1972 Bavaria is generous and features a fold-down armrest in the center.

Replacement Costs for Common Parts
2500/2800/Bavaria/3.0S/3.0Si

2500

Oil Filter	$7	
Fuel Filter	$3	
Fuel Pump	$85	
Starter (remanufactured)	$135	
Alternator (remanufactured)	$135	
Clutch	$225	
Flex Disc (Guibo)	NLA	
Front Bumper	$550	
Hood	$250	
Left Front Fender	$75	(used)
Right Rear Quarter Panel	$185	
Rear Bumper	$550	
Windshield	$230	
Tail Light Lens	$80	
Center Silencer	$100	
Rear Silencer	$100	
EGR Valve	$300	(est.)
Brake Master	NLA	
Front Rotor	$60	
Front Pads (set)	$50	
Front Shocks	$75	
Rear Shocks	$60	
Tie Rods	NLA	
Lower Control Arm/Ball Joint	NLA	

2800

Oil Filter	$7	
Fuel Filter	$3	
Fuel Pump	$85	
Starter (remanufactured)	$135	
Alternator (remanufactured)	$135	
Clutch	$225	
Flex Disc (Guibo)	$48	
Front Bumper	$550	
Hood	$250	
Left Front Fender (used)	$75	
Right Rear Quarter Panel	$185	
Rear Bumper	$550	
Windshield	$230	
Tail Light Lens	$80	
Center Silencer	$100	
Rear Silencer	$100	
EGR Valve	$300	(est.)
Brake Master	NLA	
Front Rotor	$60	
Front Pads (set)	$50	
Front Shocks	$75	
Rear Shocks	$60	
Tie Rods	NLA	
Lower Control Arm/Ball Joint	$45	

Bavaria

Oil Filter	$7	
Fuel Filter	$3	
Fuel Pump	$85	
Starter (remanufactured)	$135	
Alternator (remanufactured)	$135	
Fan Clutch	$180	
Clutch kit	$225	
Flex Disc (Guibo)	$48	
Front Bumper	$550	
Hood	$250	
Left Front Fender (used)	$75	
Right Rear Quarter Panel	$185	
Rear Bumper	$550	
Windshield	$230	
Tail Light Lens	$80	
Center Silencer	$100	
Rear Silencer	$100	
EGR Valve	$300	(est.)
Brake Master	$200	
Front Rotor	$60	
Front Pads (set)	$50	
Front Shocks	$75	
Rear Shocks	$60	
Tie Rods	$60	
Lower Control Arm/Ball Joint	$45	

3.0S/3.0Si

Oil Filter			$7	
Fuel Filter			$3	
Fuel Pump			$85	
Starter (remanufactured)			$135	
Alternator (remanufactured)			$135	
Fan Clutch			$180	
Clutch kit			$225	
Flex Disc (Guibo)			$48	
Front Bumper			$550	
Hood			$250	
Left Front Fender (used)			$75	
Right Rear Quarter Panel			$185	
Rear Bumper			$550	
Windshield			$230	
Tail Light Lens			$80	
Center Silencer			$100	
Rear Silencer			$100	
EGR Valve	New		NLA	
	Used		$300	(est.)
Thermal Reactor	Front	(new)	$880.50 NLA	
	Front	(used)	$300	(est.)
	Rear	(new)	$797.50 NLA	
	Rear	(used)	$300	(est.)
Brake Master			$200	
Front Rotor			$60	
Front Pads (set)			$50	
Front Shocks			$75	
Rear Shocks			$60	
Tie Rods			$60	
Lower Control Arm/Ball Joint			$45	

Look for rust in and around the shock towers, front and rear, as well as in the wheel arches and lower corners of the fenders and doors. Check the floorboards and in the trunk, specifically in the spare tire well, for evidence of rusting. Another common rust point is along the beltline, where the aluminum trim is attached.

The differential mounting point has a history of fatiguing and cracking. It can be repaired, but expect to spend between $400 and $700 to have it done correctly.

Lower control arm ball joints have been a problem area. If the front of the car is sagging left or right, have the ball joints checked.

While the disc brakes are generally considered excellent, watch for any pulling from side to side. Also, check the brake fluid; blackish fluid is an indication that the system has not been flushed recently. Change the fluid annually.

"Banjo" bolts that secure the oil-supply pipe to the top of the head may work loose and reduce or shut off the flow of oil. Check bolts any time a valve adjustment is performed. But note: Overtightening can crush the oil-supply pipe and cut off the oil supply.

Although the Getrag 4-speed was an improvement over the ZF manual transmission, some problems with synchronizers continued. The Borg Warner 3-speed automatic offered improved shift points, but it should be checked carefully for operation and leaking seals.

The Solex/Zenith carburetors have a reputation for being difficult to maintain and for causing drivability problems; stumbling and hesitation are common symptoms. Oftentimes the carburetors have been replaced by downdraft Webers. Check your local smog laws for information about replacing the carburetors.

The ZF 4-speed manual transmissions are known for having weak second-gear syncros. This can lead to some difficulties in shifting from first to second gear. The 3-speed ZF automatic transmissions were not considered very good. Check for leaking and proper shifting.

Look underhood for any obvious signs of fluid leakage: oil, power steering fluid (if equipped), antifreeze, and so on.

Pay attention to the various cooling system hoses, as they are known to burst. Water pumps have a tendency to fail at about 40,000 miles and thermostats can malfunction and cause overheating.

Look for rust in and around the shock towers as well as in the wheel arches and lower corners of the fenders and doors. Check the floorboards and in the trunk, specifically in the spare tire well, for evidence of rusting. Another common rust point is along the beltline, where the aluminum trim is attached.

Lower control arm ball joints have been a problem area. If the front of the car is sagging left or right, have the ball joints checked.

The rear differential mounting point tends to fatigue and crack over time. Creaking from the trunk area when power is applied could indicate a cracked differential mount.

The 3.0S and 3.0Si are the last of their models. The fuel-injected cars offer improved drivability over carbureted models, but at the expense of gas mileage. The thermal reactors could be considered the weak spot on an otherwise good-driving, well-appointed sedan.

Pay particular attention to the various cooling system hoses, as these are known to burst. Water pumps have a tendency to fail at about 40,000 miles, and thermostats can malfunction and cause overheating.

"Banjo" bolts that secure the oil-supply pipe to the top of the head may work loose and reduce or shut off the flow of oil. Check bolts any time a valve adjustment is performed. But note: Overtightening can crush the oil-supply pipe and cut off the oil supply.

The "big-six" engine family has a history of high oil consumption, even when new. While these engines are basically reliable and long-lived, do not be overly alarmed about high oil consumption: 1 quart per 1,000 miles is not unusual.

Thermal reactors crack over time, and many cars have had these removed. If you live in a state that requires original emissions equipment to be installed and functioning, be aware that a new thermal reactor costs approximately $800, two reactors are required, and they are no longer available.

A side effect of the heat required for the thermal reactors was a high rate of cracked cylinder heads on these early cars. The cure for this was to replace the damaged head with a 1980 or newer head that featured improved water passages.

Specifications
2500/2800

2500

Engine Type		SOHC Inline 6-Cylinder
Displacement cc/ci		2494/152
Compression Ratio		9.01
BHP @ rpm		170 @ 6000
Torque lbs-ft @ rpm		176 @ 3700
Carburetion		2 Solex 35/40 INAT
Fuel Requirement		Premium
Transmission	Manual	4-Speed
	Automatic	3-Speed
Steering		Worm and Roller, Optional Power Assist
Front Suspension		MacPherson Struts, Lower A-Arms, Coil Springs, Tube Shocks
Rear Suspension		Semi-Trailing Arms, Coil Springs, Tube Shocks
Wheelbase (in.)		106.0
Weight (lbs.)		3005
Wheels		14 x 6 Steel Disc
Tires		175HR-14
Brake System		4-Wheel Discs, Vacuum Assist
	Front	10.7 inch
	Rear	10.7 inch
0–60 mph, sec		10.0
Maximum Speed mph		118
EPA Estimated mpg		20.9

2800

Engine Type		SOHC Inline 6-Cylinder
Displacement cc/ci		2788/170
Compression Ratio		9.01
BHP @ rpm		192 @ 6000
Torque lbs-ft @ rpm		174 @ 3700
Carburetion		2 Solex 35/40 INAT
Fuel Requirement		Premium
Transmission	Manual	4-Speed
	Automatic	3-Speed
Steering		Worm and Roller, Optional Power Assist
Front Suspension		MacPherson Struts, Lower A-Arms, Coil Springs, Tube Shocks
Rear Suspension		Semi-Trailing Arms, Coil Springs, Tube Shocks
Wheelbase (in.)		106.0
Weight (lbs.)		3005
Wheels		14 x 6 Steel Disc
Tires		175HR-14
Brake System		4 Wheel Discs, Vacuum Assist
	Front	10.7 inch
	Rear	10.7 inch
0–60 mph, sec		10.0
Maximum Speed mph		124 (*Motor Sport*, October 1969)
EPA Estimated mpg		18.0

Specifications
Bavaria/3.0S/3.0Si

Bavaria

Engine Type		SOHC Inline 6-Cylinder
Displacement cc/ci	1972	2788/170
	1973–1975	2985/182
Compression Ratio	1972	9.01
	1973–1975	8.31
BHP @ rpm	1972	192 @ 6000
	1973–1975	190 @ 5800
Torque lbs-ft @ rpm	1972	174 @ 3700
	1973–1975	213 @ 3500
Carburetion		2 Solex 35/40 INAT
Fuel Requirement		Premium
Transmission	Manual	4-Speed
	Automatic	3-Speed
Steering		Worm and Roller, Optional Power Assist
Front Suspension		MacPherson Struts, Lower A-Arms, Coil Springs, Tube Shocks, Anti-Roll Bar
Rear Suspension		Semi-Trailing Arms, Coil Springs, Tube Shocks, Optional Anti-Roll Bar
Wheelbase (in.)		106.0
Weight (lbs.)	1972	3170
	1973–1975	3505 (*Road & Track* 2/73)
Wheels		14 x 6 Steel Disc
	Optional	14 x 6 Cast Alloy
Tires		175HR-14
Brake System		4-Wheel Discs, Vacuum Assist
	Front	10.7 inch
	Rear	10.7 inch
0–60 mph, sec	1972	9.3
	1973–1975	10.7 (*Road & Track*, February 1973)
Maximum Speed mph	1972	125 (est.)
	1973–1975	124 (*Road & Track*, February 1973)
EPA Estimated mpg	1972	18.0
	1973–1975	17.0 (*Road & Track*, February 1973)

3.0S/3.0Si

Engine Type		SOHC Inline 6-Cylinder
Displacement cc/ci		2985/182
Compression Ratio		8.11
BHP @ rpm		176 @ 5500
Torque lbs-ft @ rpm		185 @ 4500
Carburetion (3.0S)		2 Zenith or Solex Downdraft
Injection (3.0Si)		Bosch Electronic
Fuel Requirement		Premium
Emission Control (3.0Si)		Thermal Reactor, Air Injection
Transmission	Manual	4-Speed
	Automatic	3-Speed
Steering		Worm and Roller, Optional Power Assist
Front Suspension		MacPherson Struts, Lower A-Arms, Coil Springs, Tube Shocks
Rear Suspension		Semi-Trailing Arms, Coil Springs, Tube Shocks
Wheelbase (in.)		106.0
Weight (lbs.)		4140 (*Motor Trend*, November 1973)
Wheels		14 x 6 Steel Disc
Tires		175HR-14
Brake System		4-Wheel Discs, Vacuum Assist
	Front	10.7 inch
	Rear	10.7 inch
0–60 mph, sec		9.5
Maximum Speed mph	3.0S	127
	3.0Si	130
EPA Estimated mpg		17.2 (*Motor Trend*, November 1973)

What They Said About the . . .

2500

Typically German in its combination of design for fast driving and maneuverability with a low displacement, high-output engine, it also bears an unmistakable BMW personality which has been unavailable heretofore in such a spacious, luxurious car. **—Road & Track, May 1969**

2800/Bavaria

If ever a saloon deserved the tag 'sporting', the BMW 2800 is it. **—Autocar, 1970**

3.0S/3.0Si

Like all the BMW's it is essentially a driver's car, one that responds well to the enthusiast's touch and gives a lot of pleasure and satisfaction all the time. **—Autocar, February 1973**

This 1976 BMW 3.0Si features a sunroof, electric windows, metallic paint, and a leather interior.

This 1976 BMW 3.0Si's engine compartment shows the tried-and-true big six with Bosch L-Jetronic fuel injection. The brake cylinder reservoir is mounted ahead of the radiator overflow tank, and the white sticker in front of shock tower shows routing of emissions-related hoses.

DOT-mandated bumpers spoiled the clean look of the earlier 1974 Bavarias.

I Bought a . . .

1972 BMW Bavaria

We bought this car new in February 1973 and have put more than 266,400 miles on it. Several years ago, we bought a newer car and sold the Bavaria. However, Dot missed the Bavaria so much that we ended up buying it back a couple of months later. One of the things we really like about the car is its handling.

We replaced the engine with a BMW factory-rebuilt unit at 200,000 miles. The rebuilt engine is actually better than the original one—it doesn't leak or burn any oil and has an improved head design. We also replaced the mechanical fan clutch with the later- style viscous one. The automatic transmission was replaced a couple of times before we finally got one that worked. In addition, the carburetors are hard to keep right.

If we had known the problems we were going to have with the car, we might well have bought another car instead. However, we do have to admit we still do like the car and can't think of any other that we would have kept for 30 years. *—Dot and Bob Lanham, Santa Ana, California*

1976 BMW 3.0Si

Prior to buying this car new in October 1976, I owned a 1972 Bavaria (bought new), a 1986 528e (bought new), a 1973 3.0CS that I am restoring, and a 1988 528e.

I liked the styling, size, performance, and the conservative looks of the 3.0Si. It still makes me smile whenever I drive it. The cooling system and air conditioning are problem areas—one time the car overheated in Yosemite.

In the 25 years of ownership, I have replaced practically everything—the car does have over 189,000 miles on it! Last year I installed a 3.3-liter and 5-speed. I have replaced the suspension, A/C compressors (twice), alternator (twice), starter, radiator (three times), leather and carpeting, hood insulation (twice), trunk gasket, and fuel tank. I also had the car repainted and the rims refinished.

The trim parts are difficult to find, but the mechanicals are not a problem; just about all the parts are still available. *—Randy Luenebrink, Los Angeles*

1974 BMW Bavaria

Our 1974 BMW Bavaria has been in our family since my grandparents purchased it from Ocean Motors in Santa Monica. They took delivery of the car in Munich, where our family went for Christmas that year. In addition to the fact that it belonged to my grandparents and I learned to drive with it, I like the body style and the way it handles and rides—even with 219,000 miles on it!

A common problem with this series is that there is a strong smell of gasoline in the trunk that can't be traced. I would also consider it an expensive car to maintain. Mechanically, you name it, I've done it: carburetor rebuild, new radiator, complete engine rebuild. If it didn't have the sentimental value, I probably would not have gone to the expense of the engine rebuild. *—Jennifer Faneuff, Long Beach, California*

The instruments of the 1974 BMW Bavaria are large and very legible. Air conditioning controls and vents share the center console with the radio (in this example an aftermarket replacement for the original). In the lower left is the door stop. Over time, cracking will occur in the leading edge of the door skin where the door stop attaches.

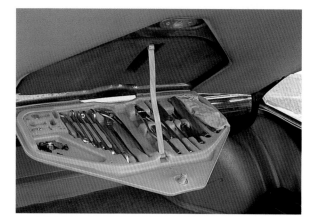

The trunk of the 1976 BMW 3.0Si contains a handy trunk-mounted dropdown tool kit that offers a selection of tools, spare bulbs and fuses, as well as a small cloth for cleaning hands and tools.

The first iteration of the timeless coupes was introduced in 1965 as the 2000CS. Powered by a 2.0-liter version of the SOHC 4-cylinder that had been used in the 1800 sedans, the 2000 coupes were offered with a 4-speed manual or a ZF 3-speed automatic.

Offering seating for four and a well-designed interior with walnut trim, the coupe drew much praise. The individual front seats were comfortable and the detailing throughout the interior was impressive.

The 2000CS's M10-based 2.0-liter 4-cylinder engine produced 135 brake horsepower at 5,800 rpm and featured two Solex 40 PHH carburetors. Smooth-running and quiet, the engine offered modest performance.

Front suspension was MacPherson struts with lower A-arms, tube shocks, coil springs, and an anti-roll bar. Rear suspension was by semi-trailing arms, tube shocks, and coil springs. Steering, although not power assisted, was rated as offering good feel.

The brakes for the 2000CS were front disc and rear drum, offering drivers adequate but not impressive stopping power, a situation that continued until 1973.

The 2000CS was replaced in 1969 by a restyled coupe featuring the 2.8-liter inline 6-cylinder from the 2800/Bavaria sedans. The use of the 6-cylinder engine meant the front of the car, from the A-pillars forward, had to be lengthened. Larger wheels and tires were also used and did a better job of filling out the wheel wells, completing the revised exterior look.

In the interior, the steering wheel and column were revised and the center console was cleaned up. The front seats were recontoured and the rear buckets were reshaped. Cloth was standard and leather was optional at extra cost.

The spare tire is hidden below the flooring of the trunk on the left and the gas tank is under the flooring on the right, both covered by nicely finished panels and carpeting. Underneath the deck lid is a drop-down tool kit.

In 1973, the M30/3.0-liter carbureted 6-cylinder replaced the 2.8-liter, and ventilated rear disc brakes were added. Also added were secondary side-marker lights front and rear, a requirement for U.S. safety regulations. The bumpers were extended slightly farther out from the body, and new bumper guards were used. The 1974 model received the 5-miles-per-hour aluminum bumpers.

The 3.0-liter engine was burdened by emissions controls that were required to meet more stringent rules. The Exhaust Gas Recirculation (EGR) equipment and retarded spark handicapped the larger engine; neither performance nor gas mileage was as good as with the 2.8-liter engine. A Getrag 4-speed manual was introduced featuring revised synchronizers. The ZF 3-speed automatic was replaced by a Borg Warner 3-speed and was generally considered to be superior to the earlier automatic.

No fuel-injected coupes were officially sold in the United States. They were available in Europe and, while you will see them for sale, they are actually European-spec coupes that have been privately imported. If you are looking at a CSi, check for the certification papers to confirm that the car can be licensed and insured. In addition, many of these cars were brought in from areas that used salt on the roads, so check carefully for rust and related repairs.

Also, beware of fake CSL coupes. Know the VIN range of the lightweight coupes. Approximately 596 left-hand drive coupes were built. None of these were made for the U.S. market, though many have been imported. Be sure to check with knowledgeable sources to verify the originality and the legitimacy of any CSL before buying.

Without question, the E9 coupes are beautiful cars. The long-lived, solid, and refined inline 6-cylinder is a jewel of an engine. The basic running gear is trouble-free and common among later model BMWs. Mechanical parts are plentiful and available through the dealerships. Find a rust-free example, keep it in a dry place, and enjoy driving it.

A single word of caution with all of these models: Rust. Clean, rust-free examples are out there, but expect to pay a premium for them.

Ratings Chart

E9 Coupes

	2000C/ 2000CS/2000CA	2800CS	3.0CS
Model Comfort/Amenities	**	**½	**½
Reliability	*½	**	**
Collectibility	***	****	****
Parts/Service Availability	**½	***	***
Est. Annual Repair Costs	****	***½	***½

A 2-liter version of the 4-cylinder engine powered the 1965 BMW 2000CA coupes. Most of this engine's parts are original, though some components have been removed and others replaced with nonoriginal components.

The trunk of the 1965 BMW 2000CA has a nice, finished appearance and offers plenty of room, but be sure to remove panels and check behind coverings for evidence of rust.

"Banjo" bolts that secure the oil-supply pipe to the top of the head may work loose and reduce or shut off the flow of oil. Check bolts any time a valve adjustment is performed. Note that Overtightening can crush the oil-supply pipe and cut off the oil supply.

The M10/2.0-liter 4-cylinder engine has many parts in common with the later 2002 and 320i; therefore, replacement parts are readily available. Do not be surprised to find that the engine has been replaced or repaired using more modern components.

Watch for worn rockers and rocker shafts, the result of the low, in-gear-at-a-stoplight idle that can reduce the flow of oil to the top end of the engine. This occurs more frequently in automatic-transmission cars. The symptom is valve gear noise once the engine is up to operating temperature.

Interior trim pieces are no longer available, and finding replacements can prove difficult and expensive. The wood trim in the interior also is hard to find. Exterior trim can be difficult to locate, and if improperly installed, can cause rust spots to appear where it attaches to the body.

Inspect the fit and finish of the taillights to the rear panel. A poor fit could be evidence of accident repair.

The differential mount under the trunk floor is known for elongating the four attaching points and also for cracking. If it is bad enough, you might see cracks in the trunk floor.

A common maintenance item in the driveline is the rubber "biscuit" coupling in the middle of the drive shaft. Many of the coupes have had the drive shaft flex disk, called a "guibo," replaced with the one from a 6-cylinder car. While this works, the disk is not as flexible as the original unit and can cause driveline vibration.

It is not unusual for the coupe's heavy doors to be misaligned, owing to the age of the cars as well as to their structural well-being. The door brake (or, as it is sometimes called, the door check) prevents the door from opening too far and can cause fatigue cracks where it attaches to the door.

A ZF 3-speed automatic transmission was an option, but it was not a good match to the engine or the character of the coupes. The standard 4-speed manual is a better match for the engine and while most praised the transmission, it is known to have weak second gear syncros.

On a good day, these carburetors were known for their stumbling part-throttle operation and hesitation. An improved design thermostat and fan-clutch were used to keep the engine in its proper operating range—not always successfully.

"Banjo" bolts that secure the oil supply pipe to the top of the head may work loose and reduce or shut off the flow of oil. Check bolts any time a valve adjustment is performed, but note: Over tightening can crush the oil supply pipe and cut off the oil supply.

The original Solex/Zenith carburetors were known for being difficult to keep adjusted properly. They also contributed to stumble, hesitation, and generally rough running. Many have been replaced by the smog-legal Weber downdrafts.

German cars of this era did not have great engine cooling systems. In an attempt to solve this, some owners may have locked-up the friction fan clutch, which results in premature failure of the water pumps. A better solution is to convert to the later style viscous fan clutch from the 5-Series.

The E9 coupes have a history of cracking where the differential mount is attached. Look at the area above where the differential mount is attached for evidence of cracking. Have the car put on a lift and have the differential mount and its surrounding area examined closely for cracking.

Before committing to a purchase of any coupe, have it examined by someone who is familiar with these cars and determine if any rust that is present is within your financial capability to repair. Rust repair can be extensive and expensive!

Make note of any shifting problems with manual transmissions. The original 4-speeds were notorious for having bad/weak second gear syncros. The 3-speed automatic transmissions were not a very good match for the engines and may have been swapped for a manual transmission.

These cars rust from the inside out. Look for rust bubbles in the tops of the front fenders, along the hood line, and where the windshield pillars join with the cowl.

Check the fit and condition of the window seals, both at the top and where they overlap the rear quarter windows. Poor fit can indicate doors that are sagging or windows that need adjusting.

The E9 coupes have a history of cracking where the differential mount is attached. Look at the area above where the differential mount is attached for evidence of cracking. Have the car put on a lift and have the differential mount and its surrounding area examined closely for cracking.

A common maintenance item in the driveline is the rubber "biscuit" coupling in the middle of the drive shaft. Called a "guibo," this rubber disk absorbs some of the driveline stresses. Drive shafts are another common failure item. Sometimes it is because of the center bearing and sometimes because of a universal joint.

"Banjo" bolts that secure the oil-supply pipe to the top of the head may work loose and reduce or shut off the flow of oil. Check bolts any time a valve adjustment is performed. But note: Overtightening can crush the oil-supply pipe and cut off the oil supply.

Watch for worn rockers and rocker shafts, the result of the low, in-gear-at-a-stoplight idle that can reduce the flow of oil to the top end of the engine. This occurs more frequently in automatic-transmission cars. The symptom is valve gear noise once the engine is up to operating temperature.

A 3-speed automatic transmission was an option on the 3.0CS, but it was not a good match to the engine or the character of the coupes. The standard 4-speed manual is a better match for the engine and, while most praised the transmission, it is known to have weak second-gear syncros.

Revised transmissions, both manual and automatic, were improvements over previous units. Perhaps one of the brightest spots was the rear brakes. In place of the rear drums, ventilated discs were fitted and the front discs were now ventilated.

U.S. emissions regulations strangled the ability of these engines to perform. These cars were equipped with exhaust-gas recirculation and had retarded spark at low engine speeds. Drivability suffered and so did gas mileage, and the refined smoothness of the six was lost.

CALIFORNIA
BZZWAX

31

Specifications
2000C/2000CS/2000CA/2800CS

2000C/2000CS/2000CA

Engine Type		SOHC Inline 4-Cylinder
Displacement cc/ci		1990/121.5
Compression Ratio		9.31
BHP @ rpm		135 @ 5800
Torque lbs-ft @ rpm		123 @ 3600
Carburetion		2 Solex 40 PHH
Fuel Requirement		Premium
Transmission	Manual	4-Speed
	Automatic	ZF 3-Speed
Steering		Worm and Roller
Front Suspension		Independent Lower A-Arms, MacPherson Struts, Coil Springs, Tube Shocks, Anti-Roll Bar
Rear Suspension		Semi-Trailing Arms, Coil Springs, Tube Shocks
Wheelbase (in.)		100.4
Weight (lbs.)	Manual	2630
	Automatic	NA
Wheels		14 x 6J
Tires		14 x 6.95
Brake System		Disc/Drum
	Front	10.8-in. Discs
	Rear	9.8-in. Drums
0–60 mph, sec	Manual	11.3
	Automatic	NA
Maximum Speed mph		115
EPA Estimated mpg		18.7

2800CS

Engine Type		SOHC Inline 6-Cylinder
Displacement cc/ci		2788/170
Compression Ratio		9.01
BHP @ rpm		192 @ 6000
Torque lbs-ft @ rpm		174 @ 3700
Carburetion		2 Solex 35/40 INAT
Fuel Requirement		Premium
Transmission	Manual	4-Speed
	Automatic	ZF 3-Speed
Steering		ZF-Gemmer Worm and Roller, Power Assisted
Front Suspension		MacPherson Struts, Lower A-Arms, Coil Springs, Tube Shocks, Anti-Roll Bar
Rear Suspension		Semi-Trailing Arms, Coil Springs, Tube Shocks, Anti-Roll Bar
Wheelbase (in.)		103.3
Weight (lbs.)	Manual	2990
	Automatic	NA
Wheels		Alloy14 x 6J
Tires		175 HR-14 Radials
Brake System		Front Disc/Rear Drum, Power Assisted
Front		10.7-in. Discs
Rear		9.8-in. Drums
0–60 mph, sec	Manual	9.3
	Automatic	NA
Maximum Speed mph		126
EPA Estimated mpg		19.0

Specifications
3.0CS

Engine Type		SOHC Inline 6-Cylinder
Displacement cc/ci		2985/182
Compression Ratio		8.31
BHP @ rpm		170 @ 5800
Torque lbs-ft @ rpm		185 @ 3500
Carburetion		2-Zenith 35/40
Fuel Requirement		Regular, 91 RON
Transmission	Manual	4-Speed
	Automatic	ZF 3-Speed
Steering		Worm and Roller, Power Assisted
Front Suspension		MacPherson Struts, Lower A-Arms, Coil Springs, Tube Shocks, Anti-Roll Bar
Rear Suspension		Semi-Trailing Arms, Coil Springs, Tube Shocks, Anti-Roll Bar
Wheelbase (in.)		103.3
Weight (lbs.)	Manual	3175
	Automatic	NA
Wheels		Alloy 14 x 6J
Tires		175 HR-14 Radials
Brake System		Front Disc/Rear Drum, Power Assisted
	Front	10.7-in. Discs
	Rear	10.7-in. Discs
0–60 mph, sec	Manual	10.0
	Automatic	NA
Maximum Speed mph		125
EPA Estimated mpg		17.0

This front view of this late-model 1973 BMW 3.0CS is a small-bumper car that features rubber "over-riders" for increased protection.

Replacement Costs for Common Parts
2000C/2000CS/2000CA/2800CS/3.0CS

2000C/2000CS/2000CA

Oil Filter	$5
Fuel Filter	$3
Fuel Pump	$85
Starter (remanufactured)	$120
Alternator (remanufactured)	$120
Clutch	$225
Flex Disc (Guibo)	NLA
Front Bumper	$550
Hood	$250
Left Front Fender (used)	$75
Right Rear Quarter Panel	$185
Rear Bumper	$550
Windshield	NLA
Tail Light Lens	$80
Center Silencer	NLA
Rear Silencer	NLA
Brake Master	NLA
Front Rotor	$30
Front Pads (set)	$35
Front Shocks	$75
Rear Shocks	$60

2800CS

Oil Filter	$7	
Fuel Filter	$3	
Fuel Pump	$85	
Starter (remanufactured)	$120	
Alternator (remanufactured)	$120	
Fan Clutch	$180	
Clutch Kit	$225	
Flex Disc (Guibo)	$55	
Front Bumper	$550	
Hood	$250	
Left Front Fender (used)	$75	(used)
Right Rear Quarter Panel	$185	
Rear Bumper	$550	
Windshield	$230	
Tail Light Lens	$80	
Center Silencer	$100	
Rear Silencer	$100	
EGR Valve	$300	(est.)
Brake Master	$200	
Front Rotor (each)	$60	
Front Pads (set)	$50	
Front Shocks (each)	$75	
Rear Shocks (each)	$60	

3.0CS

Oil Filter			$7	
Fuel Filter			$3	
Fuel Pump			$85	
Starter (remanufactured)			$120	
Alternator (remanufactured)			$120	
Fan Clutch			$180	
Clutch Kit			$250	
Flex Disc (Guibo)			$55	
Front Bumper			$550	
Hood			$250	
Left Front Fender (used)			$75	
Right Rear Quarter Panel			$185	
Rear Bumper			$550	
Windshield			$230	
Tail Light Lens			$80	
Center Silencer			$100	
Rear Silencer			$100	
EGR Valve	New		NLA	
	Used		$300	(est.)
Thermal Reactor	Front	New	$880.50	NLA
		Used	$300	(est.)
	Rear	New	$797.50	NLA
		Used	$300	(est.)
Brake Master			$200	
Front Rotor (each)			$60	
Front Pads (set)			$50	
Front Shocks (each)			$75	
Rear Shocks (each)			$60	

The wood trim in this 1965 BMW 2000CA coupe is in surprisingly good condition. Clean, functional, circular vents in the center of the dash provide fresh air, and the radio appears to be an original unit. Rocker switches control electric windows.

What They Said About the . . .

2000CS

The BMW 2000 packs more luxury, comfort, and over-the-road performance into a taut, sophisticated, beautifully-built package than anything else available within its price range. It takes aim at several well-established Grand Touring cars that don't have nearly as much to offer. —*Car and Driver,* **April 1966**

2800CS

If your neighbor looks aghast at the price tag, put him behind the wheel for 20 minutes on a nice curving road where the steering and suspension play such an important part. And tell him to try the brakes. —*Car Life,* **January 1970**

3.0CS

Soon after the test was completed it developed trouble with carburetion, engine mechanical parts, differential and many interior details, and it would seem that what is basically a great car stands a good chance of being spoiled by poor quality. —*Road & Track,* **July 1973**

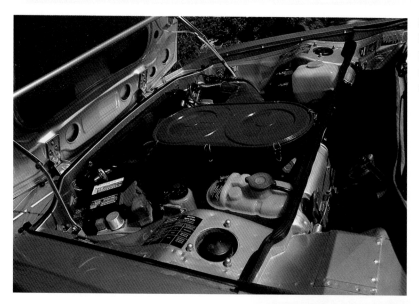

Sound-deadening materials have been removed from the inner fender panels of this 1973 BMW 3.0CS coupe. Be aware that rust can lurk under the sound-deadening material.

The instruments of the 1974 BMW 3.0CS are large and easy to read. This steering wheel is an aftermarket item, and the stowage bin below the radio indicates that this coupe is not air conditioned.

I Bought a . . .

1970 BMW 2800CS

I first saw the 2800CS in a *Road & Track* article in February 1970. I remember thinking, "I'm going to own one of these one day." Little did I know it would take 24 years to happen.

I have rebuilt the Zenith carbs to get through a California smog test, and I like them much better than the 32/36 Webers. I also have had to replace the cylinder head, which had suffered major corrosion.

Some parts can be hard to find, but unless a major restoration is planned, I do not consider these car expensive to own—especially when compared to the new BMWs.

I drive the coupe so infrequently that I have not encountered any persistent problems, but I would say water pumps are a weak item. —*B.T. Fields, Cypress, California*

1973 BMW 3.0CS

My father had a coupe back in 1973 and I have always loved the design, the wood and chrome combinations of the interior, as well as the openness of the coupes. This particular coupe just fell into my lap; I wasn't really looking for one at the time. It was low mileage and had the original Borg Warner automatic transmission in it.

I have done routine mechanical repairs—brakes, replaced the radiator and fan, valve adjustments, and so forth. I also have switched the transmission from the original to a later-style ZF 3HP 22 for better performance and reliability. I took the car apart and had it repainted.

Over the years, I have learned a great deal about this car and the coupes in general. You have to maintain them mechanically and keep them in good running order. They can be expensive in the ways of body and trim parts, but that is a one-time shot. Once you get that taken care of, though, they are just like any other car and really no more expensive to own.

I love this car and drive it every day. —*Merdad Vahid, Los Angeles*

The early coupes, like this 1974 BMW 3.0CS, still turn heads today.

Introduced to the United States in late 1976, the E21-chassis 320i is considered by most to be the logical successor to the 2002. The design of the E21 3-Series was done while Paul Bracq was still at BMW and incorporates several features that also showed up in the 5-Series and 6-Series.

The 320i's body is slightly wider and slightly lower, the wheelbase is increased by 2.5 inches, and the passenger compartment is just over 1.5 inches longer. According to BMW, the body is about 18 percent stiffer than the 2002's, and although the basic structure is lighter, the overall vehicle weight is increased by some 200 pounds, a result of U.S. specification bumpers, emissions equipment, and safety measures. As the E21 evolved during its production run, the majority of this additional weight was pared away through the use of thinner body panels and window glass, reduced noise insulation, and the use of aluminum fuel lines.

Powered by basically the same powerplant that had been in use since the mid 1960s, the 2.0-liter 4-cylinder engine used the more emissions-oriented K-Jetronic Continuous Injection System (CIS), permitting the BMW engineers to tune the engine more precisely and control emissions without having to use a catalytic converter. In place of a converter, BMW employed a combination of air-injection, Exhaust Gas Recirculation (EGR), and, in California, a thermal reactor.

As a result, the 1990-cc engine produced 110 horsepower in 49-state trim and in California, 105 brake horsepower. In 1980, a 1.8-liter engine replaced the 2.0-liter. Emission controls followed the rest of the BMW lineup, using a 3-way catalyst and Lambda sensor to monitor the air-fuel mixture. The air injection, EGR system, and thermal reactors of the earlier cars were gone completely. These changes resulted in a better-running, more fuel-efficient engine that also performed better. A downside to this was a slight reduction in torque, noticeable mostly at the low end.

The passenger compartment of the 320i benefited from improved rear headroom and legroom. The front seats offered variable-angle seatback adjustment, a headrest that can be raised or lowered, and plenty of fore–aft adjustment. Cloth or vinyl fabric was available.

The dashboard features analog-style gauges with white markings on a black background. The center of the dashboard is angled slightly towards the driver, positioning the heating and ventilation controls within easy reach. In cars equipped with the optional air conditioning, the radio is mounted vertically, making it somewhat awkward to operate but necessary to accommodate the air conditioning unit mounted inside the center console.

Options included an AM/FM stereo cassette radio, air conditioning, front fog lights, automatic transmission, a dual-operation (tilt and slide) manually operated sunroof, metallic paints, and light alloy wheels.

A sport package, called the "S" package, offered a front air dam, 5.5-inch special light alloy (cross-spoke BBS) wheels, sports suspension, a larger front anti-roll bar as well as a rear anti-roll bar, limited slip differential, electrically operated outside mirrors, halogen high-beam headlights, a very nice sport steering wheel, and Recaro sport seats. Also included in the "S" package were a leather shift knob, the deluxe toolkit (larger than the standard toolkit), fog lights, and the AM/FM stereo cassette radio. The "S" package was available in four exterior colors: henna red, black, white, and silver. The only interior color available was black in cloth or vinyl.

As far as the first-generation 3-Series goes, its cars are good drivers, and are relatively inexpensive to buy. Overall maintenance costs are not all that high, but buying parts through the dealerships still means you are paying "new car" prices for parts. A positive note is that many of the parts are still available—with the exception of the thermal reactors for cars from 1977 through 1979. The 1977–1979 2-liters offer more power than the 1980–1983 1.8-liter. However, the later cars offer better drivability and improved interior ventilation.

Ratings Chart

E21 3-Series

	320i 1977–1979	320i 1980–1983
Model Comfort/Amenities	**	**½
Reliability	**	**½
Collectibility	½	½
Parts/Service Availability	***	***
Est. Annual Repair Costs	****	***½

A rear view of a 1981 BMW 320i, perhaps the car that coined the phrase "Yuppie." The owner has taken good care of this example, and it shows.

Replacement Costs for Common Parts
320i 1977–1983

320i 1977–1979

Oil Filter				$7	
Fuel Filter				$3	
Fuel Pump				$85	
Starter (remanufactured)				$120	
Alternator (remanufactured)				$120	
Fan Clutch				$180	
Clutch Kit				$250	
Flex Disc (Guibo)				$55	
Front Bumper				$550	
Hood				$250	
Left Front Fender (used)				$75	
Right Rear Quarter Panel				$185	
Rear Bumper				$550	
Windshield				$230	
Tail Light Lens				$80	
Center Silencer				$100	
Rear Silencer				$100	
EGR Valve	New			NLA	
	Used			$300	(est.)
Thermal Reactor	Front	New	$880.50	NLA	
		Used	$300	(est.)	
	Rear	New	$797.50	NLA	
		Used	$300	(est.)	
Brake Master				$200	
Front Rotor (each)				$60	
Front Pads (set)				$50	
Front Shocks (each)				$75	
Rear Shocks (each)				$60	

320i 1980–1983

Oil Filter		$6.90	
Fuel Filter		$24	
Fuel Pump		$114	
Starter		$154,	Exchange
Alternator		$224,	Exchange
Front Bumper		$202	
Hood		$358	
Left Front Fender		$129	
Right Rear Quarter Panel		$348	
Rear Bumper		$236	
Windshield		$162	
Tail Light Housing/Lens		$45.50	
Catalyzer		$827.50	
Exhaust pipe		$261	
Muffler		$142.85	
Brake Master		$305	
Front Rotor (each)		$51.50	
Front Pads (set)		$41.50	
Front Shocks (each)	from 9/79, Boge	$67.50	
	from 9/79, Bilstein	$175	
Rear Shocks		$85	
Clutch Cylinder		$87.50	
Slave Cylinder		$48.25	
Clutch Kit		$186	Guibo
	Manual	$52.75	Guibo
	Automatic	$54.25	
Center Support Bearing		$30.50	

The dual-position sunroof of the 1981 BMW 320i can be opened conventionally, or the rear can be elevated for increased ventilation.

In 1980, the 320i's 2.0-liter engine was replaced by a 1.8-liter (1,766cc/108ci) version of the 4-cylinder engine; the K-Jetronic fuel injection was replaced with the more modern electronic L-Jetronic system; and the air-injection, EGR system, and thermal reactor were replaced with the Bosch 3-way catalyst and Lambda sensor.

Be wary of samples that have been overheated; warped heads and blown head gaskets are fairly common occurrences in vehicles that have been neglected.

Check the engine compartment fuel lines, looking for evidence of leakage. The fuel lines for the K-Jetronic system are an opaque plastic that is known to become brittle over time and may crack in the preformed bends and at the end fittings.

Thermal reactors have proved troublesome, and often cracking sets in. Thermal reactors are very expensive; many have been removed and thrown away over the years. If you live in a state that requires all original emissions equipment to be installed and functioning, used reactors can be purchased for about $400 to $500.

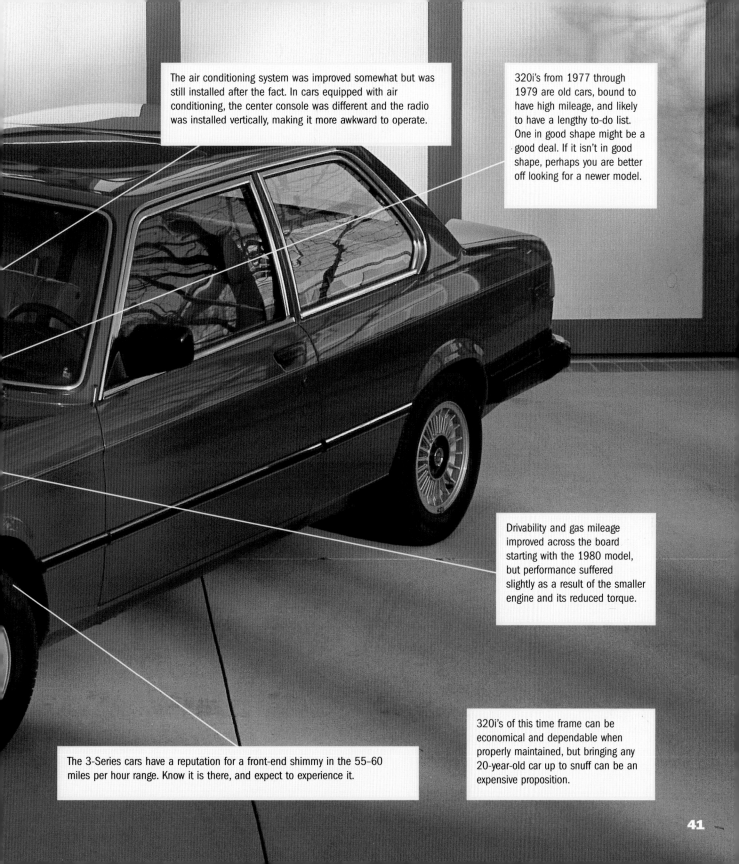

The air conditioning system was improved somewhat but was still installed after the fact. In cars equipped with air conditioning, the center console was different and the radio was installed vertically, making it more awkward to operate.

320i's from 1977 through 1979 are old cars, bound to have high mileage, and likely to have a lengthy to-do list. One in good shape might be a good deal. If it isn't in good shape, perhaps you are better off looking for a newer model.

Drivability and gas mileage improved across the board starting with the 1980 model, but performance suffered slightly as a result of the smaller engine and its reduced torque.

320i's of this time frame can be economical and dependable when properly maintained, but bringing any 20-year-old car up to snuff can be an expensive proposition.

The 3-Series cars have a reputation for a front-end shimmy in the 55–60 miles per hour range. Know it is there, and expect to experience it.

Specifications
320i 1977–1983

320i 1977-1979

Engine Type		SOHC Inline 4-Cylinder
Displacement cc/ci		1990/121
Compression Ratio		8.11
BHP @ rpm		110 @ 5800
Torque lbs-ft @ rpm		112 @ 3750
Injection Type		Bosch K-Jetronic
Fuel Requirement		Regular, 91 RON
Emission Control		Air injection, Exhaust Gas Recirculation
Transmission	Manual	4-Speed
	Automatic	3-Speed
Steering		Rack and Pinion
Front Suspension		MacPherson Struts, Lower Lateral links, Anti-Roll Bar, Coil Springs, Tube Shocks
Rear Suspension		Semi-Trailing Arms, Coil Springs, Tube Shocks, Anti-Roll Bar
Wheelbase (in.)		100.9
Weight (lbs.)		2650
Wheels		Cast Alloy 13 x 5.5J
Tires		185/70HR-13
Brake System		Front Disc/Rear Drum, Vacuum Assisted
	Front	10.0-in. Vented Discs (only in 1977), 10.0-in Solid Discs Solid Discs from 1978 on
	Rear	9.8 x 1.57-in. Drums
0–60 mph, sec		12.0 (*Road & Track*, 12/76)
Maximum Speed mph		104
MPG, City/Highway		21.5

320i 1980–1983

Engine Type		SOHC Inline 4-Cylinder
Displacement cc/ci		1766/108
Compression Ratio		8.81
BHP @ rpm		101 @ 5800
Torque lbs-ft @ rpm		100 @ 4500
Injection Type		Bosch K-Jetronic
Fuel Requirement		Unleaded, 91 RON
Emission Control		3-Way Catalyst, Lambda Sensor
Transmission	Manual	5-Speed
	Automatic	3-Speed
Steering		Rack and Pinion
Front Suspension		MacPherson Struts, Lower Lateral Links, Anti-Roll Bar, Coil Springs, Tube Shocks
Rear Suspension		Semi-Trailing Arms, Coil Springs, Tube Shocks, Anti-Roll Bar
Wheelbase (in.)		100.9
Weight (lbs.)		2435
Wheels		Cast Alloy, 13 x 5.5J
Tires		185/70HR-13
Brake System	Front	Vacuum Assisted Front 10.0-in. Discs
	Rear	9.8 x 1.57-in. Drums
0–60 mph, sec		11.1 (*Road & Track*, February 1980)
Maximum Speed mph		109 (*Road & Track*, February 1980)
EPA Estimated mpg		25.0

What They Said About the . . .

320i 1977-1979

We mourn indications that the bean counters have taken their toll even at BMW, but, on the other hand, the 320i is a genuinely excellent car. It has superb fit, finish and assembly, the quality control is right at the top for a mass-produced vehicle, and the engine is the best four-cylinder you can find. —*Road Test,* **January 1977**

320i/320is 1980-1983

An enthusiast who takes driving seriously will feel very much at home in the BMW 320i. —*Road & Track,* **February 1980**

The instruments of the 1981 BMW 320i are large and easy to read. Air conditioner installation necessitated use of a different center console, repositioning the radio vertically.

The spare tire of this 1981 BMW 320i is located under carpeting. Look for evidence of rust in wheel houses and shock towers.

I Bought a . . .

1978 BMW 320i

I purchased my 320i new in 1978. It had 70 miles on it when I picked it up. Now it has more than 150,000 miles on it. Prior to my purchase, I hadn't paid much attention to BMW until the positive comments of the enthusiast magazines caught my attention. So I drove one and then started plotting how to get the money to buy one.

The clutch hydraulics seem to fail with regularity, even with regular maintenance of the fluid. The last clutch/slave cylinders I purchased were a composite plastic instead of metal, which may last longer. Dash switches—the push button switches for the 4-ways, rear defroster, etc.—fail regularly. The button pops out and won't stay pushed in. Leaking heater control valves are supposed to be an issue, although I've only replaced it once. Front-end shimmy has been an issue with the 320i. There is no fix, although a stiffer aftermarket front suspension will usually minimize it. After all this time, rust is a serious issue for snow-belt cars.

Parts for my 320i are readily available. I've found very few things to be no longer available. Parts like EGR filters and valves are available, but very expensive. The thermal reactor for the early cars is no longer available and impossible to find used. All in all, BMW Mobile Traditions seems to be doing a very good job of keeping parts available. *—Jim Tulk, Long Beach, California*

1983 BMW 320i "S"

The 320i is a fun car to drive, gets great gas mileage—33 miles per gallon—and has been a good car for us. About the only things we don't like about the car is the famous (or infamous) 320i shimmy and the car's lack of power, especially when compared to the 1979 2-liter 320i that we owned previously. However, we have noticed that the 1983 is quieter inside than the 1979.

The most common part that we have had to replace is the emergency flasher push button. It seems to fail frequently—the push button sticks in the "On" position, and you won't notice it until your car won't start, because the battery has been drained.

The air conditioning on the cars is better than nothing, but in both our 320i's it failed frequently enough that we gave up on fixing them and have just gone without.

Would we buy another one? Yes, no question. The 320i is so easy to work on and so much fun to drive that if anything ever happened to ours, we would not hesitate to buy another one. *—Bridgette and Hani Thomas, Long Beach, California*

This is what the engine compartment should look like—all of the original panels and equipment are still in place in this a 1981 BMW 320i. The green knob on the battery terminal is aftermarket battery quick-disconnect.

Introduced to the United States in late 1983, the E30 3-Series BMW was a new chassis with improved suspension, improved brakes, and improved heating, ventilation, and air conditioning (HVAC) systems. At introduction, the revised 3-Series also had a new name badge on the rear deck lid—318i—more correctly reflecting the 1.8-liter (M10 engine family) carried over from the first-generation 3-Series.

The 1.8-liter engine used Bosch L-Jetronic electronic fuel injection and employed the latest version of Bosch's 3-way catalyst and Lambda sensor, greatly improving drivability and fuel economy in the process.

As the new 3-Series evolved through its production run, a 6-cylinder (initially the 2.7-liter M20/2.7 "eta" engine and later the M20/2.5-liter) was added as well as a 4-door sedan, a convertible, an all-wheel drive version, and the 2.3-liter, twin cam 4-valve M3.

Even though the 318i 4-cylinder cars bear the same designation, we will treat them separately because they are powered by different engines: the M10 4-cylinder in the 1984–1985 318i and the M42 in the 1991–1992 318i/is/iC. Likewise, we will separate the 325e/es from the 325i/is/iC/iX cars, as they too were equipped with different engines (the M20/2.7 "eta" engine in the 325e/es and the M20/2.5 in the 325i/is/iC/iX).

The 1984 318i was available with either a 5-speed manual or a 3-speed automatic transmission. The 325 variants were available with either the 5-speed manual or the ZF 4HP 22 4-speed automatic. The 1987–1991 M3s and the 1991–1992 318i/is cars were available only with a 5-speed manual transmission.

BMW included an onboard computer (OBC) to monitor and display the date, time, outside temperature, average speed, average mpg, and an onboard theft-prevention system. The early 318i and 325e were fitted with a version that had fewer functions. The second-iteration 318i/is/iC were fitted with a similar, basic OBC. BMW also introduced its Service Interval system (SI) to keep track of driving patterns and inform the driver when oil changes and services are due. Overhead, above the rearview mirror, BMW's "active check panel" monitors the function of various exterior lights and vital fluids, warning the driver of an unsafe condition by illuminating a warning light in the overhead panel.

An additional feature in the revised dashboards and electronics in the 318i and 325 is a fuel-consumption gauge in the lower portion of the tachometer, providing the driver with useful information regarding steady-state fuel mileage.

The second-generation 3-Series is readily available in a variety of models to choose from. You can have two doors or four doors, the basic 318i, the 325 "eta" powered cars, the sporty 325i/is, a convertible 318iC or 325iC, an all-wheel drive 325iX, or the homologation special M3.

The 1984–1985 318i, powered by the lowly 1.8-liter 4-cylinder, is considered underpowered and is usually a very basic car. The 1991–1992 318i/is/iC models offer better performance and a higher fun-to-drive quotient. Watch out for the faulty profile gasket problem. Check maintenance records before purchase for evidence of last replacement.

The 2.7-liter "eta" motor powers the 325e/es. It offers smooth running and plenty of low-end torque, but it runs out of revs quickly. There are plenty to choose from, but check maintenance records for cam belt replacement, which should be done at 40,000–60,000 mile intervals. If it snaps, expect bent or broken valves and an expensive engine rebuild.

The 325i/is/iC/iX models offer the higher-performing 2.5-liter M20 6-cylinder. Fun cars, plenty to choose from, decent performance and amenities. Check maintenance records for record of cam belt change. The electrically operated convertible top needs to be adjusted frequently. The all-wheel-drive iX has many specific-to-the-model parts and tends to be more expensive to repair.

The M3 is a limited production, homologation special—a 2.3-liter, twin-cam 16-valve rocket ship. It is very collectible, and approximately 5,300 were imported. Everything costs more to repair. Many have been driven hard, so check maintenance records closely and look for evidence of abuse. Have these cars checked closely by an expert and if all checks out, buy it.

Ratings Chart

E30 3-Series

	318i 1984–1985	318i/is/iC 1991–1992
Model Comfort/Amenities	**	***
Reliability	**	**
Collectibility	½	***½
Parts/Service Availability	***½	***½
Est. Annual Repair Costs	***½	****

	325e/es 1984–1987	325i/is 1987–1991	325iC 1984–1987
Model Comfort/Amenities	***½	***½	***
Reliability	***	***	***
Collectibility	*	***	***½
Parts/Service Availability	***½	***½2	***½
Est. Annual Repair Costs	***½	***½	***½

	325iX 1987–1991	M3
Model Comfort/Amenities	***½	***
Reliability	***	***
Collectibility	***½	****½
Parts/Service Availability	***½	***½
Est. Annual Repair Costs	****	****

The cosmoline has been completely removed from this 1991 BMW 318i's engine. Check the plastic radiator tanks closely for evidence of leaking. Check to make sure the brake fluid reservoir is clean. This can indicate whether a system has received regular maintenance.

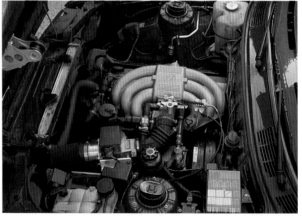

The subtle differences of the 1989 325iX BMW include a master cylinder that is farther forward and a repositioned coil and windshield washer reservoir (right rear of engine compartment). Note, too, the shock tower differences. The cone-style air cleaner is owner-installed.

Replacement Costs for Common Parts

318i 1984–1985, 325e/es 1984–1987

318i 1984–1985

Oil Filter		$6.90
Fuel Filter		$21.75
Fuel Pumps	In-Tank	$145
	External	$190
Starter		$154, Exchange
Alternator		$224, Exchange
Front Bumper		$285
Hood		$367
Left Front Fender		$185
R-R Quarter Panel	up to 2/83	$349
	from 2/83	$322
Rear Bumper		$232
Windshield		$177
Tail Light Housing/Lens		$119
Catalyzer Front Pipe		$817.50, Exchange
	from 12/84	$865
Rear Pipe/Muffler		$212
Oxygen Sensor	1984	$45
	1985	$133.35
Brake Master		$239
Front Rotor (each)		$39.50
Front Pads		$62.95
Front Shocks (each)	Boge	$77.50
	Sport, Boge	$164
	M-Technik to 3/85	$175
	M-Technik from 3/85	$125
Rear Shocks (each)	Boge Gas	$78
	Sport, Boge	$78
	M-Technik to 9/85	$58.50
Clutch Cylinder		$129.50
Slave Cylinder		$48.25
Clutch Kit		$186
Guibo		$54.25
Ctr Support Bearing		$46.50

325e/es 1984–1987

Oil Filter		$5.20
Fuel Filter		$21.75
Fuel Pumps		$233
Starter	to 12/86	$149, Exchange
	from 12/86 to 9/87	$156, Exchange
Alternator	to 11/85	$224, Exchange
	from 11/85 to 1/86	$230, Exchange
	from 1/86	$277, Exchange
Front Bumper		$285
Hood		$367
Left Front Fender		$185
Right Rear Quarter Panel		
	2-door to 9/87	$322
	2-door from 9/87	$428
	4-door to 9/87	$300
	4-door from 9/87	$284
Rear Bumper		$232
Windshield		$243
Tail Light Housing/Lens		
	to 9/87	$119
	from 9/87	$101
Header/Catalyzer	Manual Trans to 9/87	$962.50
	Manual Trans 9/87	$1,060
	Auto Trans to 9/87	$1,040
	Auto Trans from 9/87	$1,060
Rear Pipe/Muffler	to 9/87	$225
	from 9/87	$249
Oxygen Sensor		$138
Brake Master	w/o ABS	$239
	w/ABS to 5/87	$305
	w/ABS from 5/87	$239
Front Rotor (each)		$63.75
Front Pads		$62.95
Front Shocks (each)	to 9/86, Boge	$164
Sport Suspension	fr 9/87, Boge	$175
	M-Technik to 3/85, Bilstein	$152
	M-Technik from 3/85, Bilstein	$125
	325 from 9/88 on, Boge	$164
Rear Shocks (each)	to 9/87	$78
Sport Suspension	to 9/87, Boge	$78
	from 9/87, Boge	$98.25
	M-Technik to 3/85, Bilstein	$52.50
	from 3/85, Boge Gas	$78
Clutch Cylinder		$129.50
Slave Cylinder		$48.25
Clutch Kit	to 5/86	$236
	from 5/86	$239
Guibo		$54.25
Center Support Bearing		
	to 9/87	$46.50
	from 9/87	$88.50

With the top down on this 1992 BMW 325iC, the "ultimate tanning machine" beckons. Note where the third brake light is located on the convertibles.

Replacement Costs for Common Parts
325i/is/iC/iX 1987–1992, M3 1987–1991, 318i/iC 1991–1992

325i/is/iC/iX 1987–1992

Oil Filter		$5.20
Fuel Filter		$21.75
Fuel Pumps		$233
Starter		$156, Exchange
Alternator		$277, Exchange
Front Bumper	to 6/88	$285
	from 6/88	$163
Hood		$367
Left Front Fender		$185
	325iC	$301
Right Rear Quarter Panel		
	2-door to 9/87	$322
	2-door from 9/87	$428
	4-door to 9/87	$300
	4-door from 9/87	$284
	325iC	$587.50
Rear Bumper	to 6/88	$232
	from 6/88	$240
Windshield		$243
	325iC	$295
Tail Light Housing/Lens		
	to 9/87	$119
	from 9/87	$101
Header/Catalyzer	Manual Trans	$1,060
	Auto Trans	$1,060
Rear Pipe/Muffler	to 9/87	$316
	from 9/87	$257
Oxygen Sensor	to 9/87	$133.35
	from 9/87	$95
Brake Master		$239
Front Rotor (each)		$63.75
Front Pads		$62.95
Front Shocks (each)		$164
Sport Suspension from 9/87, Boge		$175
M-Technik, Bilstein		$125
325i/is	9/88 on, Boge	$164
	325iC	$139
	325iX	$175
Rear Shocks (each) 325i/is to 9/87		$78
Sport Suspension to 9/87, Boge		$78
	from 9/87, Boge	$98.25
	M-Technik	$78
	325iC	$65.50
	325iX	$99
Clutch Cylinder		$129.50
Slave Cylinder		$48.25
Clutch Kit		$239
Guibo		$54.25
Center Support Bearing		
	to 9/87	$46.50
	after 9/87	$88.50

M3 1987–1991

Oil Filter		$6
Fuel Filter		$21.75
Fuel Pumps		$233
Starter		$169, Exchange
Alternator		$299, Exchange
Distributor Cap		$186.51
Distributor Rotor		$92.50
Front Bumper		$171
Hood		$367
Left Front Fender		$341
Right Rear Quarter Panel		$857.50
Rear Bumper		$223
Windshield		$392
Tail Light Lens		$119
Header/Catalyzer		$1,895, Exchange
Rear Pipe/Muffler		$345
Oxygen Sensor		$133.35
Brake Master		$515
Front Rotor (each)		$110
Front Pads		$62.95
Front Shocks (each)		$175
Rear Shocks (each)		$112
Clutch Cylinder		$129.50
Slave Cylinder		$48.25
Clutch Kit		$381
Guibo		$67.75
Center Support Bearing		
	to 9/87	$80
	after 9/87	$88.50

318i/iC 1991–1992

Oil Filter		$6.25
Fuel Filter		$21.75
Fuel Pumps		$233
Starter		$169, Exchange
Alternator	318i (80A)	$310, Exchange
	318iC (90A)	$285, Exchange
Front Bumper		$163
Hood		$367
Left Front Fender		$185
	318iC	$301
Right Rear Quarter Panel		
	2-door	$428
	4-door	$284
	318iC	$587.50
Rear Bumper		$240
Windshield		$243
	318iC	$295
Tail Light Housing/Lens		$101
Exhaust Pipe Catalyst		$1,060, Exchange
Center Silencer		$179
Rear Silencer		$169
Oxygen Sensor		$133.35
Brake Master		$339
Front Rotor (each)		$63.75
Front Pads		$62.95
Front Shocks (each) 318i		$164
	318iC	$139
Rear Shocks (each) 318i		$78
	318iC	$78
	M-Technik	$78
Clutch Cylinder		$129.50
Slave Cylinder		$48.25
Clutch Kit		$186
Guibo		$54.25
Center Support Bearing		$46.50

Specifications
318i 1984–1985, 318i/is/iC 1991–1992

318i 1984–1985

Engine Type		Inline 4, Chain Driven SOHC, 2 Valves per Cylinder (M10 1.8)
Displacement cc/ci		1766/108
Compression Ratio		9.31
BHP @ rpm		101 @ 5800
Torque lbs-ft @ rpm		103 @ 4500
Injection Type		Bosch L-Jetronic
Fuel Requirement		Unleaded 91 RON
Emission Control		3-Way Catalytic Converter, Lambda Oxygen Sensor
Transmission	Manual	Getrag, 5-Speed
	Automatic	ZF 3-Speed
Steering		Rack and Pinion, Vehicle Speed Sensitive Power Assist
Front Suspension		Struts, Coil Springs, Lateral Lower Control Arms, Anti-Roll Bar
Rear Suspension		Semi-Trailing Arms, Coil Springs, Tube Shock Absorbers, Anti-Roll Bar
Wheelbase (in.)		101.2
Weight (lbs.)	Manual	2360
	Automatic	2380
Wheels		14 x 6J Light Alloy
Tires		195/60HR-14
Brake System		Vacuum Assist
	Front	10.2-in. Front Discs
	Rear	9.0 x 1.6-in. Self-Adjusting Drum
0–60 mph, sec	Manual	11.4
	Automatic	NA
Maximum Speed mph		113
MPG, City/Highway	Manual	27/38
	Automatic	27/34

318i/is/iC 1991-1992

Engine Type		Inline 4, Chain Driven DOHC, 4 Valves per Cylinder (M42 1.8)
Displacement cc/ci		1796/110
Compression Ratio		10.01
BHP @ rpm		134 @ 6000
Torque lbs-ft @ rpm		127 @ 4600
Injection Type		Bosch Motronic DME
Fuel Requirement		Unleaded 91 RON
Emission Control		3-Way Catalytic Converter, Lambda Oxygen Sensor
Transmission	Manual	Getrag, 5-Speed
	Automatic	NA
Steering		Rack and Pinion, Vehicle Speed Sensitive Variable Power Assist
Front Suspension		Struts, Coil Springs, Lateral Lower Control Arms, Anti-Roll Bar
Rear Suspension		Semi-Trailing Arms, Coil Springs, Tube Shock Absorbers, Anti-Roll Bar
Wheelbase (in.)		101.2
Weight (lbs.)	Manual	2635
	Automatic	NA
Wheels		14 x 6J Light Alloy
Tires		195/65HR-14
Brake System		Vacuum Assist, Antilock Braking System
Front		10.2-in. Vented Discs
Rear		10.2-in. Discs
0–60 mph, sec	Manual	10.0 (Road & Track 8/90)
	Automatic	NA
Maximum Speed mph		120
MPG, City/Highway	Manual	27/38
	Automatic	27/34

Specifications
325e/es 1984–1987, 325i/is 1987–1991

325e/es 1984–1987

Engine Type		SOHC, Inline 6, Belt Driven (M20/2.7)
Displacement cc/ci		2693/164
Compression Ratio		9.01
BHP @ rpm		121 @ 4250
Torque lbs-ft @ rpm		170 @ 3250
Injection Type		Bosch Motronic DME
Fuel Requirement		Premium Unleaded
Emission Control		3-Way Catalytic Converter, Lambda Oxygen Sensor
Transmission	Manual	Getrag, 5-Speed
	Automatic	ZF 4HP 22 4-Speed
Steering		Rack and Pinion, Vehicle Speed Sensitive Variable Power Assist
Front Suspension		MacPherson Struts, Coil Springs, Lateral Lower Control Arms, Anti-Roll Bar
Rear Suspension		Semi-Trailing Arms, Coil Springs, Tube Shock Absorbers, Anti-Roll Bar
Wheelbase (in.)		101.2
Weight (lbs.)	Manual	2654
	Automatic	2698
Wheels		14 x 6J Light Alloy
Tires		195/60HR-14
Brake System		Vacuum Assist, Antilock Braking System
	Front	10.2-in. Vented Discs
	Rear	10.2-in. Discs
0–60 mph, sec	Manual	11.4
	Automatic	NA
Maximum Speed mph		113
MPG/City/Highway	Manual	27/38
	Automatic	27/34

325i/is/1987–1991

Engine Type		SOHC, Inline 6, Belt Driven (M20/2.5)
Displacement cc/ci		2494/125.2
Compression Ratio		8.81
BHP @ rpm		168 @ 5800
Torque lbs-ft @ rpm		164 @ 4300
Injection Type		Bosch Motronic DME
Fuel Requirement		Premium Unleaded
Emission Control		3-Way Catalytic Converter, Lambda Oxygen Sensor
Transmission	Manual	Getrag, 5-Speed
	Automatic	ZF 4HP 22 4-Speed
Steering		Rack and Pinion, Vehicle Speed Sensitive Variable Power Assist
Front Suspension		MacPherson Struts, Coil Springs, Lateral Lower Control Arms, Anti-Roll Bar
Rear Suspension		Semi-Trailing Arms, Coil Springs, Tube Shock Absorbers, Anti-Roll Bar
Wheelbase (in.)		101.2
Weight (lbs.)	Manual (2dr/4dr)	2813/2811
	Automatic (2dr/4dr)	2895/2895
Wheels		14 x 6J Light Alloy (325i)
		14 x 6.5J Light Alloy (325is)
Tires		195/65VR-14
Brake System		Vacuum Assist, Antilock Braking System
	Front	10.2-in. Vented Discs
	Rear	10.2-in. Discs
0–60 mph, sec	Manual	8.5
	Automatic	10.3
Maximum Speed mph	Manual	130
	Automatic	126
MPG, City/Highway	Manual	18/23
	Automatic	18/23

Specifications
325i/iC 1987–1992, M3 1987–1991

325i/iC 1987–1992

Engine Type		SOHC, Inline 6, Belt Driven (M20/2.5)
Displacement cc/ci		2494/125.2
Compression Ratio		8.81
BHP @ rpm		168 @ 5800
Torque lbs-ft @ rpm		164 @ 4300
Injection Type		Bosch Motronic DME
Fuel Requirement		Premium Unleaded
Emission Control		3-Way Catalytic Converter, Lambda Oxygen Sensor
Transmission	Manual	Getrag, 5-Speed
	Automatic	ZF 4HP 22 4-Speed
Steering		Rack and Pinion, Vehicle Speed Sensitive Variable Power Assist
Front Suspension		MacPherson Struts, Coil Springs, Lateral Lower Control Arms, Anti-Roll Bar
Rear Suspension		Semi-Trailing Arms, Coil Springs, Tube Shock Absorbers, Anti-Roll Bar
Wheelbase (in.)		101.2
Weight (lbs.)	Manual	3015
	Automatic	NA
Wheels		14 x 6J Light Alloy
Tires		195/65VR-14
Brake System		Vacuum Assist, Antilock Braking System
	Front	10.2-in. Vented Discs
	Rear	10.2-in. Discs
0–60 mph, sec	Manual	8.6
	Automatic	10.5
Maximum Speed mph	Manual	130
	Automatic	126
MPG, City/Highway	Manual	18/23
	Automatic	18/23

M3 1987–1991

Engine Type		DOHC, Twin Cam, 4-valve Inline 4-Cylinder S14/2.3
Displacement cc/ci		2302/140
Compression Ratio		10.51
BHP @ rpm		192 @6750
Torque lbs-ft @ rpm		170 # 4750
Injection Type		Bosch Motronic DME
Fuel Requirement		Premium Unleaded
Emission Control		3-Way Catalytic Converter, Lambda Oxygen Sensor
Transmission	Manual	Getrag, 5-Speed
Steering		Rack and Pinion, Vehicle Speed Sensitive Variable Power Assist
Front Suspension		MacPherson Struts, Coil Springs, Lateral Lower Control Arms, Twin Tube Gas-Pressure Shocks, Anti-Roll Bar
Rear Suspension		Semi-Trailing Arms, Coil Springs, Twin-Tube Gas-Pressure Shock Absorbers, Anti-Roll Bar
Wheelbase (in.)		101.2
Weight (lbs.)		2865
Wheels		Cast Alloy 15 x 7.0
Tires		205/55VR 15
Brake System		Vacuum Assist, Antilock Braking System
	Front	11.0-in. Vented Discs
	Rear	11.1-in. Discs
0–60 mph, sec		7.6
Maximum Speed mph		143
MPG, City/Highway		17/29

When looking at an E30, look for evidence of body damage by checking for the presence of the factory-applied VIN stickers. Look for rust in the lower corners of the doors and in the rear valance and trunk areas. Also check the front windshield opening for rust in the lower areas.

The 1984–1985 318i is equipped with rear drum brakes, and its stopping distances will not be as good as those equipped with 4-wheel disc brakes. Still, the brakes should stop smoothly. If you feel pulsation in the pedal, suspect warped front brake rotors.

In cars that see a lot of in-town, stop-and-go driving, watch for clutch chatter. Also listen for noise from the throwout bearing. If you feel a pulsation in the clutch pedal, this may indicate a bearing that is failing. Clutch replacement runs between $700 and $1,200, parts and labor included.

Steering wheel shimmy during braking can be an indication of warped rotors. Also, make sure the amber ABS warning light comes on and doesn't remain lit. Watch for instances in which the bulb has been removed to hide a system malfunction.

Check for leaking steering racks. Leaking seals at the ends of the rack fill the rubber boots with fluid. Replacing a steering rack is expensive—about $1,100, including parts and labor.

A defective crank sensor has plagued the 325e/es. A throwout bearing fails and one of the ball bearings bounces around inside the bell housing. Occasionally, the bearing strikes the flywheel sensor and knocks the pickup off of the flywheel. The car won't start after being shut off, and the flywheel must be replaced.

A common maintenance item in the driveline is the rubber flex-disk coupling in the middle of the drive shaft. Called a "guibo," it absorbs some of the driveline stresses. Expect to spend about $300 to replace it, plus parts and labor. Drive shaft U-joints and the center support bearing are also common failure items.

The M20 6-cylinder engines in the 325e/es and 325i/is/iC/iX use a rubber timing belt that has a life expectancy of 50,000–60,000 miles. It *must* be replaced at these intervals, or it *will* break.

The engine should run smoothly, with no excessive valve noise. An engine that is idling roughly or surging could indicate a clogged or defective idle control valve. It might also indicate a malfunctioning oxygen sensor.

The 1990-1991 318i/is M42 engine uses a profile gasket to seal the head, block, and front timing cover. This gasket has a reputation of failing at 50,000-60,000-mile intervals, which causes a sudden loss of coolant, immediate overheating, and severe engine damage. Ask the seller for records indicating whether the profile gasket has been changed.

CALIFORNIA
2VFB709

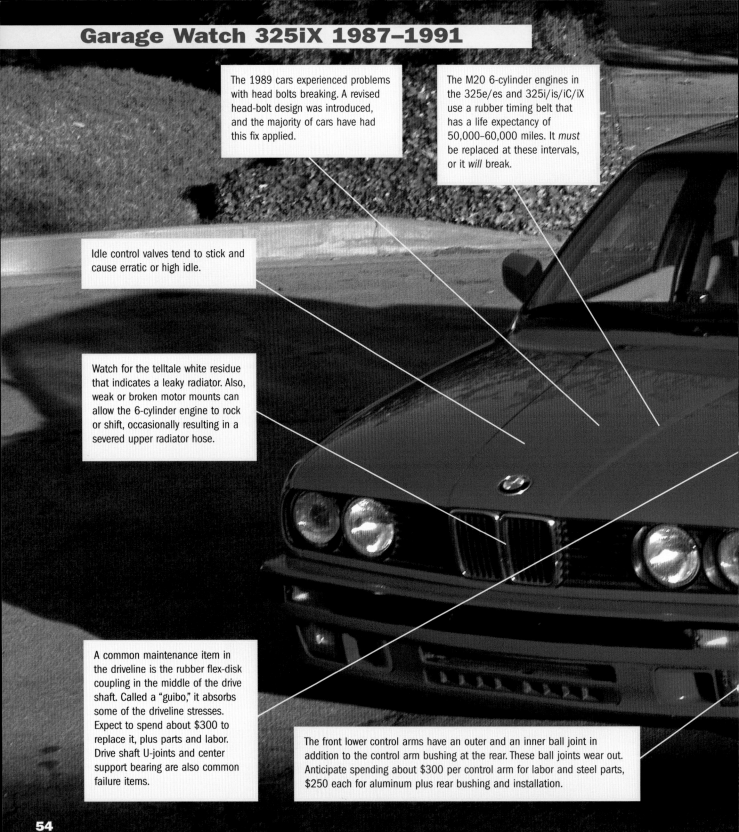

The 1989 cars experienced problems with head bolts breaking. A revised head-bolt design was introduced, and the majority of cars have had this fix applied.

The M20 6-cylinder engines in the 325e/es and 325i/is/iC/iX use a rubber timing belt that has a life expectancy of 50,000–60,000 miles. It *must* be replaced at these intervals, or it *will* break.

Idle control valves tend to stick and cause erratic or high idle.

Watch for the telltale white residue that indicates a leaky radiator. Also, weak or broken motor mounts can allow the 6-cylinder engine to rock or shift, occasionally resulting in a severed upper radiator hose.

A common maintenance item in the driveline is the rubber flex-disk coupling in the middle of the drive shaft. Called a "guibo," it absorbs some of the driveline stresses. Expect to spend about $300 to replace it, plus parts and labor. Drive shaft U-joints and center support bearing are also common failure items.

The front lower control arms have an outer and an inner ball joint in addition to the control arm bushing at the rear. These ball joints wear out. Anticipate spending about $300 per control arm for labor and steel parts, $250 each for aluminum plus rear bushing and installation.

Examine the car closely for rust and accident repairs. Be sure to have the car checked over by a mechanic familiar with these cars to verify that the complex all-wheel drive systems are mechanically sound and in proper working order.

In cars that see a lot of in-town, stop-and-go driving, watch for clutch chatter. Also listen for noise from the throwout bearing. If you feel a pulsation in the clutch pedal, this may indicate a bearing that is failing. Clutch replacement runs between $700 and $1,200, parts and labor included.

Have the suspension and driveline inspected for damage and wear. Outer ball joints generally wear out between 120,000 and 150,000 miles. The splines on the front drive shafts have shown a tendency to strip out and should be inspected at regular intervals.

Check for leaking steering racks. Leaking seals at the ends of the rack fill the rubber boots with fluid. Replacing a steering rack is expensive—about $1,100, including parts and labor.

In mid-1987, BMW replaced the "eta" engine with the M20/2.5. With the 1987 to 1989 model years, BMW did continue to produce a 4-door 3-Series powered by the "eta" engine, simply badged as the 325. The focus was clearly on the new "i" engine available in 2-door (325is), 4-door (325i), or convertible (325iC) form.

A high or erratic idle may indicate a defective idle control valve. Beginning with the 1987 325i, the idle control function was integrated into the Motronic 1.1 control unit.

The 1989 cars experienced problems with head bolts breaking. A revised head-bolt design was introduced, and the majority of cars have had this fix applied.

Ask for records of timing belt replacements. The M20/2.5 "i" engine uses a rubber timing belt that has a life expectancy of 50,000–60,000 miles. It *must* be replaced at these intervals, or it *will* break.

Watch for the telltale white residue that indicates a leaky radiator.

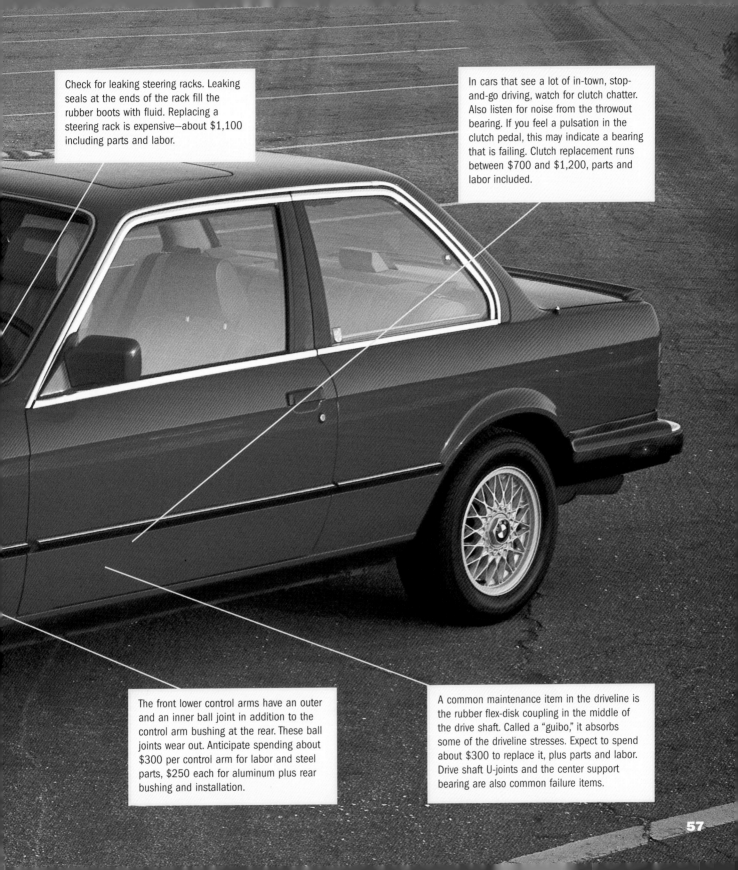

Check for leaking steering racks. Leaking seals at the ends of the rack fill the rubber boots with fluid. Replacing a steering rack is expensive—about $1,100 including parts and labor.

In cars that see a lot of in-town, stop-and-go driving, watch for clutch chatter. Also listen for noise from the throwout bearing. If you feel a pulsation in the clutch pedal, this may indicate a bearing that is failing. Clutch replacement runs between $700 and $1,200, parts and labor included.

The front lower control arms have an outer and an inner ball joint in addition to the control arm bushing at the rear. These ball joints wear out. Anticipate spending about $300 per control arm for labor and steel parts, $250 each for aluminum plus rear bushing and installation.

A common maintenance item in the driveline is the rubber flex-disk coupling in the middle of the drive shaft. Called a "guibo," it absorbs some of the driveline stresses. Expect to spend about $300 to replace it, plus parts and labor. Drive shaft U-joints and the center support bearing are also common failure items.

Look closely for any engine oil leaks. The most common one is at the pressure-relief valve on the oil filter "gooseneck." Also look for signs of leakage from the cam box and where the cylinder head bolts to the block. The rubber alternator bushings fail regularly and allow the alternator to cock sideways.

The M3 was introduced to the United States in 1987 and is powered by a 2.3-liter, twin-cam, 4-valve per cylinder 4-cylinder that produces 192 brake horsepower at 6,750 rpm and 170 lbs-ft of torque at 4,750 rpm.

The M3's water pumps, thermostats, and fan clutches tend to wear out frequently, and the plastic tank radiators are known for leaks. Look for the telltale white residue left by antifreeze.

The intake manifold gaskets deteriorate, resulting in a lumpy idle from vacuum leaks. Listen for valve noise indicating that a valve adjustment is due. The valves in the S14 engine use shims of various thicknesses, and a special tool is needed for adjustments.

The exhaust systems are specific to these cars. The catalytic converter can develop cracks, and OE replacements are expensive—$1,895 or so.

The bushings and mounts in the shift linkage wear out, and these are noted by excessive shifter rattling and buzzing, especially in third gear with the revs above 4,500.

Warped brake rotors are common in cars that see track duty.

The M3 is famous for developing cracks in the front subframe near the motor mounts. Have this area inspected closely. Motor mounts are hydraulic-filled and fail. The vibrations from the S14 can shake loose all sorts of things.

The M3 is not a car for everyone; parts and repairs tend to be more costly than for the other E30 3-Series. However, most BMW enthusiasts will agree the E30 M3 is one of the best-handling, most fun-to-drive cars ever built.

What They Said About the . . .

318i 1984–1985

If we seem to favor the Toyota at this point in the discussion, it's because in terms of absolute hardware, it offers more than the BMW – for significantly less money. *—Motor Trend, BMW 318i versus Toyota Celica GT-S, September 1983*

318is

BMW lovers: This one is worth it. *—Car and Driver, September 1990*

325e/325es

Whether attacking a stretch of sinuous pavement or droning along in lane three of the Santa Ana Freeway, the 325es exhibits impeccable decorum. *—Motor Trend, June 1986*

325i/325is

Inside all previous 3-Series models was always a finer car waiting to get out. With the 325i, it's finally here. *—Automobile Magazine, December 1987*

325iC

Maybe everybody should own a convertible sometime in his life. Maybe this is one to own all through a lifetime. *—Car and Driver, October 1987*

325iX

Of course, no car can defy the laws of physics; but the 315iX is so neutral, smooth, and capable that you can drive it much closer to its limits than you can most other cars. *— Car and Driver, February 1988*

M3

This is what driving is all about. *—Road & Track, February 1988*

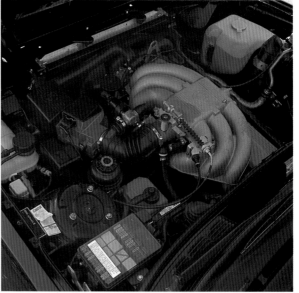

The ABS unit of this BMW 325e is in the forward, left corner of the engine compartment, which identifies it as a 1986 model. There is no sticker indicating when the timing belt was last changed. Always ask the owner for records or receipts.

Another view of the engine compartment. An engine compartment view of this 1992 BMW 325iC reveals a shock tower brace with oil service stickers as well as the independent shop stickers above the headlights that note when services were performed. Good signs, for sure!

I Bought a . . .

1991 BMW 318is

Our 318is is fun to drive, and with its great handling, it is easy to maneuver in tight places.

We had to replace the water pump as well as a few water hoses and the thermostat. The right front ball joint was bad when we bought the car—I replaced the control arm; now the left one has gone out. When we decided to autocross the car, we replaced the shocks with Tokico adjustables and replaced the front swaybar with a larger Suspension Techniques unit. I also replaced the shifter bushings (a chronic attribute). The air conditioning unit needs attention, too.

We don't really consider the 318 expensive to own. Parts are not too difficult to come by. I buy many via mail order, but the BMW dealer can order almost anything if you need it locally.

This a fun, classically cute, and competitive car. *—Shelia and Henry Botkin, Jamul, California*

1985 BMW 325e

I owned my 325e from 1985 to 1999 and put more than 200,000 miles on it. I drove it hard and it was very reliable. I didn't have any major problems with the car until the end, when the car began to give up: the transmission finally gave out, the air conditioning was failing, and the central locking system developed problems. Overall, though, the car was very good to me and I was extremely happy with it. *— Sun and David Hahn, Irvine, California*

1989 BMW 325iX

Our first test run in the snow with our new 325iX was, frankly, disappointing and uneventful. The roads were, in fact, extremely slippery. Traction and braking in the 325iX was truly awesome. From that day on, we have been believers of these cars—weather or not.

Front ball joints on the 325iX seem to need replacing at around 100,000 miles (control arms with inner and outer ball joints are about $170 each.) The weak link on the drivetrain seems to be the splines on the front driveshaft. There are several preventive steps that can be taken to minimize the risk of this happening, including adding shims to the drive shaft and properly lubricating the splines. More specific information is available at http://home.earthlink.net/~hainesinutah/iX/.

325iXs have deficiencies, as do all E30s. They are short on torque and rear seat room, and they require timing belt changes every 50,000 miles. But the 325iX makes up for this with style and incredible traction. *—Bev and Gordon Haines, St. George, Utah*

1991 BMW 325iX (2-Door)

We customized this car and made it into one that could be ready for the track in less than one hour but was still useable for weekend road trips. It is wonderful.

Mechanically, we have done all the normal repairs—timing belt/water pump, ignition/tune-up items, oxygen sensor, fuel-pump relay, wheel bearings, and brakes. There were small oil leaks everywhere. We also had to replace the front CV boots earlier than our friends with similar cars, possibly due to my constant use of cleaners and such. The most common repair item for us has been windshields. The original equipment glass is of very poor quality, and it chips and cracks easily.

All normal E30 parts are cheap and readily available. 325iX-specific items are very expensive and almost always special order.

—Julie and Malcolm Morgan, Larkspur, California

The dual exhaust tips on this 1985 BMW 325e are owner-installed. Metallic paints often experience failures of the clear-coat. Note the blisters on the quarter panel, below the window and just behind the door opening.

The 1990 and 1991 models came with an SRS airbag. This 1991 BMW 318i has large instruments that are easy to read and controls that are placed for easy reach. An optional stowage bin replaces the ashtray in this car.

I Bought a . . .

1989 BMW 325i (4-Door)

We purchased this car used, with about 60,000 miles on it. The engine performance, handling, and steering response really sold us on this car.

Parts are easy to find. We have had to replace the fuel pump twice, the air conditioning unit three times, the water pump, the engine management computer, the instrument panel circuit board (we've finally given up), and the lower control arms. We also had a broken head bolt with this car.

Although this car has not been the source of any big surprises, it has been disappointing in regard to the required maintenance.

—Kitty and Peter Birk, Fountain Valley, California

1989 BMW 325is

This is my second E30 325is. I really like the body style, its small size, and the ability to upgrade the suspension. I have found that, with a good local dealer and the availability of parts on the after-market, these cars are surprisingly not that expensive to maintain.

About the only thing I don't like about the car is that it has a timing belt instead of a timing chain. Otherwise, they are great cars, and yes, I would buy another. In fact, I did.

—Randy Waters, El Segundo, California

1988 BMW M3

When searching for an M3, look for a car with a record of maintenance that has been performed by an M3-knowledgeable mechanic. Better to have an unmaintained car than one that was butchered by someone who did not know what he was doing. I spent a lot of effort repairing damage that was caused by previous "hack" mechanics.

Also look for a straight chassis, because that is the hardest thing to fix. Minor cosmetic damage is much easier to take care of. Search for as much new rubber as you can find—hoses, bushings, mounts, and so forth. Regardless of the number of miles, all the original rubber on a 10-to-12-year-old car is going to be shot, so the less of it you have to replace, the better.

From my experience, the S14 engines of the 1988 M3 will need a certain amount of time, effort, and money, regardless of its history. **—Gustave Stroes, Beverly Hills, California**

The front view of this 1986 BMW 325e sedan shows that it is equipped with fog lights and leather interior.

A sport steering wheel replaces the original on this 1986 BMW 325e sedan. The leather interior is in good shape.

The engine is the heart and soul of the BMW M3. This 1988 model features twin cams, four valves per cylinder, 2.3-liters, and 192 brake horsepower at 6,750 rpm. The strut brace is owner-installed, which conceals the heater system pressure-relief below the strut brace in the heater hose at the rear of head.

E36 3-Series
1992-1999
Chapter 6

318i/318is/318iC/318Ti
323i/323is/323iC
325i/325is/325iC
328i/328is/328iC
M3/M3 Lightweight/M3 Cabrio

With the introduction of the third-generation 3-Series, BMW completed the makeover of its product offerings. The E30 3-Series was the last of the upright, boxy-looking cars to come from BMW. Bearing a strong family resemblance to the 5- and 7-Series, the E36 3-Series offered improved aerodynamics, a stronger body structure, a refined interior, and an all-new engine design, the M50, which was a 2.5-liter inline 6-cylinder.

Sitting on a 106.3-inch wheelbase, fully 5 inches more than the E30, the new 325 sedans showed the results of wind-tunnel work with its enclosed headlights and bumpers that were tastefully integrated into the design. The steeply raked windshield and rear glass were bonded to the structure for an even more rigid shell. Flush-fitting side windows and underbody panels were also used to smooth out the airflow over and under the cars. The traditional BMW kidney grills were smaller and neatly incorporated into a hood that hinged at the rear.

Suspension was traditional MacPherson struts in front, while at the rear the familiar semi-trailing arms were a further developed version of the "Z-axle" design first shown in the European-only Z1 sports car.

Through its seven-year production run, the E36 3-Series evolved into a sophisticated and polished road car featuring good handling, satisfying performance, and the largest number of models of the entire BMW line. In 1997, there were nine different models of the E36 3-Series available for sale.

The third-generation E36 3-Series cars are excellent values and will provide drivers with competent handling, outstanding performance, safety, and comfort. They are available in a variety of body styles to fit just about any need buyers have, from the 318Ti 3-door hatchback to the 4-door M3. Some are new enough to be available through BMW's Certified Pre-Owned program. The early cars are getting high in mileage and will show results of deferred maintenance.

The 1992–1995 318s powered by the M42/1.8-liter are subject to profile gasket failure problem, and unexpected and catastrophic loss of engine coolant can lead to overheating and expensive repairs. Routine repair for this costs in the range of $1,000. There is an improved design available, and the 1996 model-year cars as well as the 318s that are powered by the M44/1.8-liter are not subject to profile gasket problems.

Early M50/2.5-liter 6-cylinder water pumps had a high failure rate—the plastic impeller fails and the engine overheats. BMW improved the design, and most have been replaced. Model year 1993 introduced the M50TU VANOS engine with improved performance.

The 325 models were dropped at the end of 1995 and replaced by the 328 models powered by a M52/2.8-liter 6-cylinder. The 323 models in 1998 and 1999 use the same engine as 325 models. The 328 models offer slightly more performance and additional amenities over 323 models; otherwise, they are basically the same cars.

The M3 models were introduced in 1995 to recapture the performance market. Specific to the U.S. model was the S50US/3.0-liter 6-cylinder, better brakes, and better handling. The M3 Lightweight is very collectible—approximately 125 were sold in the United States and had no air conditioning, no sunroof, limited sound deadening, and aluminum panels. They were definitely targeted at racers wanting to build a race car. The S52US/3.2-liter engine was available in 1996 and offered even more power. These were available in 1997–1998 with four doors and in 1998–1999 as convertibles. The early cars had some problems with drivers selecting second gear instead of fourth gear on upshifts, resulting in many cases of engine damage. Later cars seem less prone to this error. Rear subframe mounts are showing a tendency to fatigue and break on cars that have seen hard usage.

Best buy: Convertibles are always a good bet, though generally speaking, convertibles are more expensive because owners need to factor in replacement of the top in long-term maintenance costs. The 318Ti is a great, fun-to-drive hatchback. The M3 4-door with the 5-speed automatic Steptronic transmission is a great all-around sedan that offers comfort, performance, and stealth looks.

Watch for cars that have not been maintained according to schedule. They will have low-cost appeal but could lead to expensive repair bills. Generally speaking, the cars are reliable and had only a couple of problem areas to watch for.

If the grills in the lower right corner of the windshield are packed with loose debris, water can get into the underhood compartment and short out the Digital Motor Electronics (DME) computer. Make sure this area is clean and unobstructed; the engine management computer brain costs about $1,200 to replace.

The 1992–1995 318i/is/iC cars' M42 engine design was known for having a profile gasket failure problem, usually between 40,000 and 60,000 miles. The majority of cars have an improved gasket installed. As this is a routine maintenance item, ask for documentation of when this item was last performed. The 1996–1999 M44 engine design is different and does not experience profile gasket problems.

The heated throttle body experienced problems with debris clogging the flow of coolant, which can cause water vapor to create an icing condition inside the throttle body in cold ambient temperatures, and the throttle plate may not completely close. Most have been replaced with a modified throttle body heater.

Underhood heat dries out the rubber fuel lines, and over time the lines will harden and crack. When pressurized, the fuel lines can leak and allow fuel to spray around the engine compartment. The majority of cars with this defect were updated during routine dealer servicing.

The convertible-top mechanisms had a better design than on the earlier E30 cars. However, damaged or torn convertible tops are expensive to replace and should be factored into the purchase price and routine maintenance costs for the cars.

If you hear a banging noise from the rear of the car when driving over bumps and driveways, suspect that the rear shock mounts need replacing. Using the stronger convertible or M3 shock mounts is a cost-effective solution . The M3 mounts retail for about $35 each.

Substantial improvements in rustproofing were used for the E36 chassis. If rust is noted, check for evidence of crash repairs. Also check for missing VIN stickers, another indication of crash repair.

The thermostat housings and radiator tanks are made of plastic; they become brittle with age and can rupture or break. Look for the telltale white residue in and around both.

Warped or cracked cylinder heads and blown head gaskets are the results of overheating. Remove the engine oil filler cap and look for any evidence of a chocolate-colored milk shake, which is an indication of engine oil and coolant mixing together.

Ignition coils used in the 325s are prone to failure. If not corrected, this can lead to damage to the engine's electronic control module.

Underhood heat dries out the rubber fuel lines, and over time the lines harden and crack. When pressurized, the fuel lines can leak and allow fuel to spray around the engine compartment. This problem was noted, and the majority of cars were updated during routine dealer servicing.

The plastic impellers used in the water pumps tend to come apart unexpectedly. When this occurs, the flow of coolant stops and the engines can overheat in a matter of minutes. Original-equipment replacement water pumps use metal impellers to solve this problem.

If the grills in the lower right corner of the windshield are packed with loose debris, water can get into the underhood compartment and short out the Digital Motor Electronics (DME) computer. Make sure this area is clean and unobstructed; the engine management computer brain costs about $1,200 to replace.

Check for cracking where the rear subframe mounts to the chassis under the rear seats. There have been reports of the mounting points breaking apart and, in extreme cases, pulling completely away from the underpan.

There have been reports of the automatic transmissions locking in fourth gear on later cars. When this happens, a "transmission program" light illuminates in the dashboard display. Recycle the engine (shut down and restart the engine). If the light goes out, you may need to upgrade the transmission EPROM.

The earliest cars suffered from a variety of quality-control problems, primarily with interior trim items. By the time the 2-door coupe was introduced in mid-1992, BMW was addressing these quality problems with improved materials.

Modified cars—in particular the M3 2-door and 4-door—should be inspected closely to determine whether the modifications were made properly and are ones you can live with.

Check for cracking where the rear subframe mounts to the chassis under the rear seats. There have been reports of the mounting points breaking apart and, in extreme cases, pulling completely away from the underpan.

Owing to a combination of driver error and design flaw, some drivers have selected second gear instead of fourth on the upshift from third. The rear wheels spin the engine above the safe operating range and cause valve-to-piston contact. The usual result is bent and broken valves and a huge repair bill.

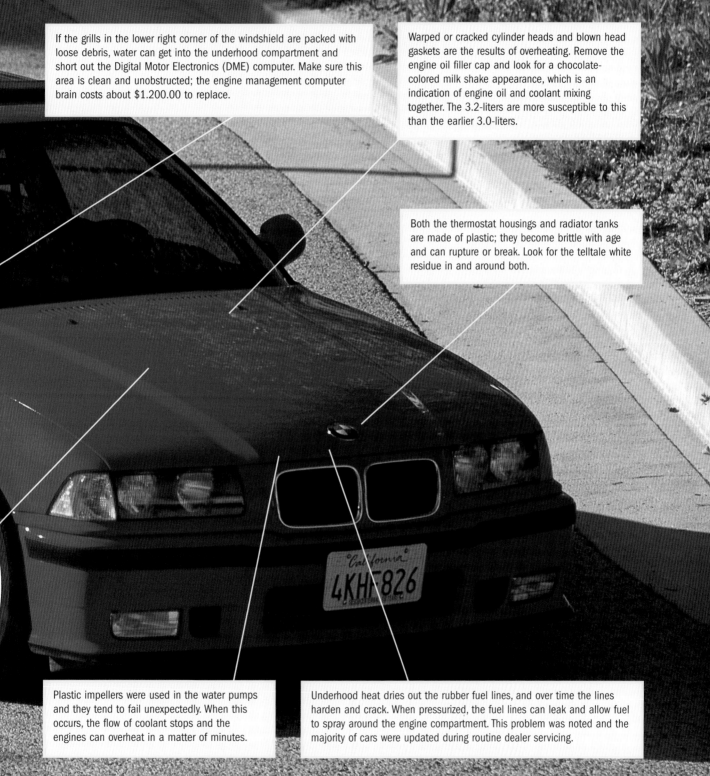

If the grills in the lower right corner of the windshield are packed with loose debris, water can get into the underhood compartment and short out the Digital Motor Electronics (DME) computer. Make sure this area is clean and unobstructed; the engine management computer brain costs about $1.200.00 to replace.

Warped or cracked cylinder heads and blown head gaskets are the results of overheating. Remove the engine oil filler cap and look for a chocolate-colored milk shake appearance, which is an indication of engine oil and coolant mixing together. The 3.2-liters are more susceptible to this than the earlier 3.0-liters.

Both the thermostat housings and radiator tanks are made of plastic; they become brittle with age and can rupture or break. Look for the telltale white residue in and around both.

Plastic impellers were used in the water pumps and they tend to fail unexpectedly. When this occurs, the flow of coolant stops and the engines can overheat in a matter of minutes.

Underhood heat dries out the rubber fuel lines, and over time the lines harden and crack. When pressurized, the fuel lines can leak and allow fuel to spray around the engine compartment. This problem was noted and the majority of cars were updated during routine dealer servicing.

Ratings Chart

E-36 3-Series

	318i/is	318iC	318Ti
Model Comfort/Amenities	***	***	***
Reliability	**	**	**
Collectibility	**	**½	***½
Parts/Service Availability	***½	***½	***½
Est. Annual Repair Costs	***	***	***

	323i/is	323iC	325i/is
Model Comfort/Amenities	***½	***½	***
Reliability	***	***	***
Collectibility	**½	***	**½
Parts/Service Availability	***½	***½	***½
Est. Annual Repair Costs	***	***	***

	325iC	328i/is	328iC
Model Comfort/Amenities	***	***	***
Reliability	***	***	***
Collectibility	***	**½	***
Parts/Service Availability	***½	***½	***½
Est. Annual Repair Costs	***	***	***

	M3 2-door	M3 4-door
Model Comfort/Amenities	***	***
Reliability	***	***
Collectibility	***½	***½
Parts/Service Availability	***½	***½
Est. Annual Repair Costs	***½	***½

	M3 Cabrio	M3 Lightweight
Model Comfort/Amenities	***	**½
Reliability	***	***
Collectibility	***½	****½
Parts/Service Availability	***½	***½
Est. Annual Repair Costs	***½	***½

Specifications
318i/is/iC (M42/1.8) 1992–1995

Engine Type			1.8-Liter DOHC 16-Valve Inline 4-Cylinder
Displacement cc/ci			1796/110
Compression Ratio			10.01
BHP @ rpm			138 @ 6000
Torque lbs-ft @ rpm			129 @ 4500
Engine Management			Bosch ML-Motronic w/Knock Control (2 Sensors)
Fuel Requirement			Unleaded Premium
Emission Control			3-Way Catalytic Converter, Oxygen Sensor, Closed-Loop Mixture Control
Transmission	Manual		Getrag Type C, 5-Speed
	Automatic		THM R1, 4-Speed w/Electronic Control
Steering			Rack and Pinion, Vehicle Speed Sensitive Power Assist
Front Suspension			MacPherson Struts, Arc-Shaped Lower Control Arms, Coil Springs, Twin-Tube Gas-Pressure Shock Absorbers, Anti-Roll Bar (Sport Calibration Optional)
Rear Suspension			Multi-Link System with Central, Links, Coil Springs, Twin-Tube, Gas-Pressure Shock Absorbers, Anti-RollBar, (Sport Calibration Optional)
Wheelbase (in.)			106.3
Weight (lbs.)	Manual	1993/1994	2866 318i/iC 1995 2933/3120
	Automatic	1993/1994	2955
		1995 318i/iC	2933/3208
Wheels	Standard		Steel, 15 x 6.0J
	Optional		Cast Alloy, 15 x 7.0J (Standard on 318is/iC)
Tires	Standard		185/65R-15 88T
	Optional		205/60HR-15 91H (Standard on 318is/iC)
Brake System			Vaccum Assist, ABS Standard
	Front		11.3-in. Vented Discs
	Rear		11.0-in. Solid Discs
0–60 mph, sec	Manual	318i/is 1993–1995	9.9
		318iC	10.6
	Automatic	318i/is 1993	11.4
		318i/is 1994–1995	10.8
		318iC	11.6
Maximum Speed mph	318i/is 1993		128
	318i/is/iC 1994–1995		116 (electronically limited)
MPG, City/Highway	Manual	318i/is 1993–1994	22/30
		318i/is 1995	22/32
		318iC	22/31
	Automatic	318i/is 1993–1994	22/30
		318i/is/iC 1995	21/29

Specifications
318i/is/iC (M44/1.9) 1996-1998

Engine Type			1.9-liter DOHC 16-valve Inline 4-Cylinder
Displacement cc/ci			1895/116
Compression Ratio			10.01
BHP @ rpm			138 @ 6000
Torque lbs-ft @ rpm			133 @ 4300
Engine management			Bosch HFM-Motronic 5.2 w/knock Control
Fuel Requirement			Unleaded Premium
Transmission	Manual		Getrag Type C, 5-Speed
	Automatic		THM R1, 4-Speed
Steering			Rack and Pinion, Vehicle Speed Sensitive Power Assist
Front Suspension			MacPherson Struts, Arc-Shaped, Lower Control Arms, Coil Springs, Twin-Tube Gas-Pressure Shock, Absorbers, Anti-Roll Bar (Sport Calibration Optional on 318i/is.)
Rear Suspension			Multi-Link System with Central Links, Coil springs, Twin-Tube, Gas-Pressure Shock Absorbers, Anti-Roll Bar, (Sport Calibration Optional on 318i/is)
Wheelbase (in.)			106.3
Weight (lbs.)	Manual	318i/iC 1996–1997	2976/3131
		318i Sedan 1998	2954
	Automatic	318i/iC 1996–1997	3064/3219
		318i Sedan 1998	3042
Wheels	Standard		Steel, 15 x 6.0J
	Optional		Cast Alloy, 15 x 7.0J (Standard on 318is/iC), 16 x 7.0J on 1998 318i Sedan
Tires	Standard		185/65R-15 88T
	Optional		205/60HR-15 91H (Standard on 318is/iC), 225/50ZR-16 on 1998 318i Sedan
Brake System			Vaccum Assist, ABS Standard
	Front		11.3-in. Vented Discs Front
	Rear		11.0-in, Solid Discs Rear
0–60 mph, sec	Manual		9.9
		318iC	10.6
	Automatic		10.8
		318iC	11.6
Maximum Speed mph			116 (electronically limited)
MPG, City/Highway	Manual		23/31
		318i Sedan 1998	23/32
	Automatic		22/31

Specifications
318Ti (M42/1.8) 1992-1995

Engine Type		1.8-Liter DOHC 16-Valve Inline 4-Cylinder
Displacement cc/ci		1796/110
Compression Ratio		10.01
BHP @ rpm		138 @ 6000
Torque lbs-ft @ rpm		129 @ 4500
Engine management		Bosch ML-Motronic w/Knock Control (2 Sensors)
Fuel Requirement		Unleaded Premium
Emission Control		3-Way Catalytic Converter, Oxygen Sensor, closed-loop mixure Control (50 states)
Transmission	Manual	Getrag Type C, 5-Speed
	Automatic	THM R1, 4-Speed
Steering		Rack and Pinion, Vehicle Speed Sensitive Power Assist
Front Suspension		Struts, Arc-Shaped Lower Control Arms, Coil Springs, Twin-Tube Gas-Pressure Shock Absorbers, Anti-Roll Bar (Sport Calibration Optional)
Rear Suspension		Semi-Trailing Arms, Coil Springs, Twin-Tube, Gas-Pressure Shock Asorbers, Anti-Roll Bar (Sport Calibration Optional)
Wheelbase (in.)		106.3
Weight (lbs.)	Manual	2734
	Automatic	2822
Wheels	Standard	Steel, 15 x 6.0J
	Optional	Cast Alloy, 15 x 7.0J
Tires	Standard	185/65R-15 88T
	Optional	205/60HR-15 91H
Brake System		Vaccum Assist, ABS Standard
	Front	11.3-in. Discs Front
	Rear	10.7-in, Discs Rear
0–60 mph, sec	Manual	9.3
	Automatic	10.3
Maximum Speed mph		116
MPG, City/Highway	Manual	22/32
	Automatic	21/29

The 1993 BMW 325i contains a refined and smooth-running M50 6-cylinder. Be aware that the plastic radiator tanks become brittle and crack and that the thermostat housing is also plastic. The jump start connector is located in the right side of the engine

Specifications
318Ti (M44/1.9) 1996–1999

Engine Type		1.9-Liter DOHC 16-Valve Inline 4-Cylinder
Displacement cc/ci		1895/116
Compression Ratio		10.01
BHP @ rpm		138 @ 6000
Torque lbs-ft @ rpm		133 @ 4300
Engine management		Bosch Motronic M5.2 w/knock Control (2 Sensors)
Fuel Requirement		Unleaded Premium
Emission Control		3-Way Catalytic Converter, Dual Lambda Oxygen Sensors, Closed-Loop Mixture Control (50 states)
Transmission	Manual	Getrag Type B, 5-Speed
	Automatic	THM R1, 4-Speed, 3 Shift Modes
Steering		Rack and Pinion, Vehicle Speed Sensitive Variable Power Assist
Front Suspension		MacPherson Struts, Arc-Shaped Lower Control Arms, Coil Springs, Twin-Tube Gas-Pressure Shock Absorbers, Anti-Roll Bar Sport Calibration Standard on Ti Sport
Rear Suspension		Semi-Trailing Arms, Coil Springs, Twin-Tube, Gas-Pressure Shock Absorbers, Anti-Roll Bar Sport Calibration Standard on Ti Sport
Wheelbase (in.)		106.3
Weight (lbs.)	Manual	2778
	Automatic	2866
Wheels	Standard	Steel Disc, 15 x 6.0J
	Optional	Cast Alloy, 15 x 7.0J or 16 x 7.0J (Standard on Ti Sport)
Tires	Standard	185/65R-15 88T
	Optional	205/60HR-15-91T or 225/50ZR-16 (Standard on Ti Sport)
Brake System		Vaccum Assist, ABS Standard
	Front	11.3-in. Discs Front
	Rear	10.7-in, Discs Rear
0–60 mph, sec	Manual	9.3
	Ti Sport	8.3
	Automatic	10.3
	Ti Sport	9.6
Maximum Speed mph		116 (electronically limited)
MPG, City/Highway	Manual	23/32
	Automatic	22/31

Black/Hurricane cloth upholstery is lighter than leather. The seats in this 1995 BMW M3 Lightweight are manually adjustable. The carbon-fiber trim pieces above the glovebox and around the center console and ashtray are Lightweight-specific pieces.

Specifications
323i/is/iC 1998–1999

Engine Type			DOHC Inline 6, 4 Valves per Cylinder, Variable Valve Timing
Displacement cc/ci			2494/152
Compression Ratio			10.51
BHP @ rpm			168 @ 5500
Torque lbs-ft @ rpm			181 @ 3950
Engine Management	1998		Siemens MS 41.1 w/Knock Control (2 Sensors)
	1999		Siemens MS 42 w/Knock Control (2 Sensors)
Fuel Requirement			Unleaded Premium
Emissions Control			3-Way Catalytic Converter Dual Lambda Oxygen Sensors, Closed-Loop Mixture Control (50 states)
Transmission	Manual	1998	ZF Type C, 5-Speed
		1999	ZF Type B, 5-Speed
	Automatic		THM R1, 4-Speed, 3 shift modes (E, S, M via switch)
Steering			Rack and Pinion, Engine Speed Sensitive Steering, Variable Power Assist
Front Suspension			Struts, Arc-Shaped Lower Control Arms, Coil Springs, Twin-Tube Gas-Pressure Shock Absorbers, Anti-Roll Bar(Sport Calibration on 323is Coupe.)
Rear Suspension			Multi-Link System with Central Links, Coil Springs, Twin-Tube Gas-Pressure Shock Absorbers,Anti-Roll Bar (Sport Calibration on 323is Coupe)
Wheelbase (in.)			106.3
Weight (lbs.)	is/iC Manual		3075/3296
	is/iC Automatic		3175/3373
Wheels	Standard		Cast Alloy, 15 x 7.0J
	Optional		Cast Alloy, 16 x 7.0J
Tires	Standard		205/60HR-15 91H
	Optional		225/50ZR-16
Brake System			Vacuum Assist, ABS Standard
Front			11.3-in. Vented Discs Front
Rear			11.0-in, Solid Discs Rear (323iC–Vented)
0–60 mph, sec	Manual (iC)		7.1 (7.7)
	Automatic (iC)		8.2 (8.8)
Maximum Speed mph			128 (electronically limited)
MPG, City/Highway	Manual		20/30
	Automatic		19/27

The cone filter and cold-air box in this 1995 BMW M3 Lightweight are owner installed. A front strut upper crossbrace works with an underbody crossbrace to stiffen the front body structure. Installing the braces voids the new-car warranty.

Specifications
325i/is/iC 1993–1995

Engine Type			DOHC Inline 6, 4 Valves per Cylinder, Variable Valve Timing
Displacement cc/ci			2494/152
Compression Ratio			10.51
BHP @ rpm			189 @ 5900
Torque lbs-ft @ rpm			181 @ 4200
Engine Management	1993		Bosch MH-Motronic/DME
	1994–1995		Bosch HFM-Motronic with 2 Knock Sensors
Fuel Requirement			Unleaded Premium
Transmission	Manual		Getrag Type C, 5-Speed
	Automatic		THM R1, 4-Speed w/Electronic Control
Steering			Rack and Pinion, Vehicle Speed Sensitive Power Assist
Front Suspension			MacPherson Struts, Arc-Shaped Lower Control Arms, Coil Springs, Twin-Tube Gas-Pressure Shock Absorbers, Anti-Roll Bar (Sport Calibration Optional on 325i/is)
Rear Suspension			Multi-Link System with Central Links, Coil Springs, Twin-Tube Gas-Pressure Shock Absorbers, Anti-Roll Bar (Sport Calibration Optional on 325i/is)
Wheelbase (in.) (in)			106.3
Weight (lbs.)	Manual	1993 325i/is	2866
		1994 325i/is	3087
		1994 325iC	3351
		1995 325i/is	3086
		1995 325iC	3352
	Automatic	1993 325i/is	2955
		1994 325i/is	3164
		1994 325iC	3428
		1995 325i/is	3164
		1995 325iC	3429
Wheels	Standard		Cast Alloy, 15 x 7.0J
	Optional		Cast Alloy, 16 x 7.0J
Tires	Standard		205/60HR-15 91H
	Optional		225/60R-15 92V (Sports Package)
		1995 325i/is/iC	225/50ZR-16
Brake System			Vacuum Assist, ABS Standard
	Front		11.3-in. Vented Discs Front
	Rear		11.0-in, Solid Discs Rear
0–60 mph, sec	Manual	325i/is 1993–1995	7.8
		325iC 1994–1995	8.3
	Automatic	325i/is 1993	8.8
		325i/is 1994–1995	8.2
		325iC 1995	8.9
Maximum Speed mph			128 (electronically limited)
MPG, City/Highway	Manual	325i/is 1993–1995	19/28
		325iC 1994	19/27
		325iC 1995	19/28
	Automatic	325i/is/iC 1993–1995	20/28

Specifications
328i/is/iC 1996–1999

Engine Type			DOHC Inline 6, 4 Valves per Cylinder, Variable Valve Timing
Displacement cc/ci			2793/170
Compression Ratio			10.21
BHP @ rpm			190 @ 5300
Torque lbs-ft @ rpm			206 @ 3950
Engine Management	328i/is/iC 1996–1998		Siemens MS 41.0 w/Knock Control (2 Sensors)
	328i/is/iC 1999		Siemens MS 42 w/Knock Control (2 Sensors)
Fuel Requirement			Unleaded Premium
Emissions Control			3-Way Catalytic Converter Dual Lambda Oxygen Sensors, Closed-Loop Mixture Control (50 states)
Transmission	Manual		ZF Type C, 5-Speed
	Automatic	328i/is/iC 1996–1998	THM R1, 4-Speed
		328i/is/iC 1999	THM R1, 4-Speed, 3 shift modes (E, S, & M via switch)
Steering			Rack and Pinion, Engine Speed Sensitive Variable Power Assist
Front Suspension			MacPherson Struts, Arc-Shaped Lower Control Arms, Coil Springs, Twin-Tube Gas-Pressure Shock Absorbers, Anti-Roll Bar (sport calibration optional on 328is Coupe.)
Rear Suspension			Multi-Link System with Central Links, Coil Springs, Twin-Tube Gas-Pressure Shock Absorbers, Anti-Roll Bar (sport calibration optional on 328is Coupe)
Wheelbase (in.)			106.3
Weight (lbs.)	Manual	328i/is 1996–1997	3120
		328iC 1996–1997	3362
		328iC 1998–1999	3395
		328i/is 1999	3142
	Automatic	328i/is 1996–1997	3197
		328iC 1996–1997	3439
		328i 1998	3208
		328is 1999	3230
		328iC 1998–1999	3472
Wheels	Standard		Cast Alloy, 15 x 7.0J
	Optional		Cast Alloy, 16 x 7.0J
Tires	Standard		205/60HR-15 91H
	Optional		225/50ZR-16
Brake System			Vacuum Assist, ABS Standard
	Front		11.3-in. Vented Discs
	Rear		11.0-in. Solid Discs
		328iC 1999	11.0-in. Vented Discs
0–60 mph, sec	Manual	328i/is 1996	7.0
		328iC 1996–1997	7.3
		328i/is 1997–1999	6.6
		328iC 1998–1999	6.9
	Automatic	328i/is 1996	7.7
		328iC 1996–1997	8.2
		328i/is 1997–1999	7.2
		328iC 1998–1999	7.5
Maximum Speed mph			128 (electronically limited)
MPG, City/Highway	Manual	328i/is/iC 1996–1999	20/29
	Automatic	328i/is/iC 1996	20/27
		328i/is/iC 1997	19/27
		328i/is/iC 1998	18/26
		328i/is/iC 1999	20/27

Specifications
M3 1995–1999

Engine Type			DOHC 24-Valve Inline 6-Cylinder; VANOS Variable Valve Timing
Displacement cc/ci	1995		2900/182
	1996–1997		3201/195
	1999		3152/192
Compression Ratio			10.51
BHP @ rpm			240 @ 6000
Torque lbs-ft @ rpm	1995		225 @ 4250
	1996		240 @ 4000
	1997–1999		236 @ 3800 (Automatic trans–225 @ 3800)
Injection Type	1995		Bosch HFM Motronic with Knock Control
	1996–1997		Siemens MS 41.0 with Knock Control
	1998		Siemens MS 41.1 with Knock Control
	1999		Siemens MS 41.2 with Knock Control
Fuel Requirement			Unleaded Premium
Emission Control			3-Way Catalytic Converter, Dual Lambda Oxygen Sensors, Closed-Loop Emission Control (50 states)
Transmission	Manual		ZF Type C, 5-Speed
	Automatic	1995	ZF 5HP 18, 5-Speed
		1996	NA
		1997	ZF 5HP 18, 5-Speed
		1998	ZF 5HP 18, 5-Speed, 3 shift modes (E,S & M via switch)
		1999	ZF 5HP 18, 5-Speed (M3 Convertible only)
Steering			Rack and Pinion, Engine Speed Sensitive Variable Power Assist
Front Suspension			MacPherson Struts, Arc-Shaped Lower Arms with Cast-in Lightening Holes, Coil Springs, Twin-Tube Gas Pressure Shocks, Anti-Roll Bar, BMW M-Sports Suspension Calibration
Rear Suspension			Multi-Link with Central Links, Upper and Lower Lateral Links, Coil Springs, Twin-Tube Gas-Pressure Shocks, Anti-Roll Bar, BMW M-Sports Suspension Calibration
Wheelbase (in.)			106.3
Weight (lbs.)	Manual	1995–1999	3175
		1999 Convertible	3494
	Automatic	1995	3241
		1996	NA
		1997–1998	3241
		1999 Convertible	3560
Wheels	Standard	1995	Cast Alloy 17 x 7.5J
		1996–1999	Cast Alloy 17 x 7.5J Front/ 17 x 8.5 Rear
	Optional	1995	Cast or Forged Alloy 17 x 7.5J
		1996–1999	Cast or Forged Alloy 17 x 7.5J f/ 17 x 8.5 r
Tires	Standard	1995	235/40ZR-17
		1996–1999	225/45ZR-17 Front, 245/40ZR-17 Rear
Brake System			Vacuum Assist, Antilock Braking System
	Front		12.4-in. Vented Discs
	Rear		12.3-in. Vented Discs
0–60 mph, sec	Manual	1995	6.1
		1996	5.9
		1997–1998	5.7
		1999 Convertible	5.8
	Automatic	1995	6.9
		1996	NA
		1997–1998	6.4
		1999Convertible	6.6
Maximum Speed mph			137 (electronically limited)
MPG, City/Highway	Manual	1995–1996	19/27
		1997–1998	20/28
		1999	19/26
	Automatic	1995	19/28
		1996	NA
		1997–1998	19/28
		1999 Convertible	17/25

Replacement Costs for Common Parts
318i/is/iC/Ti 1992–1995 (M42/1.8)
318i/is/iC/Ti 1996–1998 (M44/1.9)

318i/is/iC/Ti 1992–1995 (M42/1.8)

Oil Filter		$6.50
Fuel Filter		$21
Fuel Pump(s)		$159
Starter		$166, Exchange
Alternator		$310, Exchange
Clutch		$239
Water Pump		$TBS
Front Bumper		$214
Hood	2-door	$390
	4-door	$436
Left Front Fender	2-door	$267
	4-door	$235
Right Rear Quarter Panel		
	2-door	$377
	4-door	$284
	Convertible	$550
	318Ti	$287
Rear Bumper	2-door	$460
	4-door	$460
	Convertible	$460
	318Ti	$226
Windshield	2-door	$295
	4-door	$304
	Convertible	$295
	318Ti	$304
Tail Light Housing/Lens		
	2-door/4-door/iC	$178
	318Ti	
	Side	$89
	Hatch	$42.50
Rear Muffler	318i/is/iC	$415
	318Ti	$369
Catalytic Converter		$1,050, Exchange
Oxygen Sensor		$133.35
Brake Master	318i/is/iC	$339
	318Ti	$305
Front Rotor (each)	318i/is/iC	$65.75
	318Ti	$47
Front Pads (set)		$65.75
Front Shocks (each)	318i/is/Ti, Boge	$154
	318iC, Boge	$175
	M-Technik i/is/iC/Ti	$218
	Motorsports i/is, Bilstein	$315
Rear Shocks	318i/is, Boge	$66.75
	318Ti	$64
	318iC, Boge M-Technik	$74.25
	318i/is/iC/Ti, Boge	$74.25
	Motorsports i/is, Bilstein	$74.25

318i/is/iC/Ti 1996–1998 (M44/1.9)

Oil Filter		$6.25
Fuel Filter		$21
Fuel Pump(s)		$159
Starter		$166, Exchange
Alternator		$310, Exchange
Clutch		$239
Water Pump		$TBS
Front Bumper		$214
Hood	2-door	$390
	4-door	$436
Left Front Fender	2-door	$267
	4-door	$235
Right Rear Quarter Panel		
	2-door	$377
	4-door	$284
	Convertible	$550
	318Ti	$287
Rear Bumper	2-door	$460
	4-door	$460
	Convertible	$460
	318Ti	$226
Windshield	2-door	$295
	4-door	$304
	Convertible	$295
	318Ti	$304
Tail Light Housing/Lens		
	2-door/4-door/iC	
	318Ti	$178
	Side	$89
	Hatch	$42.50
Header/Catalyst		$825, Exchange
Rear Muffler	318i/is/iC	$415
	318Ti	$369
Oxygen Sensor	Regulating	$133.35
	Monitoring	$62
Brake Master		$307
Front Rotor (each)	318i/is/iC	$65.75
	318Ti	$47
Front Pads (set)		$61.50
Front Shocks (each)	318i/is/Ti, Boge	$154
	318iC, Boge	$175
	M-Technik i/is/iC/Ti	$218
	Motorsports–i/is Bilstein	$315
Rear Shocks	318i/is, Boge	$66.75
	318Ti	$64
	318iC, Boge	$74.25
	M-Technik 318i/is/iC/Ti, Boge	$74.25
	Motorsports–i/is, Bilstein	$74.25

Replacement Costs for Common Parts
323i/is/iC 1998–1999, 325i/is/iC 1992–1995

323i/is/iC 1998-1999

Oil Filter		$8.50
Fuel Filter		$21
Fuel Pump(s)		$117
Starter		$166, Exchange
Alternator (80 amp)		$310, Exchange
Clutch		$239
Water Pump		$TBS
Front Bumper		$214
Hood		$390
Left Front Fender		$267
Right Rear Quarter Panel		$550
Rear Bumper		$460
Windshield		$295
Tail Light Housing/Lens		$184
Header/Catalyst Exchange		$1,275,
Real Pipe/Muffler		$695
Oxygen Sensor	Regulating	$133.35
	Monitoring	$133.35
Brake Master		$305
Front Rotor		$65.75
Front Pads (set)		$61.50
Front Shocks	Standard	$175
	M-Technik	$218
Rear Shocks	Standard	
	323is	$66.75
	323iC	$74.25
	M-Technik	$75.25

325i/is/iC 1992-1995

Oil Filter		$8.50
Fuel Filter		$21.75
Fuel Pump(s)		$117
Starter		$156, Exchange
Alternator	80 amp	$310, Exchange
	140 amp	$378, Exchange
Clutch		$239
Water Pump		$TBS
Front Bumper		$247
Hood	2-door	$390
	4-door	$436
Left Front Fender	2-door	$267
	4-door	$235
Right Rear Quarter Panel		
	2-door	$377
	4-door	$284
	Convertible	$550
Rear Bumper		$460
Windshield	2-door/Convertible	$295
	4-door	$304
Tail Light Housing/Lens		
	2-door/Convertible	$184
	4-door	$178
Header/Catalyst Exchange		$1,150,
Real Pipe/Muffler	to 3/93	$335
	from 3/93	$325
Oxygen Sensor		$133.35
Brake Master		$339
Front Rotor		$65.75
Front Pads (set)		$61.50
Front Shocks	325i/is to 6/92	$198
	325i/is from 6/92	$175
	325iC	$158
	Motorsport–i/is, Bilstein	$218
	M-Technik i/is/iC from 6/92	$218
Rear Shocks Standard	325i/is, Boge	$66.75
	325iC, Boge	$74.25
	M-Technik	$75.25

Flush-fitting glass is apparent in this photo of a 1999 BMW 323is. The trunk lid opens to full-vertical for ease of access.

Replacement Costs for Common Parts
328i/is/iC 1996–1999, M3 1995–1999

328i/is/iC 1996-1999

Oil Filter		$8.50
Fuel Filter		$21.75
Fuel Pump(s)		$117
Starter		$156, Exchange
Alternator	80 amp	$310, Exchange
	140 amp	$378, Exchange
Clutch		$239
Water Pump		$TBS
Front Bumper		$247
Hood	2-door	$390
	4-door	$436
Left Front Fender	2-door	$267
	4-door	$235
Right Rear Quarter Panel		
	2-door	$377
	4-door	$284
	Convertible	$550
Rear Bumper		$460
Windshield	2-door/Convertible	$295
	4-door	$304
Tail Light Housing/Lens		
	2-door/Convertible	$184
	4-door	$178
Header/Catalyst		$965, Exchange
Real Pipe/Muffler		$695
Oxygen Sensor		$133.35
Brake Master		$339
Front Rotor (each)		$65.75
Front Pads (set)		$61.50
Front Shocks	328i/is/iC	$175
	Motorsport–i/is/Ic, Bilstein	$315
	M-Technik i/is/iC	$218
Rear Shocks	Standard	
	328i/is, Boge	$74.25
	328iC, Boge	$74.25
	M-Technik	$75.25

M3 1995-1999

Oil Filter		$8.50
Fuel Filter		$21.75
Fuel Pump(s)		$117
Starter		$156, Exchange
Alternator		$TBS
Clutch		$239
Water Pump		$TBS
Front Bumper		$TBS
Hood	2-door	$390
	4-door	$436
Left Front Fender	2-door	$267
	4-door	$235
Right Rear Quarter Panel		
	2-door	$377
	4-door	$284
	Convertible	$550
Rear Bumper		$TBS
Windshield	2-door/Convertible	$295
	4-door	$304
Tail Light Housing/Lens		
	2-door/Convertible	$184
	4-door	$178
Header/Catalyst		$965, Exchange
Real Pipe/Muffler		$695
Oxygen Sensor		$133.35
Brake Master		$339
Front Rotor		$65.75
Front Pads (set)		$61.50
Front Shocks		$TBS
Rear Shocks		$TBS

A front view of the beautiful 1998 BMW M3 Convertible.

What They Said About the . . .

318i/318is/318iC

If you delight in the subjective pleasures of driving, the 318is will keep a smile on your face. —*Car and Driver,* **August 1992**

318ti

A sporty, affordable hatch for the young and the restless. —*Motor Trend,* **February 1995**

323is/iC

The 323is may enjoy fractionally reduced steering effort on account of its heavier engine (in place of the former 318is' 4-cylinder engine), but it still boasts big brakes, near-perfect weight distribution, and phenomenal rear-wheel drive chassis dynamics. —*Automobile,* **February 1998**

325i/is/iC

It's roomy enough for family-car use and quick enough on its feet to plaster a grin on your face when you go up-tempo on two-lanes. Its twin-cam six emits a lusty cry. And the 325i looks almost as pricey as it is. In short, it has soul. —*Car and Driver,* **September 1991**

325is

The wonderful song of its engine, and the responsiveness of its chassis leave little doubt that the BMW is a driver's car. —*Road & Track,* **August 1992**

325iC

If you're in the market for a four-seat convertible, with impressive handling and powertrain credentials, you just found it. —*Motor Trend,* **September 1993**

328i

The twin-cam six is so sweet and eager, the five-speed so perfectly slick, the chassis so hunkered down and trustworthy, think about it—what if there is no afterlife? This may be as good as it ever gets." —*Car and Driver,* **May 1998**

328is

The 328is continues to reign as the sport driving king of its class. —*Motor Trend,* **May 1998**

328iC

The 328i convertible makes few compromises in real-world usefulness while giving the enthusiastic driver a wonderful tool for the full enjoyment of those hours we all spend behind the wheel. —*Road & Track,* **July 1999**

M3

Its dual personality allows you to drive it as a comfortable, torquey sedan, or to dip into reserves of revs, power and roadholding for a scorching run up the road. —*Road & Track,* **1995**

The M44/1.9-liter engine is a feature of 1996 and newer BMW models, like this 1997 318ti. Profile gasket problems of earlier M42 engines are a thing of the past.

The spare tire for the 1997 BMW 318ti is under the floor, and the security panel can be removed and the seats folded down to offer an amazing amount of room.

I Bought a . . .

1999 BMW 323is

I am very impressed with the overall reliability of this daily driver. It has a very smooth ride and handles exceptionally well. The ASC (anti-skid control) is fantastic.

The clutch pedal was quite heavy to push repeatedly, but this was solved with the replacement of the clutch assembly at 61,000 miles. The car had a new flex disk installed at 29,000 miles, and a week later had the entire driveshaft replaced because it vibrated so much at different rpm. Also, the rear shock tower mount bushings were replaced at 25,000 miles. The air conditioner's fan blower motor has been replaced three times because it squealed at low speeds. The gas gauge float has been replaced a couple of times. I also had the front brake rotors and pads replaced.

Amazingly, the 323is has better lower-end torque, without much loss at the higher rpm, than its comparable M50 325is predecessor. Overall, I think the E36 323is is the best BMW bang for your buck, as it offers a low-maintenance, silky inline six-cylinder performance engine, ASC, cruise control, —*Craig Alviso, Artesia, California*

1995 BMW 318iC

The affordability is what attracted me to the 318i convertible, and the fact that I like driving with the top down.

Beyond regular, scheduled maintenance, I have not had any long-term problems with this car. Getting parts has not been a problem, and there have not been any particular parts that have had to be replaced more often than others.

The 318iC could use more power. I really enjoy owning it, but for the money I think I could have found a more powerful car. —*Donna Jimenez, Los Angeles*

1995 BMW M3

Here are some problems I have experienced with my M3: Due to an early-production irregularity early in the car's life the transmission was replaced because it stuck in gear. The problem has not recurred.

The plastic impeller water pump went at 60,000 miles and was replaced with the later, metal impeller version. The rear shock mounts have been replaced two times. The rear toe bushings have gone out three times.

The original 235/40/17 Michelin MXX3s on 17x7.5 alloys repeatedly cracked their inner sidewalls. The cracking eventually led to several flat tires and one total delamination. Michelin replaced all of the tires at no charge, but the problem persisted until I changed to an aftermarket rim in an 8.5-inch width.

The plastic aerodynamic cowling and splashguards under and behind the front spoiler have broken and detached four times. Eventually, the broken cowling will drop below the car, often taking other plastic parts with it. Some owners remove these plastic parts, but this can cause aerodynamic problems, cooling problems, and even warped brake rotors due to misaligned brake ducts. —*Juan Bruce, Cupertino, California*

1998 M3 Cabrio

We took delivery of this car in Europe and drove it on the Autobahn and in the Alps. We love the styling, handling, steering response, and engine performance. The confidence the car inspires when it is driven quickly over winding mountain roads is just incredible.

The only repairs that have been needed so far have been the fuel gauge sending unit, the lighted shift knob, and a seatbelt flapping problem. —*Kitty and Peter Birk, Fountain Valley, California*

It is important to examine the plastic radiator tanks of the 1998 BMW M3 Convertible for evidence of leaking. Also check the drains at the lower corners of the windshield for debris that is blocking drainage.

E46 3-Series
1999-2001
Chapter 7

323i/323Ci
325i/325Ci/325Xi
328i/328Ci
330i/330Ci/330Xi
M3

Although a completely new design, the fourth-generation E-46 chassis 3-Series is not a dramatic visual change from the third-generation chassis. Displaying the same clean, rounded look, the E46 chassis is more aerodynamic, slightly larger, barely heavier, and offers more interior room than its predecessor.

Following a pattern established with the preceding 3-Series, BMW introduced the four-door models first, selling the new design alongside the soon-to-be-discontinued E36-chassis 3-Series. By 2000, 2-door coupes joined the sedans, followed in 2001 by a convertible as well as all-wheel-drive versions of the sedan and Sports Wagon. Also introduced in 2001 were the much-anticipated M3 coupe and convertibles.

BMW also reengined the 3-Series for the 2001 model year, with revised versions of their inline six, designated the M54, available in 2.5- and 3.0-liter form and featuring dual-VANOS, fully electronic throttles (replacing the electromechanical design of the M52 engines), a new intake manifold, and electronically controlled engine cooling.

The new chassis offers increased structural rigidity, improved impact energy management, and shows the benefits of the ever-expanding use of CAD/CAM design techniques. Increased use of high-strength steel—by weight, more than 50 percent of the body shell—resulted in the new chassis's resistance to torsion (twisting) being almost twice that of the E36 chassis. To guard against corrosion, 85 percent of the E46 body panels are stamped from galvanized steel.

Front suspension is a refined version of the MacPherson strut and arc-shaped lower control arm used in the E36 chassis. Detail improvements include forged aluminum lower control arms and a hydraulic-cushioned bushing for lighter weight and reduced road vibrations. The rear suspension is a refined and lighter-weight version of the multilink design used in the previous 3-Series chassis.

The brake system is a mix of traditional BMW—ventilated discs front and rear—and new technology, incorporating electronic brake proportioning with the ABS system to monitor and adjust brake pressures at each wheel for more balanced braking.

Traction control is a standard feature, and for the E46 it includes a new feature, Motor Speed Regulation (MSR), which helps reduce the possibility of the rear wheels skidding when lifting off the throttle on slippery surfaces. Dynamic Stability Control (DSC) became standard equipment and a special version, DSC-X, is used in the all-wheel drive models. Dynamic Brake Control (DBC) appears in cars built after September 2000.

There have been a couple of recalls on the engine auxiliary cooling fans. Problems with the fan malfunctioning and causing engine overheating as well as reports of the wiring for the fans overheating and causing problems are commonplace. The majority of cars affected have been recalled and repairs have been made.

Other recalls for the E46 cars include the following:

- A retaining clip on the brake booster pushrod that may not have been properly installed. Dealers are inspecting and correcting this during normal services.
- The head protection system (HPS) and side airbags on the early cars experienced some inadvertent deployments; dealers reprogrammed the central computer control module to reduce sensitivity to everyday potholes and bumps.
- Small screws that attach the M3's parking brake cable mounting hardware to the rear brake backing plates are being checked during normal service. Some have been reported to have come out and could become lodged in the parking brake drum.

The fourth-generation 3-Series is a thoroughly competent car offering buyers a variety of body styles and performance capabilities. For those living in snow-belt areas, all-wheel-drive is available, making the 3-Series an even more versatile and useful vehicle. If you want the open-air feeling with seating for four, the convertible will suit your desires. If stunning performance is your preference, the new M3 delivers mind-boggling acceleration, handling, and braking.

Ratings Chart

E46 3-Series

	323i	323Ci	325i
Model Comfort/Amenities	★★★½	★★★½	★★★½
Reliability	★★★	★★★	★★★
Collectibility	★★	★★	★★
Parts/Service Availability	★★★½	★★★½	★★★½
Est. Annual Repair Costs	★★★	★★★	★★★

	325Ci	325Xi	328i
Model Comfort/Amenities	★★★½	★★★½	★★★½
Reliability	★★★	★★★	★★★
Collectibility	★★	★★½	★★
Parts/Service Availability	★★★½	★★★½	★★★½
Est. Annual Repair Costs	★★★	★★★	★★★

	328Ci	330i	330Ci
Model Comfort/Amenities	★★★½	★★★½	★★★½
Reliability	★★★	★★★	★★★
Collectibility	★★	★★	★★
Parts/Service Availability	★★★½	★★★½	★★★½
Est. Annual Repair Costs	★★★	★★★	★★★

	330Xi	M3
Model Comfort/Amenities	★★★½	★★★½
Reliability	★★★	★★★
Collectibility	★★½	★★★★
Parts/Service Availability	★★★½	★★★½
Est. Annual Repair Costs	★★★	★★★½

The Sport Package's 17-inch wheels are attractive and really set off this 2000 BMW 323 Sport Wagon.

The new-generation water-based paints are susceptible to chipping, particularly on the nose sections, where they are subject to more damage.

The dashboard displays for mileage and messages have experienced problems with display pixels "dropping out" (not displaying).

The engine cooling systems need to be properly maintained. Reports of radiator plastic tanks leaking and plastic hose-necks breaking continue. The coolant and heater hoses are subject to extreme underhood heat and should be checked routinely for cracking or leaking.

There have been several reports of the engine thermostats failing, and with the electronically controlled system, this may be a long-term problem area to be watched.

In both the 323i/Ci and 328/Ci models, a 5-speed automatic transmission was optional and featured Adaptive Transmission Control (ATC) that "learns" and adapts its shifting characteristics to how the car is driven. The 2000 models offered a Steptronic version of this transmission, allowing drivers to engage a Manual/Sport (M/S) mode.

Door seals, particularly around the sedan's rear doors, tend to dry out and squeak. Rattles in the dash area and especially in the sunroofs have been difficult to isolate and resolve.

The E46 323i/Ci and 328i/Ci are still relatively new cars, and not many specific problems areas have surfaced yet. Over the long term, additional problem areas may be revealed because of the electronic controls and built-in monitoring systems.

When evaluating an E46 323i/Ci or 328i/Ci, prospective buyers should look for maintenance records indicating that all scheduled services have been done and that any outstanding recalls have been attended to.

The 325/330 was introduced in 2001. The 325-model line replaced the 323-model range. Joining the sedans and coupes in 2001 are convertibles and the Sport Wagon. A new engine, the M54 series, replaced the previous M52TU engines.

The dashboard displays for mileage and messages have experienced problems with display pixels "dropping out" (not displaying).

The new-generation water-based paints are susceptible to chipping, particularly on the nose sections where they are subject to more damage.

The engine cooling systems need to be properly maintained. Reports of radiator plastic tanks leaking and plastic hose-necks breaking continue. The coolant and heater hoses are subject to extreme underhood heat and should be checked routinely for cracking or leaking.

There have been several reports of the engine thermostats failing, and with the electronically controlled system this may be a long-term problem area to be watched.

Door seals, particularly the sedan's rear doors, tend to dry out and squeak. Rattles in the dash area and especially in the sunroofs have been difficult to isolate and resolve.

The 325i/Ci offered an improved Getrag 5-speed manual transmission, while the all-wheel drive 325Xi models used a ZF 5-speed manual. The 330i/Xi and 330Ci offered a ZF 5-speed manual transmission.

The 325i/Ci/Xi and 330i/Ci/Xi models are new cars as of this writing. Not very many specific problems areas have surfaced yet. With the electronic controls and built-in monitoring systems, additional problem areas may be uncovered over the long term.

When evaluating an E46 325i/Ci/Xi or 328i/Ci/Xi, prospective buyers should look for maintenance records indicating that all scheduled services have been done and that any outstanding recalls have been attended to.

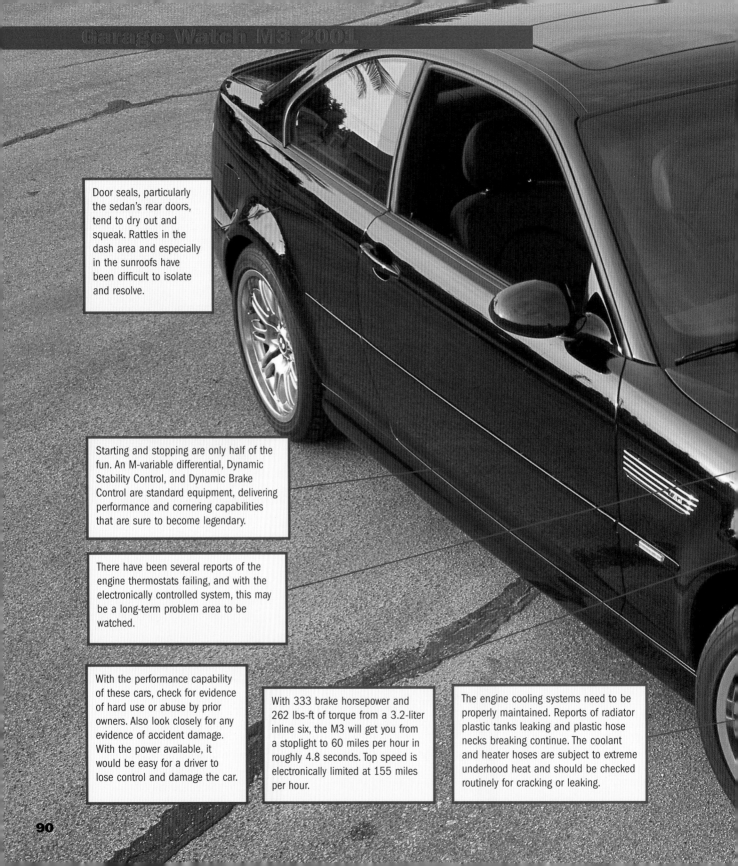

Door seals, particularly the sedan's rear doors, tend to dry out and squeak. Rattles in the dash area and especially in the sunroofs have been difficult to isolate and resolve.

Starting and stopping are only half of the fun. An M-variable differential, Dynamic Stability Control, and Dynamic Brake Control are standard equipment, delivering performance and cornering capabilities that are sure to become legendary.

There have been several reports of the engine thermostats failing, and with the electronically controlled system, this may be a long-term problem area to be watched.

With the performance capability of these cars, check for evidence of hard use or abuse by prior owners. Also look closely for any evidence of accident damage. With the power available, it would be easy for a driver to lose control and damage the car.

With 333 brake horsepower and 262 lbs-ft of torque from a 3.2-liter inline six, the M3 will get you from a stoplight to 60 miles per hour in roughly 4.8 seconds. Top speed is electronically limited at 155 miles per hour.

The engine cooling systems need to be properly maintained. Reports of radiator plastic tanks leaking and plastic hose necks breaking continue. The coolant and heater hoses are subject to extreme underhood heat and should be checked routinely for cracking or leaking.

The dashboard displays for mileage and messages have experienced problems with display pixels "dropping out" (not displaying).

Check for any shifting difficulties in the transmission, clutch, and driveline. Watch for problems with warped brake rotors and possibly damaged or bent wheels.

A 6-speed manual transmission is standard, and in late 2001 a 6-speed Sequential Manual Gearbox (SMG) became an extra cost option.

The new-generation water-based paints are susceptible to chipping, particularly on the nose sections where they are subject to more damage.

Specifications
323i/Ci 2000–2001

Engine Type			DOHC Inline 6, 24-Valve Double; VANOS Steplessly Variable Valve Timing
Displacement cc/ci			2494/152
Compression Ratio			10.51
BHP @ rpm			170 @ 5500
Torque lbs-ft @ rpm			181 @ 3500
Injection Type			Siemens MS 42 with Adaptive Control (2 Sensor)
Fuel Requirement			Unleaded Premium
Emission Control Sensors, Secondary Air Injection,			3-Way Catalytic Converter, Dual Oxygen Closed-Loop Mixture Control (50 states)
Transmission	Manual		Getrag Type B, 5-Speed
	Automatic		GM 5, 5-Speed
Steering Variable Power Assist			Rack and Pinion, Vehicle Speed Sensitive
Front Suspension			Struts, Arc-Shaped Forged-Aluminum Lower Arms with Hydraulic Rear Cushion, Coil Springs, Twin-Tube Gas Pressure Shocks, Anti-Roll Bar, Sport Package and Coupe Models with Sport Suspension Calibration
Rear Suspension			Multi-Link System with Central Links, Upper and Lower Lateral Links (upper link of cast aluminum), Coil Springs, Twin-Tube Gas Pressure Shocks, Anti-Roll Bar, Sport Package and Coupe Models with Sport Suspension Calibration
Wheelbase (in.)			107.3
Weight (lbs.)	Manual		3153
	Automatic		3213
Wheels	Standard	323i 1999	Steel, 15 x 6.5
		323i 2000	Cast Alloy, 15 x 6.5
		323Ci 2000	Cast Alloy, 16 x 7.0 (Sport Package)
	Optional	323i 1999	LBS. (Lightweight Forged Alloy) 15 x 6.5 or Cast Alloy, 16 x 7.0
		323i 2000	Cast Alloy, 16 x 7.0 (Premium Package)
		323Ci 2000	Cast Alloy, 16 x 7.0 (Sport Package)
Tires	Standard	323i 1999	195/65R-15H All-Season
		323i 2000	195/65R-15 91H All-Season
		323Ci 2000	205/55R-15 91H
	Optional	323i 1999	205/55R-16H All-Season, 225/50R-16W
	Performance	323i 2000	205/55R-16 91H (Premium Package)
		323i 2000	225/50R-16 92W (Sport Package)
		323Ci 2000	225/45R-17 91W (Sport Package
Brake System	1999		Antilock Braking System (ABS), All-Season Traction (AST), and Cornering Brake Control (CBC)
	2000		ABS, AST, and Dynamic Stability Control (DSC)
		Front	11.3 x 0.87-inch
		Rear	10.9 x 0.75-in.
0–60 mph, sec	Manual		7.1
	Automatic (2000)		7.7 (8.2)
Maximum Speed mph			128 (electronically limited)
MPG, City/Highway	Manual		20/29
	Automatic (2000)		19/28 (19/27)

Specifications
325i/Ci/Xi 2000–2001

Engine Type			DOHC Inline 6, 24-Valve, Double-VANOS Steplessly Variable Valve Timing
Displacement cc/ci			2494/152
Compression Ratio			10.51
BHP @ rpm			184 @ 6000
Torque lbs-ft @ rpm			175 @ 3500
Injection Type			Siemens MS 43 with Adaptive Control (2 Sensors)
Fuel Requirement			Unleaded Premium
Emission Control			3-Way Catalytic Converter, Dual Oxygen Sensors, Secondary Air Injection, Closed-Loop Mixture Control (50 States)
Transmission	Manual	325i/Wagon/Ci	Getrag Type B, 5-Speed
		325xi Sedan/Wagon	ZF C (All-Wheel Drive)
	Automatic		5-Speed Steptronic with Adaptive Transmission Control and Selectable Sport Mode
		325i/Wagon/Ci	ZF 5 HP 19
		325xi Sedan/Wagon	GM 5, 5-Speed
Steering			Rack and Pinion, Vehicle Speed Sensitive Power Assist
Front Suspension			Arc-Shaped Forged-Aluminum Lower Arms with Hydraulic Cushion, Coil Springs, Twin-Tube Gas Pressure Shocks, Anti-Roll Bar, Sport Package and Coupe Models with Sport Suspension Calibration (not on AWD Sport Packages)
Rear Suspension			Multi-Link System with Central Links, Upper and Lower Lateral Links (Upper Link of Cast Aluminum), Coil Springs, Twin-Tube Gas-Pressure Shocks, Anti-Roll Bar, Sport Package and Coupe Models with Sport Suspension Calibration (not on AWD Sport Packages)
Wheelbase (in.)			107.3
Weight (lbs.)	Manual/Automatic	325i Sedan	3241/3318
		325xi Sedan	3494/3560
		325i Sport Wagon	3384/3428
		325xi Sport Wagon	3627/3693
		325Ci Coupe	3252/3340
		325Ci Convertible	3560/3627
Wheels	Standard		Cast Alloy, 16 x 7.0
	Optional	325i Sedan/Sport Wagon	Cast Alloy, 17 x 8.0 Sport Package
		325xi Sedan/Sport Wagon	Cast Alloy, 17 x 7.0 Sport Package
		325Ci Coupe/Convertible	Cast Alloy, 17 x 8.0 Sport Package
Tires	Standard		205/55R-16 91H All-Season
	Optional		205/50R-17 91H All-Season (Sport Package)
			225/45R-17 91W (Sport Package)
Brake System			Antilock Braking System (ABS), All-Season Traction (AST), and Dynamic Stability Control (DSC)
	Front		11.8-inch. Front
	Rear		11.6-inch. Rear
0–60 mph, sec	Manual/Automatic	325i Sedan	7.1/8.1
		325xi Sedan	7.6/8.8
		325i Sport Wagon	7.4/8.5
		325xi Sport Wagon	7.8/9.0
		325Ci Coupe	7.1/8.1
		325Ci Convertible	7.7/8.9
MPG, City/Highway			128 (electronically limited)
	Manual	325i Sedan	20/29
		325xi Sedan	19/27
		325i Sport Wagon	20/29
		325xi Sport Wagon	19/26
		325Ci Coupe	20/29
		325Ci Convertible	19/27
	Automatic	325i Sedan	19/27
		325xi Sedan	19/26
		325i Sport Wagon	19/27
		325xi Sport Wagon	19/26
		325Ci Coupe	19/27
		325Ci Convertible	19/26

Specifications
328i/Ci 1999–2000

Engine Type			DOHC Inline 6, 24-Valve, Double-VANOS Steplessly Variable Valve Timing
Displacement cc/ci			2793/170
Compression Ratio			10.21
BHP @ rpm			193 @ 5500
Torque lbs-ft @ rpm			206 @ 3500
Injection Type			Siemens MS 42 with Adaptive Control (2 Sensors)
Fuel Requirement			Unleaded Premium
Emission Control Air Injection, Closed-			3-Way Catalytic Converter, Dual Oxygen Sensors, Secondary Loop Mixture Control (50 states)
Transmission	Manual		ZF C, 5-Speed
	Automatic		GM 5, 5-Speed with Adaptive Transmission Control and Selectable Sport Mode or Steptronic
Steering			Rack and Pinion, Vehicle Speed Sensitive Power Assist
Front Suspension			MacPherson Struts, Arc-Shaped Forged-Aluminum Lower Arms with Hydraulic Rear Cushion, Coil Springs, Twin-Tube Gas Pressure Shocks, Anti Roll Bar, Sport Package and Coupe Models with Sport Suspension Calibration
Rear Suspension			Multi-Link System with Central Links, Upper and Lower Lateral Links (Upper Link of Cast Aluminum), Coil Springs, Twin-Tube Gas-Pressure Shocks, Anti-Roll Bar, Sport Package and Coupe Models with Sport Suspension Calibration
Wheelbase (in.)			107.3
Weight (lbs.)	Manual		3197
	Automatic		3256
Wheels	Standard	328i/Ci 1999-2000	Cast Alloy, 16 x 7.0
	Optional	328i 1999	Cast Alloy, 16 x 8.0
		328i 2000	Cast Alloy, 17 x 8.0 (Sport Package)
		328Ci 2000	Cast Alloy, 17 x 7.5 Front (Sport Package) Cast Alloy, 17 x 8.5 Rear (Sport Package)
Tires	Standard	328i/Ci 1999-2000	205/55R-16 91H All-Season
	Optional	328i 1999	225/45R-17W
Performance		328i 2000	225/45R-17 91W (Sport Package)
		328Ci 2000	
	Front		225/45ZR-17 (Sport Package)
	Rear		245/40ZR-17 (Sport Package)
Brake System		1999	Antilock Braking System (ABS), All-Season Traction (AST) and Cornering Brake Control (CBC)
		2000	ABS, AST, and Dynamic Stability Control (DSC)
		Front	11.8 x 0.87-inch
		Rear	11.6 x 0.75-inch
0–60 mph, sec	Manual		6.6
	Automatic		7.2
MPG, City/Highway			128 (electronically limited)
	Manual (2000)		20/29 (21/29)
	Automatic (2000)		19/27 (18/27)

Specifications
330i/Ci/Xi 2000–2001

Engine Type			DOHC Inline 6, 24-Valve, Double-VANOS Steplessly Variable Valve Timing
Displacement cc/ci			2979/182
Compression Ratio			10.21
BHP @ rpm			225 @ 5900
Torque lbs-ft @ rpm			214 @ 3500
Injection Type			Siemens MS 43 with Adaptive Control (2 Sensors)
Fuel Requirement			Unleaded Premium
Emission Control			3-Way Catalytic Converter, Dual Oxygen Sensors, Secondary Air Injection, Closed-Loop Mixture Control (50 states)
Transmission	Manual		ZF Type C, 5-Speed
	Automatic		ZF 5 HP 19
		330ix Sedan	GM 5-Speed, All-Wheel Drive
Steering			Rack and Pinion, Vehicle Speed Sensitive Variable Power Assist
Front Suspension			Struts, Arc-Shaped Forged-Aluminum Lower Arms with Hydraulic Rear Cushion, Coil Springs, Twin-Tube Gas Pressure Shocks, Anti-Roll Bar; Sport Package and Coupe Models with Sport Suspension Calibration
Rear Suspension			Multi-Link System with Central Links, Upper and Lower Lateral Links (Upper Link of Cast Aluminum), Coil Springs, Twin-Tube Gas-Pressure Shocks, Anti-Roll Bar; Sport Package and Coupe Models with Sport Suspension Calibration
Wheelbase (in.)			107.3
Weight (lbs.)	Manual	330i Sedan	3318
		330xi Sedan	3527
		330Ci Coupe	3351
		330Ci Convertible	3627
	Automatic	330i Sedan	3373
		330xi Sedan	3583
		330Ci Coupe	3395
		330Ci Convertible	3704
Wheels	Standard		17 x 7.0 Cast Alloy
	Optional Sports Package		17 x 7.5 Front, 17 x 8.5 Rear
Tires	Standard		205/50R-17 91H All-Season
	Optional Sports Package		225/45ZR-17 Front, 245/40ZR-17 Rear
Brake System			Antilock Braking System (ABS), All-Season Traction (AST), and Dynamic Stability Control (DSC)
	Front		12.8-in. Ventilated Discs
	Rear		12.6-in. Ventilated Discs
0–60 mph, sec	Manual	330i Sedan	6.4
		330xi Sedan	6.9
		330Ci Coupe	6.4
		330Ci Convertible	6.9
	Automatic	330i Sedan	7.0
		330xi Sedan	7.5
		330Ci Coupe	7.0
		330Ci Convertible	7.5
MPG, City/Highway			128 (electronically limited)
	Manual	330i Sedan	21/30
		330xi Sedan	20/27
		330Ci Coupe	21/30
		330Ci Convertible	20/28
	Automatic	330i Sedan	19/27
		330xi Sedan	17/25
		330Ci Coupe	19/27
		330Ci Convertible	18/26

Specifications
M3 2000–2001

Engine Type		DOHC Inline 6, 24-Valve, Double-VANOS Steplessly Variable Valve Timing
Displacement cc/ci		3246/198
Compression Ratio		11.51
BHP @ rpm		333 @ 7900
Torque lbs-ft @ rpm		262 @ 4900
Injection Type		Siemens MS 42 with Adaptive Control (2 Sensors)
Fuel Requirement		Unleaded Premium
Emission Control		3-Way Catalytic Converter, Dual Oxygen Sensors, Secondary Air Injection, Closed Loop Mixture Control (50 states)
Transmission	Manual	6-Speed
	Automatic	NA
Steering		Rack and Pinion, Vehicle Speed Sensitive Variable Power Assist
Front Suspension		MacPherson Struts, Double-Pivot Lower L Arms, Coil Springs, Twin-Tube Gas Pressure Shocks, Anti-Roll Bar
Rear Suspension		Multi-Link System with Central Links, Upper and Lower Lateral Links, Coil Springs, Twin-Tube Gas-Pressure Shocks, Anti-Roll Bar
Wheelbase (in.)		107.5
Weight (lbs.)	Manual	3415
	Automatic	6-speed SMG
Wheels	Front	18 x 8.0 Cast Alloy
	Rear	18 x 9.0 Cast Alloy
Tires	Front	225/45ZR-18
	Rear	255/40ZR-18
Brake System		4-wheel Disc, Vacuum-Assisted, ABS with Dynamic Brake Control
	Front	12.8-in. Vented
	Rear	12.9-in. Vented
0–60 mph, sec	Manual	4.8
	Automatic	NA
		155 (electronically limited)
MPG, City/Highway	Manual	16/24
	Automatic	NA

The 2001 BMW 330Ci features numerous creature comforts, including electrically adjustable seats, dual airbags, side-impact airbags, and a 5-speed Steptronic automatic transmission.

Replacement Costs for Common Parts
323i/Ci 1999–2000, 325i/Ci/Xi 2000–2001

323i/Ci 1999-2000

Oil Filter		$8.50
Fuel Filter		$21
Fuel Pump(s)		$152
Starter		$190 Exchange
Alternator		$384
Clutch		$221
Spark Plugs		$12.80
Front Bumper		$239
Hood	2-door	$378
	4-door	$363
Left Front Fender		$249
Right Rear Quarter Panel		
	2-door	$338
	4-door	$284
	Convertible	$389
Rear Bumper		$339
Windshield		$254
Tail Light Housing/Lens		$127
Header/Catalyst Assembly		$760
Oxygen	Regulating(2 required)	
		$133.35
	Monitoring(2 required)	
		$133.35
	Brake Master w/ DSC	$305
	w/o DSC	$339
Front Rotor (each)		$65.75
Front Pads (set)		$61.50
	+ Sensor	$15.50
Front Shocks	Sports package (each)	$176
	Convertible	$175
Rear Shocks	Sports Package	$85.75
	Convertible	$75.25
	w/ Sports Package	$92.50
	323i 4-door	$69
	w/ Sports Package	$85.75
Rear Shocks (each)		$69–85.75

325i/Ci/Xi/ 2000-2001

Oil Filter		$8.50
Fuel Filter		$52.75
Fuel Pump(s)		$152
Starter		$190, Exchange
Alternator	90 Amp	$307, Exchange
	120 Amp	$384, Exchange
Clutch		$221
Spark Plugs (each)		$12.80
Front Bumper	2-door	$239
	4-door	$226
Hood	2-door	$378
	4-door	$363
Left Front Fender		$249
Right Rear Quarter Panel		
	2-door	$338
	4-door	$284
	Convertible	$389
Rear Bumper		$339
Windshield		$254–327
Tail Light Housing/Lens		$127
Header/Catalyst		$760
Center Silencer		$225
	325Ci	$560
Oxygen Sensor	Regulating (2 required)	
		$133.35
	Sensor Monitoring (2 required)	
		$133.35
Brake Master	325i	$275
	325Ci w/ DSC	$305
	325iX	$305
Front Rotor (each)		$59
Front Pads (set)		$61.50
	+ Sensor	$15.50
Front Shocks (each)		$175–176
Rear Shocks (each)		$69–85.75

Sequential Manual Gearbox (SMG) paddles (– and +) behind the steering wheel of this 2000 BMW M3 give drivers the option of shifting F-1-style. The sound system face swings out for access to cassette tapes.

Replacement Costs for Common Parts
328i/Ci 1999–2000, 330i/Ci/Xi 2000–2001

328i/Ci 1999–2000

Oil Filter		$8.50
Fuel Filter		$21
Fuel Pump(s)		$152
Starter		$190, Exchange
Alternator		$384, Exchange
Clutch		$221
Spark Plugs (each)		$12.80
Front Bumper	2-door	$239
	4-door	$226
Hood	2-door	$378
	4-door	$363
Left Front Fender	2-door	$249
	4-door	$235
Right Rear Quarter Panel		
	2-door	$338
	4-door	$284
Rear Bumper		$339
Windshield		$254–327
Tail Light Housing/Lens		$127
Header/Catalyst/Center Silencer		$384
Oxygen Sensor		
Regulating (2 required)		$133.35
Monitoring (2 required)		$133.35
	w/ DSC	$305
	w/o DSC	$339
Front Rotor (each)		$65.75
Front Pads (set)		$61.50 + Sensor
		$15.50
Front Shocks (each)	Sports Package	$176
	Convertible	$175
Rear Shocks	Sports Package	$85.75
	Convertible	$75.25
	w/ Sports Package	$92.50
	323i 4-door	$69
	w/ Sports Package	$85.75

330i/Ci/Xi 2000–2001

Oil Filter		$8.50
Fuel Filter		$55
Fuel Pump(s)		$152
Starter		$190, Exchange
Alternator	90 Amp	$307, Exchange
	120 Amp	$384, Exchange
Clutch		$344
	330iX	$451
Spark Plugs (each)		$12.80
Front Bumper	2-door	$239
	4-door	$226
Hood	2-door	$378
	4-door	$363
Left Front Fender		$235–$249
Right Rear Quarter Panel		
	2-door	$338
	4-door	$284
	Convertible	$389
Rear Bumper		$339
Windshield		$254–327
Tail Light Housing/Lens		$127
Front Muffler/Catalyst		$249–298
Center Muffler		$225
Rear Muffler		$495–595
Oxygen	Regulating	$133.35
		(2 required)
	Monitoring	$133.35
		(2 required)
Brake Master	330i	$275
	330Ci w/ DSC	$305
	330iX	$305
Front Rotor		$59
Front Pads (set)		$50 + Sensor
		$15.50
Front Shocks (each)		$154–176
Rear Shocks (each)		$69–85.75

Replacement Costs for Common Parts
M3 2000–2001

Oil Filter		$8.50
Air Filter		$15
Fuel Filter		$30
Fuel Pump		$218
Starter		$225, Exchange
Alternator		$387, Exchange
Clutch		$381
Spark Plugs (each)		$24
Front Bumper		$293
Hood		$495
Left Front Fender		$249
Right Rear Quarter Panel		
	2-door	$455
	Cabrio	$394
Rear Bumper		$339
Windshield		$254–327
Tail Light Housing/Lens		$127
Header/Catalyst		$383
Center Silencer		$469
Rear Silencer		$775
Oxygen Sensor		
Regulating (2 required)		$133.35
Monitoring (2 required)		$133.35
Brake Master		$305
Front Rotor (each)		$117
Front Pads (set)		$98.25 + Sensor
		$15.50
Front Shocks		$198
Rear Shocks	Coupe/Cabrio	
	to 9/01	$155
	after 9/01	$159
Alloy Wheels	18 x 8.0	$632
	18 x 9.0	$652
	Painted	
	19 x 8.0	$735
	19 x 9.5	$775

The electronically controlled thermostats of the 2002 BMW 325Ci's M52/2.5-liter six have caused problems, and the auxiliary fans have been subject of multiple recalls.

The 2001 BMW M3's S54/3.2-liter features double-VANOS, drive-by-wire throttle, and six individual throttle butterflies.

Be sure to check a 2000 BMW 323i's records to confirm that auxiliary fan recall repairs have been performed.

What They Said About the . . .

323i Sport Wagon

If you're one of the hip new breed of sport wagon enthusiasts, put this new BMW on your 'must drive' list. *—Motor Trend,* **December 1999**

323Ci

By anyone's account, the 3-Series is a handsome car, and it takes to the convertible treatment like UV rays to George Hamilton. *—Road & Track,* **June 2000**

325i/Ci

Yea, we're earlobe deep in talent here at *C/D,* but this BMW never stops flattering. *—Car and Driver,* **January 2001**

325Xi

At around $35,000 with some necessary options, it's expensive, yes, but you get a superbly finished and finely engineered machine for your money. *—Bimmer Magazine,* **April 2002**

328i/Ci

Before the comparison test, we took the 328i on a 2,000-mile, three-day trip, the sort of journey that uncovers flaws you don't find in casual driving. But none surfaced. *—Car and Driver,* **November 1998**

328i Sport

It may cost a little more, but delivers the most good stuff in one package. There's a reason why the others are wannabes. *—Motor Trend,* **September 2000**

330i/xi/Ci

Now, with more than three decades of building seriously driver-focused sedans and coupes, the E46 (as this chassis type is internally known) represents the 3-Series pinnacle. *—Road & Track,* **January 2001**

M3

I think I may need to get one. *—BMWPower,* **Spring 2001**

Wind tunnel work on the 2002 BMW 325Ci resulted in clean lines, smooth sides, flush windows, and plenty of detail work.

I Bought a . . .

2001 BMW 325i Sedan

Three things attracted me to this car: handling, styling, and safety. The 325i handles superbly and inspires confidence and a feeling of security on the road. The styling is modern with classic lines and projects a trendy yet respectable image.

The steering wheel was misaligned when I took delivery of the car, but this was fixed rather quickly. The keys could not be programmed and had to be taken care of on a subsequent visit. I've heard about the high repair costs, but I have yet to spend a dime.

I like the car so far. We'll see how things go with reliability in the long term, but I am sure that I will be happy as long as it is reliable.

—*Scott S. Uyeunten, Torrance, California*

2001 BMW 330i

We ordered our 330i in the spring of 2000, and it arrived in late summer.

Maintenance is included with my car, but the engine is nearly maintenance-free. No valve adjustments, 7,500-mile oil changes, a timing chain instead of a belt. However, tires can be expensive, especially with the Sports Package and its 17-inch wheels. A new set could easily run between $800 and $1,000.

The transmission is wonderful, but the clutch is annoying. There is no feel of engagement, no resistance under your left foot as you let it out. As a result, launches are often far from smooth and occasionally embarrassing.

There is a feeling you get sitting behind the wheel of a BMW that other manufacturers have not been able to duplicate. It is a feeling of confidence, control, and safety. No matter how many cars I look at and drive, my BMW still feels most natural to me.

—*Michele and Michael Harley, Thousand Oaks, California*

2001 BMW M3

We really love this car. The entire package is nearly perfect, the new engine is awesome, and the 333 horsepower and 8,000-rpm redline are extremely addicting. It feels as if the power will never end! The brakes are awesome and the seats are the best. For a 2-door, the rear seat room and accessibility are very good.

One complaint is that the rear passenger seats don't have grab handles. They need them. We previously owned a 1998 M3 four-door sedan. While the 2001's gas mileage isn't as high, it's no wonder with that addictive redline. Also, the nose does not tuck in as smartly when lifting the throttle in a turn, but the initial turn-in is sharper and more responsive. The 1998 was a great car, but this one is significantly improved in most areas, including a firmer but less harsh ride. —*Lisa and Shannon Yauchzee, Anaheim Hills, California*

2001 330Ci—rear view. The electrically operated top of this 2001 BMW 330Ci is covered up by tight-fitting and nicely finished panels, a nice touch of the smooth-looking 3-series convertibles.

E12 5-Series
1975-1981
Chapter 8

The E12-chassis 530i sedan began arriving in the United States in 1975 and bridged the gap between the New Class sedan and the larger Bavaria/3.0Si sedan. This new design brought with it some good and some bad.

At introduction, the same 2,985-cc engine used in the 3.0Si powered the 530i. Developing 176 brake horsepower at 5,500 rpm and featuring Bosch L-Jetronic fuel injection, the M30/3.0-liter six was equipped with dual thermal reactors and ran on leaded fuel. All of this required running a rich fuel mixture and retarded spark to meet emissions requirements. Unfortunately, terrible throttle response, below-average gas mileage, and lots of underhood heat were side effects of the reactors. Performance was considered to be lacking, especially in those cars equipped with the optional 3-speed automatic transmissions.

BMW adjusted quickly, offering two versions of the 530i in 1976, one to meet California's stricter emissions standards and a 49-state version that offered a different tuning calibration for better throttle response and better gas mileage that rated at 19 miles per gallon versus the California car's 12 to 15 miles per gallon real-world average.

In 1979, BMW made a significant improvement to the 5-Series by adopting the 3-way catalytic converter and Lambda sensor to control emissions and reduced the engine capacity to 2.8 liters. During the 1980 model year, a 5-speed manual transmission was available.

The "big six" engines are robust. It is not unusual to see one go well over 100,000 miles with nothing more than oil changes and tune-ups.

The manual transmissions are fairly sturdy. As the mileage increases, the second-gear syncros tend to go bad, a condition usually noted by balkiness in selecting second gear and an occasional grinding of gears. If it is difficult to change gears, ask when the transmission fluid was last changed. If it was changed recently, some stiffness is to be expected. Usually the fresh gear oil is the culprit, and it will loosen up as the miles increase.

Automatic transmissions have a reputation for being problematic. The ZF transmission is less troublesome than the Borg Warner model. Rust can be a problem, showing up in the lower corners of the doors and fenders and around the front shock towers. Another area to check is at the lower corners of the rear windshield. Also watch for rust in the battery compartment.

Named by *Road & Track* magazine as one of the "Ten Best Cars for a Changing World" (June 1975 and June 1978), there is a lot to like about this mid-sized BMW. Featuring common-sense styling with a low beltline and a tall greenhouse providing excellent visibility, the 5-Series also featured the federally mandated safety bumpers that some felt distracted from an otherwise clean design.

The E12 5-Series was evolved and improved throughout its production run. In 1977, the front received a facelift, the fuel filler was relocated to the right rear quarter panel, and the taillights were enlarged. The ventilation and air conditioning were improved, the sound insulation increased, and the outside rear view mirror relocated from the door to the lower edge of the driver's side window. Alloy wheels became standard, and ventilated front disc brakes were added.

This first-generation 5-Series is a solid performer, an excellent driver, and is relatively inexpensive to buy. Overall maintenance costs are on the high side—buying parts through the dealerships still means you are paying new-car prices for parts. A positive note is that many of the parts are still available, with the exception of the thermal reactors for the 1975 through 1978 cars.

Ratings Chart

E12 5-Series

	530i	528i
Model Comfort/Amenities	★★½	★★½
Reliability	★★	★★½
Collectibility	★	★
Parts/Service Availability	★★	★★
Est. Annual Repair Costs	★★★★	★★★

The colored vacuum lines on this 1977 BMW 530i are for the various emissions equipment. The brake system reservoir is remotely located on the inner fender panel.

The 530i's rich fuel mixture killed the gas mileage, and its retarded spark killed performance. As a result, the 530i was sluggish, returned terrible gas mileage, and had a history of overheating and cracking cylinder heads.

Water pumps usually leak at 25,000-mile intervals and, if not tended to, this can lead to overheating. One the first things to do when purchasing a 530i is to replace the radiator and heater hoses as preventive maintenance.

Thermal reactors crack over time, and many cars have had these removed. If you live in a state that requires original emissions equipment to be installed and functioning, be aware that a new thermal reactor costs approximately $800, two reactors are required, and they are no longer available.

"Banjo" bolts that secure the oil-supply pipe to the top of the head may loosen, and the rocker arms may get oil starved. Check bolts annually. If loose, dry and clean the bolts and heads, apply a light coating of Loctite, and reinstall. Don't overtighten, or you might crush the oil-supply pipe.

Check the fuel lines and fuel injectors whenever the oil level is checked (weekly), looking for any signs of seepage or leakage. Fuel is delivered under about 40 PSI, and if the fuel lines are cracked, they may leak and spray fuel onto the exhaust system.

Fuel tanks can rust through along the horizontal seam and where the gas filler neck connects. Also watch for rust in the front shock towers, at the lower forward corner of the rear wheel well, and in the lower corners of the rear window.

Over time, as the drivetrain is loaded and unloaded (power on, power off), the stresses generated can lead to the rear differential mounting point fatiguing and cracking. Be sure to put the car on a lift and examine this area carefully.

A common maintenance item in the driveline is the rubber flex-disk coupling in the middle of the drive shaft. Called a "guibo," it absorbs some of the driveline stresses. Expect to spend about $300 to replace it, plus parts and labor.

Drive shafts can and do fail. Sometimes it is the center bearing and sometimes it is a universal joint. Available through the aftermarket as rebuilt units, expect to pay in the range of $500–$900 to replace a drive shaft.

The "big-six" engine is known to be an oil consumer; some may use as much as 1 quart per 1,000 miles.

The "big-six" engine is known to be an oil consumer; some may use as much as 1 quart per 1,000 miles.

Although the motoring press liked the 530i and praised its clean styling and silky-smooth 3.0-liter six, with the introduction of the 2.8-liter engine in the 1979 528i, BMW hit the mark.

Check the fuel lines and fuel injectors whenever the oil level is checked (weekly), looking for any signs of seepage or leakage. Fuel is delivered under about 40 PSI, and if the fuel lines are cracked, they may leak and spray fuel onto the exhaust system.

Water pumps usually leak at 25,000-mile intervals and if not tended to, this can lead to overheating. One the first things to do when purchasing a 528i is to replace the radiator and heater hoses as preventive maintenance.

Fuel tanks can rust through along the horizontal seam and where the gas filler neck connects. Also, watch for rust in the front shock towers and at the lower forward corner of the rear wheel well and in the lower corners of the rear window.

A common maintenance item in the driveline is the rubber flex-disk coupling in the middle of the drive shaft. Called a "guibo," it absorbs some of the driveline stresses. Expect to spend about $300 to replace it, plus parts and labor.

Drive shafts can and do fail. Sometimes it is the center bearing and sometimes it is a universal joint. Available through the aftermarket as rebuilt units, expect to pay in the range of $500–$900 to replace a drive shaft.

"Banjo" bolts that secure the oil-supply pipe to the top of the head may loosen, and the rocker arms may get oil starved. Check bolts annually. If loose, dry and clean bolts and heads, apply a light coating of Loctite, and reinstall. Don't overtighten, or you may crush the oil-supply pipe.

Over time, as the drivetrain is loaded and unloaded (power on, power off), the stresses generated can lead to the rear differential mounting point fatiguing and cracking. Be sure to put the car on a lift and examine this area carefully.

Replacement Costs for Common Parts
530i 1975–1978, 528i/is 1979–1981

530i 1975–1978

Oil Filter		$6
Fuel Filter		$18.60
Fuel Pump		
In-Tank		$127.50
External		$190
Starter		$134, Exchange
Alternator		$192
Clutch Kit	Clutch Disk	$105
	Pressure Plate	$117
	Throwout Bearing	$36.25
Water Pump		$71.25
Front Bumper (w/o rubber trim)		
		$347
Hood		$555
Left Front Fender		$221
Right Rear Quarter Panel		
		$374
Rear Bumper (w/o rubber trim)		
		$439
Windshield		$243
Tail Light Housing/Lens Early (small) Style		$90.50
	Later (larger) Style	$138
Front Silencer	from 9/76	$412
Rear Muffler	from 9/76	$316
Thermal Reactor	Front	$882.50 NLA
	Rear	$797.50 NLA
EGR System	Valve	NLA
	Filter	137
Brake Master		$245
Front Rotor (each)	to 2/76	$108
	2/76 to 9/76	$57
	from 9/76	$59
2 Front Pads (set)	up to 9/76	$73.25
	9/76 on	$58.75
Rear Rotor (each)		$49
Rear Pads		$43.50
Front Shocks	to 9/79 (each)	$164
	from 9/79 (each)	$162
Rear Shocks (each)		$142
Gas Tank	to 8/76	$277
	8/76 to 2/78	$297 NLA
	2/78 and up	$238 NLA

528i/is 1979–1981

Oil Filter		$5.20
Fuel Filter		$21.75
Fuel Pump		
	In-Tank	$127.50
	External	$190
Starter		$134, Exchange
Alternator		$169
Clutch Kit	Clutch Disk	$105
	Pressure Plate	$117
	Throwout Bearing	$36.25
Water Pump		$75
Front Bumper (w/o Rubber Trim)		$347
Hood		$555
Left Front Fender		$221
Right Rear Quarter Panel		$374
Rear Bumper (w/o rubber trim)		$439
Windshield		$243
Tail Light Housing/Lens		$138
Front Silencer		$322
Rear Muffler		$258
Oxygen Sensor		$45
Catalytic Converter	to 9/79	$1090
	from 9/79	$907.50
Brake Master		$245
Front Rotor (each)		$59
Front Pads (set)		$58.75
Rear Rotor (each)		$49
Rear Pads		$43.50
Front Shocks (each)		$162
Rear Shocks (each)		$142
Gas Tank		$276

Specifications
530i 1975–1978, 528i 1979–1981

530i 1975–1978

Engine Type		SOHC Inline 6
Displacement cc/ci		2985/182
Compression Ratio		8.11
BHP @ rpm		176@5500
Torque lbs-ft @ rpm		185@4500
Injection Type		Bosch L-Jetronic
Fuel Requirement		Regular, 91 Octane
Emission Control		Thermal Reactor, Air-Injection
Transmission	Manual	4-Speed
	Automatic	3 Speed ZF 3HP20 or Borg Warner 65
Steering		Recirculating Ball, Variable Power Assist
Front Suspension		MacPherson Struts, Lower Lateral Arms, Coil Springs, Tube Shocks, Anti-Roll Bar
Rear Suspension		Tube Shocks, Coil Springs, Semi-Trailing Arms, Anti-Roll Bars
Wheelbase (in.)		103.8
Weight (lbs.)		4340
Wheels		14 x 6 Steel
	Optional	14 x 6 Alloy
Tires		195/70HR Steel Belted Radials
Brake System	Front	10.7-in. Vented Discs to 9/76
		11.0-in. Vented from 9/76
	Rear	10.7-in. Vented Discs
0–60 mph, sec		9.0 (Manual Transmission)
Maximum Speed mph		124 (Automatic 120)
MPG, City/Highway		19.0

528i 1979–1981

Engine Type		SOHC Inline 6
Displacement cc/ci		2788/170.1
Compression Ratio		8.21
BHP @ rpm		169@5500
Torque lbs-ft @ rpm		170@4500
Injection Type		Bosch L-Jetronic
Fuel Requirement		Unleaded, 91 Octane
Emission Control		3-Way Catalytst, Lambda Sensor
Transmission	Manual	5-Speed
	Automatic	3 Speed ZF HP22
Steering		Recirculating Ball, Variable Power Assist
Front Suspension		MacPherson Struts, Lower Lateral Arms, Coil Springs, Tube Shocks, Anti-Roll Bar
Rear Suspension		Semi Trailing Arm, Coil Springs, Tube Shocks, Anti-Roll Bar
Wheelbase (in.)		103.8
Weight (lbs.)		4210
Wheels	Standard	14 x 6 Steel Disk
	Optional	14 x 6 Cast Alloy
Tires		195/70HR Steel Belted Radials
Brake System	Front	11.0-in. Vented Discs
	Rear	10.7-in. Solid Discs
0–60 mph, sec		8.2
Maximum Speed mph		125
MPG, City/Highway		22.0

What They Said About the . . .

530i

The 530i is everything a luxury sports sedan should be. It's comfortable, practical in the extreme and with a good measure of performance, ride and handling thrown in. It's no wonder we had little trouble choosing it as one of the world's ten best cars. —*Road & Track,* **June 1975**

528i

This 528i never ceases to thrill a car connoisseur with the mighty surge of its small but smooth engine and the sheer roadability built into its steering and suspension. —*Car and Driver,* **February 1979**

The steering wheel on this 1981 BMW 528i has been replaced with one from a 320iS. The binnacle at the top center of the dash is the seat belt warning light and oxygen sensor warning light. The analog clock of earlier models has been replaced by a digital display (in center of fan speed switch). This radio is an aftermarket unit.

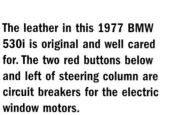

The leather in this 1977 BMW 530i is original and well cared for. The two red buttons below and left of steering column are circuit breakers for the electric window motors.

I Bought a . . .

1977 BMW 530i

The best feature of the car is its balance of performance and comfort. The M30 six-cylinder makes great sounds and is bulletproof. It's great to open all the windows and sunroof and go cruising on a winding road, and I love the big leather seats.

The worse feature of my car is the gas mileage. I knew going in that this car has thermal reactors and that the gas mileage is terrible. It averages 13 to 17 miles per gallon. Also, the car is a little noisy at high-speed cruising (4,000 rpm at 80 miles per hour), although that's not something a 5-speed couldn't solve.

I ended up selling my 530i to a fellow enthusiast who was looking for an exceptional E12. After I sold the car, I had a major bout of seller's remorse. But luckily, I recently solved that with the purchase of a 1980 Polaris Silver 528i. —*Eric Quon, Anaheim Hills, California*

1981 BMW 528i

When I bought this car, I was looking for an inexpensive second car. I wanted a 5-Series, but the E28s were too expensive. I found this car and liked it immediately, especially the body style and lines. The car is not as boxy as the E28 5-series and it looks smaller, even though they are about the same size. I also like the great visibility from the driver's seat. In fact, the car doesn't have any real faults to speak of, and there isn't anything I don't like about it.

I wouldn't really consider the car any more expensive to own than any other. BMW parts can be a bit pricier, but usually they are similar to those for American cars. The fact that this car is older and simpler than its newer counterparts helps to keep part costs down. I find many parts at junkyards, and if I'm not able to find a part through other sources, the dealers can get just about anything I need. —*James Hineline, Romona, California*

The 1981 BMW 528i saw the brake system reservoir colocated with the brake master cylinder. The dual relay is the aluminum rectangle with two plugs at the bottom. Insulation for the wiring harness has deteriorated over time.

E28 5-Series
1982-1989
Chapter 9

524td
528e
533i
535i/535is
M5

Introduced in 1982, the updated 5-Series was met with mixed reviews. The magazines were impressed with the improvements made in the ride and comfort of the new chassis as well as with the technological improvements. However, they were underwhelmed by the cosmetic changes as well as disappointed in the loss of performance delivered by the 2,693-cc "eta" engine.

The improved ride was a result of a complete reengineering of both the front and rear suspensions. Up front, a double-pivot system incorporating a single upper-pivot point and two lower-pivot points allowed engineers to improve directional stability and reduce dive during braking. These improvements also allowed bigger brakes (11.8-inch diameter discs at all four corners) to be fitted. In the rear, the traditional semi-trailing arm remained, but the pivot-axis angle of the arms was reduced from 20 degrees to 13 degrees and raised slightly. Incorporated into the design is a Trac-Link bushing attached to each semi-trailing arm's outboard pivot. This is an elegant and complex method of refining the traditional BMW semi-trailing arm design for improved ride and at the same time further taming the traditional BMW tendency towards trailing-throttle oversteer at the limit.

These improvements were clothed in a slightly smaller body that featured reduced drag and lift. Stability in crosswinds was also improved. The second-generation 5-Series offered improved interior room with a new dash, new design seats front and rear, increased leg and headroom, as well as greatly improved heating, ventilation, and air conditioning (HVAC).

With the introduction of the service interval (SI) indicator system, BMW also introduced owners to a new way of determining when their cars were due for service. In normal operation, the SI lights illuminate when the ignition switch is turned to the "ON" position and then go out as the starter is engaged.

The E28 5-Series offered a 3-speed ZF HP-22 automatic transmission as an option up through the 1986-year model. These transmissions, if properly cared for, will deliver good service and last a long time. Regular fluid changes are a must. In 1987, the ZF 4-speed automatic was offered as an option. The E28 5-Series transmission did have some problems, particularly with regard to the California emissions testing requiring a 2,500-rpm test in neutral. The ZF 4-speed transmissions experienced a series of premature failures directly related to this emission test. Subsequently this requirement was waived for all BMWs fitted with this transmission.

The E28 5-Series may be considered a dated, redundant design by some, but even today it delivers reliable and economical service provided the common maintenance needs of timing belts, thrust rod bushings, brake rotors, and cooling system are taken care of properly. The M30 inline six has been around since the Bavarias of the early 1970s. It is a robust engine that will last well over 100,000 miles when cared for in a reasonable manner. The "big six" is known to be an oil consumer; some may use as much as 1 quart per 1,000 miles.

The E28 5-Series cars are readily available and are relatively inexpensive to buy. Overall maintenance costs are still on the high side—buying parts through the dealerships still means you are paying new-car prices for parts. A positive note is that many of the parts are still available.

The 524td diesel is there if you really must have one, and while not as quick as the 528e, the 524td still managed to register 0-to-60-mph times of under 12 seconds and a top speed of 107 miles per hour. The 528e is a good, basic starter BMW; the 533i offers great performance and typical BMW longevity. The 535i and 535is are nearly the same but with upgraded power and handling. The M5 is the limited-production rocket ship, highly desirable for its performance but costly to maintain and repair.

Ratings Chart

E28 5-Series

	524td	528e	533i
Model Comfort/Amenities	***	***	***
Reliability	**	***	***
Collectibility	*	*	*
Parts/Service Availability	**	***	***
Est. Annual Repair Costs	****	***	***

	535i	535is	M5
Model Comfort/Amenities	***	***	***
Reliability	***	***	***
Collectibility	*	*	****½
Parts/Service Availability	***	***	***
Est. Annual Repair Costs	***	***	***½

Visible in this photo of a 1987 BMW 535is interior are switchable transmission modes, an original radio, and onboard computer (OBC) service interval system (SI) light display that is centered in the instrument cluster, just above the left and right turn signal arrows.

The Motorsports steering wheel of the 1988 BMW M5 differs from the 535is design. Visible in this photo is the M-logo in the tachometer face, the service interval system (SI) indicator lights (center dash), and onboard computer (OBC) The lower dash, center console, and door panels are leather-covered.

The 528e's M20 engine featured the latest in Bosch engine-management systems. Digital Motor Electronics (DME) incorporated a microprocessor that measured several variables (engine speed, temperature, exhaust gases flowing past the Lambda sensor) to constantly adjust the air/fuel mixture and timing to maintain proper emissions figures.

Check the fuel lines and fuel injectors whenever the oil level is checked (weekly), looking for any signs of seepage or leakage. Fuel is delivered under about 40 PSI, and if the fuel lines are cracked, they may leak and spray fuel onto the exhaust system.

Look specifically for any records of the cam belt replacement in the 528e. The M20 engine utilizes a rubber cam/timing belt in place of the traditional BMW timing chain. It should be changed between 50,000 and 60,000 miles and is perhaps the single most critical item to check for in a 528e.

The diesel injection pump in the 524td is the weakest link in the system and tends to be more troublesome. Replacement injection pumps are available; however, they retail for approximately $2,000. Pumps can be rebuilt for much less.

Look for any evidence of rust in the major structure. Also check the dipstick for any evidence of coolant in the oil. If the dipstick has a milk shake brown coating instead of the expected clear or black oil, this could be an indication of a head that has cracked at the cam journal.

"Banjo" bolts that secure the oil-supply pipe to the top of the head may loosen, and the rocker arms may get oil starved. Check bolts annually. If loose, dry and clean bolts and heads, apply a light coating of Loctite, and reinstall. Don't overtighten, or you may crush the oil-supply pipe.

A common maintenance item in the driveline is the rubber flex-disk coupling in the middle of the drive shaft. Called a "guibo," it absorbs some of the driveline stresses. Expect to spend about $300 to replace it, plus parts and labor.

Do you feel any "seat-of-the-pants" vibration at low speeds, when you drive away from a stop? This may indicate either a center support bearing or failed or failing drive shaft U-joints.

Test-drive the car. Is the brake pedal "hard," indicating a possible problem with the hydraulic brake accumulator? A shimmy or shake in the steering may indicate that the thrust rod bushings are worn, either as a result of normal wear and tear or as a result of warped rotors transmitting additional stress to the bushings.

The 524td uses a timing belt. Check the maintenance records to see when it was replaced last. The recommendation is that the belt be inspected at each major service and replaced at 30,000–50,000-mile intervals.

Garage Watch 533i 1983–1985
535i/535is 1985–1989

The 4-speed electronically controlled transmissions did have some problems. Check for any evidence of leaking (especially after a test drive, when the fluid is hot and seals have expanded), slipping, and that the switchable shift programs function.

Available with either the Getrag 5-speed manual transmission or the ZF 4 speed automatic with electronic/hydraulic (EH) control (offering three distinct shifting programs), the 535i/is replaced the 533i in a lineup that also included the 528e and the M5.

"Banjo" bolts that secure the oil-supply pipe to the top of the head may loosen, and the rocker arms may get oil starved. Check bolts annually. If loose, dry and clean bolts and heads, apply a light coating of Loctite, and reinstall. Don't overtighten, or you may crush the oil-supply pipe.

While the aluminum radiators transfer heat more efficiently, the plastic tanks become brittle, and it is not unusual for the tanks to rupture or the hose necks to break off. New radiators are available, but expect to pay from $250 to $400 for a factory-replacement aluminum radiator.

Worn-out thrust rod bushings and warped brake rotors are common maintenance problems in the E28 5-Series.

The brake accumulator reservoir is a common failure item. Symptoms of a failed accumulator include stiff steering and a hard brake pedal. The brake accumulator reservoir is still available from BMW, and there are two switches that should also be replaced at the same time.

The 533i featured the familiar 3,210-cc engine, which produced 181-brake horsepower at a 6,500 rpm redline and 195 lbs-ft of torque at 4,000 rpm. This was a welcome relief from the 528e's sluggish performance.

A common maintenance item in the driveline is the rubber flex-disk coupling in the middle of the drive shaft. Called a "guibo," it absorbs some of the driveline stresses. Expect to spend about $300 to replace it, plus parts and labor.

Check the fuel lines and fuel injectors whenever the oil level is checked (weekly), looking for any signs of seepage or leakage. Fuel is delivered under about 40 PSI, and if the fuel lines are cracked, they may leak and spray fuel onto the exhaust system.

The TRX size tires have not proven to be a popular size and are becoming harder to find and expensive. Many owners have replaced the original TRX wheels and tires with aftermarket rims and tires in standard sizes.

The M5 has specific-to-the-model suspension and brakes that will be more expensive to replace than those in the other E28 5 series. Other than the engine, suspension, and brake upgrades, the M5 shares all the good attributes of the E28 chassis as well as the common problem areas.

A common maintenance item in the driveline is the rubber flex-disk coupling in the middle of the drive shaft. Called a "guibo," it absorbs some of the driveline stresses. Expect to spend about $300 to replace it, plus parts and labor.

Worn-out thrust rod bushings and warped brake rotors are common maintenance problems in the E28 5-Series.

The 1987 BMW 5-Series brochure describes this car as "A nice, practical 150-mph family sedan." Subtle description for a car that even today is considered a benchmark for performance sedans. Each one produced was literally hand-assembled by a two-person team at BMW Motorsports facility.

While the aluminum radiators transfer heat more efficiently, the plastic tanks become brittle, and it is not unusual for the tanks to rupture or the hose necks to break off. New radiators are available, but expect to pay from $250 to $400 for a factory-replacement aluminum radiator.

When considering an E28 M5, examine the maintenance records carefully. The engines are both a strong point and a weak point. When maintained properly, the M88 engine can be a reliable and relatively trouble-free powerplant. If it has not been maintained correctly, repairs *will* be expensive.

The brake accumulator reservoir is a common failure item. Symptoms of a failed accumulator include stiff steering and a hard brake pedal. The brake accumulator reservoir is still available from BMW, and there are two switches that should also be replaced at the same time.

Check the fuel lines and fuel injectors whenever the oil level is checked (weekly), looking for any signs of seepage or leakage. Fuel is delivered under about 40 PSI, and if the fuel lines are cracked, they may leak and spray fuel onto the exhaust system.

Specifications
524td, 528e

524td

Engine Type		SOHC 6-Cylinder Diesel,
Turbocharger		AiResearch T3 Turbo, 11.6 psi boost
Engine Designation		M21 D24
Displacement cc/ci		2443/149
Compression Ratio		22.01
BHP @ rpm		115 @ 4800
Torque lbs-ft @ rpm		155 @ 2400
Injection Type		Bosch Electronic
Fuel Requirement		Diesel
Transmission	Manual	5-Speed Manual
	Automatic	4-Speed Automatic
Steering		Recirculating Ball, Engine-Speed Sensitive Variable Power Assist
Front Suspension		MacPherson Struts, Double-Pivot Lower Arms, Coil Springs, Tube Shocks, Anti-Roll Bar
Rear Suspension		Semi-Trailing Arms, Coil Springs, Tube Shocks
Wheelbase (in.)		103.3 inch
Weight (lbs.)		3268
Wheels		14 x 6J
Tires		195/70 HR
Brake System		Vacuum Assist, Antilock Braking System
	Front	11.2-in. Discs
	Rear	11.2-in. Discs
0–60 mph, sec		11.7
Maximum Speed mph		107

528e

Engine Type		SOHC Inline 6
Displacement cc/ci		2693/164
Compression Ratio		9.01
BHP @ rpm		121 @ 4250
Torque lbs-ft @ rpm		170 @ 3250
Injection Type		Bosch L-Jetronic
Fuel Requirement		Unleaded, 91 Octane
Transmission	Manual	5-Speed Manual
	Automatic	4-Speed Automatic
Steering		Recirculating Ball, Engine-Speed Sensitive Variable Power Assist
Front Suspension		MacPherson Struts, Lower Lateral links, Coil Springs, Tube Shocks, Anti-Roll Bar
Rear Suspension		Semi-Trailing Arms, Coil Springs, Tube Shocks, Anti-Roll Bar
Wheelbase (in.)		103.3 in.
Weight (lbs.)	Manual	3100
	Automatic	3140
Wheels		14 x 6.5J
Tires		195/70 HR-14
Brake System		Vacuum Assist
	Front	11.8-in. Vented Discs
	Rear	11.8-in. Solid Discs
0–60 mph, sec	Manual	10.3
Maximum Speed mph		114

Specifications
533i, 535i/is

533i

Engine Type		SOHC Inline 6
Displacement cc/ci		3210/196
Compression Ratio		8.81
BHP @ rpm		181 @ 6000
Torque lbs-ft @ rpm		195 @ 4000
Injection Type		Bosch L-Jetronic
Fuel Requirement		Unleaded, 91 Octane
Transmission	Manual	5-Speed Manual
	Automatic	4-Speed Automatic
Steering		Recirculating Ball, Engine-Speed Sensitive Variable Power Assist
Front Suspension		MacPherson Struts, Lower LateralLinks, Coil Springs, Tube Shocks, Anti-Roll Bar
Rear Suspension		Semi-Trailing Arms, Coil Springs, Tube Shocks, Anti-Roll Bar
Wheelbase (in.)		103.3 in.
Weight (lbs.)	Manual	3120
Wheels		165 TR 390
Tires		200/60 x 390
Brake System		Dual-Circuit with Hydraulic Booster
	Front	11.8-in. Vented Discs
	Rear	11.8-in. Solid Discs
0–60 mph, sec	Manual	10.3
Maximum Speed mph		114

535i/is

Engine Type		SOHC Inline 6
Displacement cc/ci		3210/196
Compression Ratio		8.81
BHP @ rpm		182 @ 5400
Torque lbs-ft @ rpm		214 @ 4000
Injection Type		Bosch L-Jetronic
Fuel Requirement		Unleaded, 91 Octane
Transmission	Manual	5-Speed Manual
	Automatic	4-Speed Automatic
Steering		Recirculating Ball, Engine-Speed Sensitive Variable Power Assist
Front Suspension		MacPherson Struts, Lower Lateral Links, Coil Springs, Tube Shocks, Anti-Roll Bar
Rear Suspension		Semi-Trailing Arms, Coil Springs, Tube Shocks, Anti-Roll Bar
Wheelbase (in.)		103.3 inch
Weight (lbs.)	Manual	3270
	Automatic	3310
Wheels		165 TR 390
Tires		200/60 x 390
Brake System		Dual-Circuit with Hydraulic Booster, Antilock Brake System
	Front	11.8-in. Vented Discs
	Rear	11.8-in. Solid Discs
0–60 mph, sec	Manual	7.7
	Automatic	9.4
Maximum Speed mph	Manual	134
	Automatic	130

Specifications
M5 1987–1988

Engine Type	SOHC Inline 6
Displacement cc/ci	3453/211
Compression Ratio	9.81
BHP @ rpm	256 @ 6500
Torque lbs-ft @ rpm	243 @ 4500
Injection Type	Bosch Motronic
Fuel Requirement	Unleaded, 95 Octane
Transmission	5-Speed Manual
Steering	Recirculating Ball, Engine-Speed Sensitive Variable Power Assist
Front Suspension	MacPherson Struts, Lower Lateral links, Coil Springs, Tube Shocks, Anti-Roll Bar
Rear Suspension	Semi-Trailing Arms, Coil Springs, Hydraulic Self-Levelling, Anti-Roll Bar
Wheelbase (in.)	103.3 in.
Weight (lbs.)	3420
Wheels	16 x 7.5J
Tires	225/50 VR 16
Brake System	Dual-Circuit with Hydraulic Booster, Antilock
Front	11.8-in. Vented Discs
Rear	11.8-in. Solid Discs
0–60 mph, sec	6.7
Maximum Speed mph	150

The 1988 BMW 528e's M20 engine's single weakest point is the timing belt. Ask for records of the most recent change. Also, look closely at plastic radiator tanks for any signs of leaking.

The engine of this 1988 BMW M5 tells you that this is not your average 4-door sedan.

Replacement Costs for Common Parts
524td, 528e

524td

Oil Filter		$14.90
Fuel Filter		$23
Fuel Pump		
In-Tank		$127.50
External		$190
Starter		$134, Exchange
Alternator		$169
Clutch Kit	Clutch Disk	$105
	Pressure Plate	$117
	Throwout Bearing	$36.25
Water Pump		$75
Turbocharger		$1,265,
Exchange		
Injection pump		$1,489,
Exchange		
Front Bumper (w/o rubber trim)		$286
Hood		$312
Left Front Fender		$210
Right Rear Quarter Panel		$292
Rear Bumper (w/o rubber trim)		$339
Windshield		$195
Tail Light Housing/Lens		$254
Front Silencer		$136
Rear Muffler		$191
Brake Master		$319
Front Rotor (each)		$61
Front Pads (set)		$62.95
Rear Rotor (each)		$39.50
Rear Pads		$62.95
Brake Accumulator		$169
	Switch	$26.75
	Switch	$22.75
Front Shocks (each) to 2/85		$115
from 2/85		$165
Rear Shocks (each)		$149.50
(each)		
Gas Tank		$276

528e

Oil Filter		$5.20
Fuel Filter		$21.75
Fuel Pump	In-Tank	$127.50
	External	$190
Starter		$125, Exchange
Alternator		$229
Clutch Kit		$236
Water Pump		$55.75
Timing Belt		$14.60
Tensioner		$23.75
Front Bumper (w/o rubber trim)		$286
Hood		$312
Left Front Fender		$210
Right Rear Quarter Panel		$292
Rear Bumper (w/o rubber trim)		$339
Windshield		$195
Tail Light Housing/Lens		$254
Muffler and Pipe	to 3/87	$208
	from 3/87	$361
Catalytic Converter	Manual Transmission	
	to 9/87	$1,375
	from 9/87	$1,421
	Automatic Transmission	
	to 9/83	$1,375
	from 9/83	$1,421
Oxygen Sensor	to 3/87	$45
	from 3/87	$133.35
Brake Master	w/o ABS	$305
	w/ ABS	$239
Front Rotor (each)		$61
Front Pads (set)		$62.95
Rear Rotor (each)		$39.50
Rear Pads		$54.75
2 Brake Accumulator		$169
	Switch	$26.75
	Switch	$22.75
Front Shocks (each)		$115
Rear Shocks (each) to 9/82		$165
	from 9/82	$149.50
Gas Tank		$276

Greatly improved HVAC is a feature of the E28-Series. Visible in this photo of a 1988 BMW 528e are the front armrests, and electric seat controls, an aftermarket radio, and onboard computer (OBC). A miles-per-gallon gauge is in the lower portion of the tachometer.

Replacement Costs for Common Parts
533i, M5, 535i/is

533i

Oil Filter		$5.20
Fuel Filter		$21.75
Fuel Pump	In-Tank	$127.50
	External	$190
Starter		$134 Exchange
Alternator		$183
Clutch Kit		$290
Water Pump		$71.25
Front Bumper (w/o rubber trim)		$347
Hood		$555
Left Front Fender		$221
Right Rear Quarter Panel		$374
Rear Bumper (w/o rubber trim)		$439
Windshield		$243
Tail Light Housing/Lens		$138
Pipe/Muffler		$650
Oxygen Sensor		$45
Catalytic Converter	Manual Transmission	$1,355
	Automatic Transmission	
	to 9/83	$1,355
	from 9/83	$1,440
Brake Master		$305
	w/ ABS	$239
Front Rotor (each)		$61
Front Pads (set)		$62.95
Rear Rotor (each)		$39.50
Rear Pads		$54.75
Brake Accumulator		$169
	Switch	$26.75
	Switch	$22.75
Front Shocks (each)		$115
Rear Shocks (each)	to 9/82	$165
Gas Tank		$276

M5

Oil Filter		$5.20
Fuel Filter		$21.75
Fuel Pump	In-Tank	$127.50
	External	$190
Starter		$134, Exchange
Alternator		$310, Exchange
Clutch Kit		$446
Water Pump		$71.25
Front Bumper (w/o rubber trim)		$356
Hood		$312
Left Front Fender		$210
Right Rear Quarter Panel		$292
Rear Bumper (w/o rubber trim)		$411
Windshield		$195
Tail Light Housing/Lens		$248
Pipe/Muffler		$730
Oxygen Sensor		$133.35
Catalytic Converter;		$1,500, Exchange
Brake Master		$239
Front Rotor (each)		$100
Front Pads (set)		$62.95
Rear Rotor (each)		$39.50
Rear Pads		$62.95
Brake Accumulator		$169
	Switch	$26.75
	Switch	$22.75
Front Shocks(each)		$196
Rear Shocks(each)		$298
Gas Tank		$276

535i/is

Oil Filter		$5.20
Fuel Filter		$21.75
Fuel Pump	In-Tank	$127.50
	External	$190
Starter		$134, Exchange
Alternator	to 1/86	$183
	from 1/86	$287
Clutch Kit		$290
Water Pump		$71.25
Front Bumper (w/o rubber trim)		$347
Front Air Dam		$449
Hood		$555
Left Front Fender		$221
Right Rear Quarter Panel		$374
Rear Bumper (w/o rubber trim)		$439
Windshield		$243
Tail Light Housing/Lens		$138
Pipe/Muffler		$560
Oxygen Sensor	to 9/86	$138
	from 9/86	$95
Catalytic Converter	Manual Transmission	$1,421
	Automatic Transmission	$1,695
Brake Master		$305
	w/ ABS	$239
Front Rotor (each)		$61
Front Pads (set)		$62.95
Rear Rotor (each)		$39.50
Rear Pads		$54.75
Brake Accumulator		$169
	Switch	$26.75
	Switch	$22.75
Front Shocks (each)	M-Technic	$165
	Bilstein	$125
Rear Shocks (each)	to 9/82	$149
	Bilstein	$135
Gas Tank		$276

The M30/3.4-liter, as shown in this 1987 BMW 535is, is a robust engine. Check the plastic radiator tanks for signs of leaking. Note the absence of a VIN sticker on the fender and a DOT-R sticker on hood (one o'clock position) that indicates repairs.

What They Said About the . . .

524td

Well, it ain't all that bad. It goes pretty good. (For a diesel.) It's impressively quiet. (For a diesel.) And it handles *exactly* like a BMW. It's lacking only one ingredient: *performance,* the need for which has definitely been established. **—Roundel, August 1985**

528e

At the heart of our feelings about the 528e is the fact that this latest 5-Series BMW is an excellent automobile, one of the best in its class. **—Road & Track, February 1982**

533i

Wake the neighbors, throw out the cat, pull on your Jim Clark driving gloves, and get down to your BMW store. Then, just like Superman, ask them to stand aside, please, and blast off. **—Car and Driver, February 1983**

535i/is

The ideal luxury sedan, it'll carry grandparents or kids in a comfortable manner, but gives dad enough power to enjoy the drive too. **—Road & Track, October 1985**

M5

The M5 is a no-compromises, foot-to-the-floor screamer built for those who demand the ultimate in speed and refinement. The few who can afford it are going to have a ball. **—Car and Driver, December 1987**

Closeup of the M88 engine in a 1988 BMW M5, which shows an airflow meter, throttle bodies, and thermostat.

Blacked-out trim, black anodized bumpers, and the M5 badge on the deck lid of this 1988 BMW M5 tell you that this is the real thing.

I Bought a . . .

1988 BMW 528e

You really need to follow the maintenance guidelines with this model. Change the timing belt every four years or 50,000 miles and the water pump while you're at it. Immediately after purchase, I brought this car up to standard: tune-up, timing-belt replacement, water pump, suspension repairs, and repair of the faulty central locking module. Other than these maintenance items, I have not experienced any other repairs, and the car has not been down for any extended time.

In spite of being underpowered, I like the car. I had owned a 1986 BMW 528e previously, and it was extremely reliable with great gas mileage. While it does not offer the greatest performance, the 528e is an inexpensive, no-fuss, drive-it-anywhere, leave-it-anywhere BMW. *—Randy Luenebrink, Los Angeles*

1984 BMW 533i

We wanted an inexpensive, reliable car for my wife. This car was available and the price was right.

The fact that the 533i is easy to maintain and that I am pretty familiar with it helped. We also liked the styling, its color combination (graphite exterior/black interior). It handles almost as well as my modified Bavaria and is a quieter cruising car. I do feel that rear seat legroom is lacking and that the front suspension and steering parts are underdesigned.

Mechanically, we have replaced the front control arms and center link, the in-tank fuel pump, air conditioning hoses, an alternator, a water pump, and the radiator. Common replacement items seem to be the plastic-chrome window trim, the service interval system (SI) boards, and the thrust rod bushings. That's not bad for a car with such high mileage. These cars will run forever with reasonable maintenance. *—Jim Stansfield, Costa Mesa, California*

1985 BMW 535i

I bought my 1988 BMW 535i new. Now it has just over 106,000 miles on it. I was interested in a BMW with plenty of power and more room than the 3-Series. The 535i 5-speed had those attributes and also provided the sports-car feel I was looking for.

I was not impressed with the stock TRX wheels and tires. The tires were expensive and only offered by one manufacture (Michelin). Maintenance can be expensive; however, the M30 engine is very robust and will likely last many years with minimal service. If something internal should break, figure that the bill will likely be in the $2,000 to $3,000 range. The Inspection Service II will likely cost you about $600 to $700, which can be a shock if not expected.

The car has only been down to replace the water pump and the front control arms. *—Brad Herrin, Lake Forest, California*

1987 BMW 535is

I purchased my 535is used in September 2000. It had about 94,000 miles on it when I purchased it, and I drive it every day, on average between 100 and 150 miles, and it currently has 114,000 miles on it. I get many compliments on the car from everyday people who aren't BMW nuts.

My worst experience with this car was when my wife called me telling me that there was a lot of smoke coming from under the hood. My heart went right to my stomach! It turned out that the thermostat had seen better days. Needless to say, I was happy it was a relatively simple repair.

During my ownership, I have had the following mechanical repairs done:

Replaced the front and rear pads and rotors; replaced the tires; the thrust rod bushings (used the 750i bushings); and the tie rod ends. The air conditioning unit has been recharged, and as mentioned earlier, the thermostat has been replaced. *—Lori and Robbie Adelson, San Diego, California*

1988 BMW M5

I have had many great experiences with this car. However, my first close-up look at the car on the day it was delivered, followed by my first drive around the block, was probably the most thrilling. I knew I had made the right choice.

When I first got the M5 it had a brake problem—a sticking caliper that resulted in the brakes locking up. The brake problems were the only time during my ownership that the car was out of service for any length of time. During the time I have owned this car, I have replaced the front rotors (they warp easily), installed new calipers, a new brake master cylinder, front shocks, front end bushings, the "dog-bones" in the rear suspension, the fuel pre-pump, and the service interval system (SI) board—three times. Next I will replace the rear self-leveling with Bilstein shocks.

Parts seem readily available, but because the car is unique and has the M insignia, they can be pricey. Another drawback is that there is no real service manual for this car.

My favorite part of the M5 is the power/torque in all gears, the way it handles, and its roomy comfort. While you can still feel the road, you are insulated enough that long trips are comfortable. I also like the look of the car. While in some ways the M5 is a sleeper, it also has the appearance and sound of a machine with bad intentions. No question, I would buy another one. *—Lisa and Alan Clark, Pacific Palisades, California*

525i/525i Touring
535i
530i/530i Touring
540i/540i Sport
M5

E34 5-Series
1989-1996
Chapter 10

When the E28 5-Series was introduced in 1982, BMW took a good deal of flack from critics who complained that the new car did not look different enough from the old car. The third-generation 5-Series, with its steeply raked windshield and rear window, wedge-shaped profile, and longer wheelbase left no doubt in anyone's mind that the design and engineering teams had listened.

Designated the E34 chassis, the 1989 5-Series bears a strong resemblance to the E32 7-Series. Computer-aided design techniques resulted in a 30 percent stiffer body shell. The front and rear windscreens contributed to this by being bonded into their openings. Side windows were very nearly flush with the doorframes. By weight, 45 percent of the body shell was zinc-coated for improved corrosion resistance. Front and rear bumpers were now gracefully integrated into the overall design, and BMW chose to standardize these bumpers for all markets.

Technically, the E34 5-Series was a night-and-day difference from its predecessor. A new design body, redesigned suspension front and rear (although traditional BMW in that it is based on MacPherson struts and semi-trailing arms), improved braking (larger rotors and calipers), more efficient heating and air conditioning, and increased passenger room were all features. This is a car that set new standards and raised the bar for all the other manufacturers.

When introduced in 1989, the 5-Series offered two engine choices—the smaller, M20/2.5-liter six, as used in the E30 325i/is; and the traditional M30/3.4-liter inline six, as used in the previous generation 5-Series, the 6-Series, and 7-Series cars.

In 1990, BMW introduced a revised small six, the M50/2.5-liter, and kept the 525i designation. By 1993, an updated engine, the M50TU/2.5, was in use. In 1993, BMW introduced V-8 engines to the 5-Series lineup, retaining the 525i and Touring models but replacing the 535i model with a 530i and a 540i, both of which were powered by alloy block, DOHC 4-valve per cylinder V-8 engines.

Late in 1995, a more sporting version of the 5-Series sedan was offered. Known as the 540i Sport and sometimes called an M 540i, this car featured the cosmetics, suspension, and brakes from the M5 with the 4.0-liter V-8. Two hundred of these cars were imported, 135 equipped with the 6-speed manual transmission and 65 equipped with the 5-speed automatic.

The 1991–1993 M5 shares major body and chassis components with the rest of the E34 5-Series but has its own set of unique problems. Powered by a DOHC, 4-valve S38/3.6-liter inline six, watch for even seemingly minor engine problems, as they can quickly get very expensive. This highly desirable package of supercar performance and subtle looks is expensive to maintain but may be the finest example of the breed.

In short, the E34 5-Series is quicker, quieter, roomier, more comfortable, and more economical than the previous generation and is available with a variety of engines, from the 2.5-liter inline 6-cylinder to the 4.0-liter V-8 to the DOHC 310 horsepower M5. Watch out for the 1994 and 1995 V-8 powered cars and their problems with the Nikasil blocks. The V-8s from 1996 on are not problematic because they use Alusil blocks.

The versatile E34 5-Series also offers a number of models, and the prices of the cars dip to the level of serious affordability. Thus, this third-generation 5-Series offers buyers the opportunity to own a luxurious, competent, good-handling sports sedan. If solid transportation is your desire, there are several models to meet those needs. If your desire is to carry four adults in luxury and yet still have the quintessential race car in disguise, then the M5 will meet—and in most cases exceed—your expectations.

The 525i Touring uses self-leveling rear suspension to help compensate for the anticipated load that can be carried in a station wagon-type vehicle. The system should be checked carefully for leaks and for proper operation.

Introduced alongside the larger-engined 535i, the 1989 525i offered buyers the choice of a less expensive version of the fourth-generation 5-Series.

Engine compartment heat has a tendency to cause problems for fuel and coolant hoses. The radiator hoses should be checked closely and replaced at two- to- three-year intervals. The fuel lines also can harden and crack over time. In 1994, there was a recall issued to examine and replace any fuel lines showing evidence of deterioration.

A recall was issued for a sticking throttle valve shaft. This can happen when the engine reaches normal operating temperatures and it is below 40 degrees outside. The expansion rates of the different materials used for the throttle valve shaft and the throttle housing may result in the throttle shaft hanging up and the throttle not closing.

The M50/2.5-liter engine water pumps had plastic impellers that are known for failing. An improved design was introduced, and by now most engines have had water pumps replaced. The thermostat and fan clutch are also common failure items.

There is a fusible link in the engine compartment that can weaken as a result of age and heat. The 525i's were recalled so this could be checked and replaced if necessary.

From 1993 on, the DOHC M50/2.5 engine, which uses a timing chain instead of a belt, was used in the 525i sedan and Touring. Basically trouble-free, listen for valve clatter at startup. If the noise lasts more than a couple of minutes, a lifter may be malfunctioning. These engines have also experienced occasional failures of engine ignition coils.

"Banjo" bolts that secure the oil-supply pipe to the top of the head may loosen, and the rocker arms may get oil starved. Check bolts annually. If loose, dry and clean bolts and heads, apply a light coating of Loctite, and reinstall. Don't overtighten, or you may crush the oil-supply pipe.

There have been reports of problems with the 5-speed automatic transmissions going into "limp-home" mode and locking in fourth gear. Sometimes shutting off the car and restarting it—like rebooting a computer—can resolve this problem.

Introduced alongside the smaller-engined 525i sedan, the 535i had an outstanding design, excellent fit and finish, and a proven engine-transmission combined to deliver style and performance.

Cooling systems need to be maintained properly. The plastic tank radiators are known for developing cracks and for the hose necks breaking off. Also common are defective thermostats and failed fan clutches. All can lead to overheating and serious engine damage.

Check the condition of the fuel lines frequently. There was a recall for possible leaks at the connector to the main fuel rail.

The 1989 to 1993 535i uses the M30/3.4-liter inline six that has been around for years. It is a robust engine that will last well over 100,000 miles when cared for in a reasonable manner. The big-six is known to be an oil consumer; some may use as much as 1 quart per 1,000 miles.

Sunroofs may jam on post-1991 cars, and central locking actuators may malfunction. Wires leading to the rear license plate where they pass from the trunk area to the trunk lid have a tendency to fatigue and break. This can cause the license plate lights to remain illuminated and can drain the battery.

Primary weak spots in the chassis and suspension are the rear subframe mount bushings. Ball joints and steering components wear out and can lead to vagueness in the steering. The E34 chassis also uses thrust rod bushings, which when worn out can cause vibrations in the steering wheel. Warped front brake rotors can also lead to steering wheel vibrations.

There have been reports of problems with the 5-speed automatic transmissions going into "limp-home" mode and locking in fourth gear. Sometimes shutting off the car and restarting it—like rebooting a computer—can resolve this.

Look for leaky valve cover gaskets, which are also a common problem. Look for signs of radiators or coolant hose leaks. Also known to fail are the engine thermostats and fan clutches.

Listen for a whistle-like sound coming from the rear of the engine block. There is a "vacuum plate" under the shrouding that can fail. Test by removing the oil filler cap with the engine running. If the plate has failed, the vacuum will be strong enough to suck the cap right back down. Replacement part is $150 and requires four hours of labor.

The motor mounts are hydraulic oil–filled to help dampen any engine vibrations. They do fail over time and the oil will leak out. This will result in normal engine vibrations being transmitted to the car.

In 1994, the big news for the 5-Series was the replacement of the 3.5-liter inline six with the DOHC, 32-valve V-8. Available in two different displacements—a 3.0-liter or 4.0-liter—this gave buyers a choice of several different models: the 525i sedan, the 525i Touring, the 530i sedan, the 530i Touring, and the top-of-the-line 540i sedan.

High-sulphur-content gas tends to damage the cylinder bores of the Nikasil M60 V-8 engines, causing a loss of compression. Before purchasing any BMW with one of these engines, take it to an authorized BMW mechanic and request an idle quality check, which will help determine if the engine is one that is affected.

Check the condition of the fuel lines frequently. There was a recall for possible leaks at the connector to the main fuel rail.

Unleashed on the U.S. market as a 1991 model, the E34 M5 picked up where the E28 M5 left off. Subtle, more sophisticated, with more power, better handling, and better amenities.

Exact numbers vary, but between 1,500 and 1,700 of these cars were imported from 1991 to 1993. This car is rare and expensive to own and operate. Find the best one you can, and set aside a second monthly payment to cover maintenance costs.

The unusual-looking wheels are expensive to replace if damaged. The 1991 and 1992 covers are awkward looking but effective in cooling the brakes.

The M5s were equipped with self-leveling rear suspensions. Look for leaks in the rear shocks and in the trunk-mounted reservoir. The system is expensive to repair, and many owners have removed the system completely, converting it to normal shocks and springs.

Interior door panels, primarily on cars with black interior, have a history of delaminating.

The 1993 models were equipped with Servotronic power steering. This system is reported to be less accurate and offers less road feel than the earlier models.

The engines have a tendency to leak oil from the cylinder head gasket area and from the front cover.

Water pumps seem to fail at four year/50,000-mile intervals. Engine drive belts (water pump, power steering, alternator) fail on a regular basis. Change all belts at 24 to 36 month intervals to be safe.

Second- and third-gear syncros are known to be weak points.

Ratings Chart

E34 5-Series

	525i	525i Touring	530i
Model Comfort/Amenities	★★★	★★★	★★★
Reliability	★★★	★★★	★★★
Collectibility	★	★	★
Parts/Service Availability	★★★½	★★★½	★★★½
Est. Annual Repair Costs	★★★	★★★	★★★

	530i Touring	535i	540i
Model Comfort/Amenities	★★★	★★★	★★★
Reliability	★★★	★★★	★★★
Collectibility	★	★	★
Parts/Service Availability	★★★½	★★★½	★★★½
Est. Annual Repair Costs	★★★	★★★	★★★

	540i Sport	M5
Model Comfort/Amenities	★★★	★★★
Reliability	★★★	★★★
Collectibility	★★★★½	★★★★★
Parts/Service Availability	★★★½	★★★
Est. Annual Repair Costs	★★★	★★★★

The S38/3.5-liter of the 1991 BMW M5 develops 310 brake horsepower and will push the M5 to a top speed of 155 miles per hour. Weak points are radiator hoses and accessory drive belts.

Specifications
525i/525i Touring 1989–1995, 535i 1989–1993

525i/525i Touring 1989–1995

Engine Type				DOHC Inline 6, Variable Valve Timing
Displacement cc/ci				2494/152
Compression Ratio				10.51
BHP @ rpm				189 @ 5900
Torque lbs-ft @ rpm				184 @ 4200
Injection Type				Bosch HFM-Motronic with Adaptive Knock Control
Fuel Requirement				Unleaded Premium
Transmission	Manual	525i		Getrag Type C, 5-Speed
		525i Touring		NA
	Automatic			THM R1, 4-Speed with Electronic Control
Steering				Recirculating Ball, Engine-Speed Sensitive Variable Power Assist
Front Suspension				MacPherson Struts, Double-Pivot Lower Arms, Coil Springs, Twin-Tube Gas Pressure Shocks, Anti-Roll Bar
Rear Suspension				Semi-Trailing Arms, Track Links, Coil Springs, Twin-Tube Gas-Pressure Shocks, Anti-Roll Bar
Wheelbase (in.)				108.7
Weight (lbs.)	Manual	525i		3483
	Automatic	525i		3560
		525i Touring		3759
Wheels				Cast Alloy 15 x 7.J
Tires				205/65R-15 94 H,
Brake System				Vacuum Assist, Antilock Braking System
	Front			11.9-in. Vented Disks
	Rear			11.8-in. Solid Disks
0–60 mph, sec	Manual	525i		8.6
	Automatic	525i	1993	9.7
			1994–1995	9.1
		525i Touring	1993	10.4
			1994–1995	9.7
MPG, City/Highway				128 (electronically limited)
	Manual	525i		19/28
	Automatic			18/25

535i 1989–1993

Engine Type			SOHC Inline 6
Displacement cc/ci			3430/209
Compression Ratio			9.01
BHP @ rpm			208 @ 5700
Torque lbs-ft @ rpm			225 @ 4000
Injection Type			Bosch ML-Motronic DME
Fuel Requirement			Unleaded Regular
Transmission	Manual		Getrag 260/6 5-Speed
	Automatic		ZP 4HP 22N EH 4-Speed with Electronic Control
Steering			Recirculating Ball, Engine-Speed Sensitive Variable Power Assist
Front Suspension			MacPherson Struts, Double-Pivot Lower Arms, Coil Springs, Twin-Tube Gas Pressure Shocks, Anti-Roll Bar
Rear Suspension			Semi-Trailing Arms, Track Links, Coil Springs, Twin-Tube Gas-Pressure Shocks, Anti-Roll Bar
Wheelbase (in.)			108.7
Weight (lbs.)	Manual		3570
	Automatic		3615
Wheels			Cross Spoke Cast Alloy 15 x 7.J
Tires			225/60R-15 95 V, Steel Belted Radial
Brake System			Vacuum Assist, Antilock Braking System
	Front		11.9-in. Vented Discs
	Rear		11.8-in. Solid Discs
0–60 mph, sec	Manual		7.6
	Automatic		8.7
Maximum Speed mph	Manual		143
	Automatic		142
MPG, City/Highway	Manual		15/23
	Automatic		16/22

Specifications
530i/530i Touring 1994–1995

Engine Type				DOHC V-8
Displacement cc/ci				2997/183
Compression Ratio				10.51
BHP @ rpm				215 @ 5800
Torque lbs-ft @ rpm				214 @ 4500
Injection Type				Bosch HFM-Motronic with Adaptive Knock Control
Fuel Requirement				Unleaded Premium
Transmission	Manual	530i		Getrag Type C, 5-Speed
		530i Touring		NA
	Automatic			ZF 5 HP 18 EH, 5-Speed
Steering				Recirculating Ball, Engine-Speed Sensitive Variable Power Assist
Front Suspension				MacPherson Struts, Double-Pivot Lower Arms, Coil Springs, Twin-Tube Gas Pressure Shocks, Anti-Roll Bar
Rear Suspension				Semi-Trailing Arms, Track Links, Coil Springs, Twin-Tube Gas-Pressure Shocks, Anti-Roll Bar
Wheelbase (in.)				108.7
Weight (lbs.)	Manual	530i		3627
		530i Touring		NA
	Automatic	530i		3693
		530i Touring		3880
Wheels				Cast Alloy 15 x 7.0J
Tires				225/60ZR-15 96H
Brake System				Vacuum Assist, Antilock Braking System
Front				11.9-in. Vented Discs
	Rear			11.8-in. Solid Discs
0–60 mph, sec	Manual	530i		7.5
		530i Touring		NA
	Automatic	530i		8.8
		530i Touring		9.1
Maximum Speed mph				128 (electronically limited)
MPG, City/Highway	Manual	530i	16/24	
		530i Touring		NA
	Automatic	530i	1994	16/23
			1995	17/26
		530i Touring	1994	16/25
			1995	17/26

An engine view of the 1991 BMW 535i. The airbox in the lower right leads to an airflow meter with a flexible duct that leads to an intake plenum. Idle control valve (ICV) mounts are at a 90° angle to intake boot. The battery terminal has a red "+" sign on the cover. Ahead of that is the service interval system (SI) reset port (round, size of soda can), which is attached to left strut mount.

Specifications
540i/540i Sport 1994–1995, M5 1991–1993

540i/540i Sport 1994–1995

Engine Type			DOHC V-8
Displacement cc/ci			3982/243
Compression Ratio			10.01
BHP @ rpm			282 @ 5800
Torque lbs-ft @ rpm			295 @ 4500
Injection Type			Bosch HFM-Motronic with Adaptive Knock Control
Fuel Requirement			Unleaded Premium
Transmission	Manual	1994	NA
		1995	Getrag Type D, 6-Speed
	Automatic		ZF 5 HP 30 EH, 5-Speed
Steering			Recirculating Ball, Engine-Speed Sensitive Variable Power Assist
Front Suspension			MacPherson Struts, Double-Pivot Lower Arms, Coil Springs, Twin-Tube Gas Pressure Shocks, Anti-Roll Bar, With Manual Transmission, Sports Suspension Calibration
Rear Suspension			Semi-Trailing Arms, Track Links, Coil Springs, Twin-Tube Gas-Pressure Shocks, Anti-Roll Bar, with Manual Transmission Sports Suspension Calibration
Wheelbase (in.)			108.7
Weight (lbs.)	Manual	1994	NA
		1995	3693
	Automatic		3803
Wheels			Cast Alloy 15 x 7.0J
Tires			225/60R-15 96H
Brake System			Vacuum Assist, Antilock Braking System
	Front		11.9-in. Vented Discs
	Rear		11.8-in. Vented Discs
0–60 mph, sec	Manual	1994	NA
		1995	6.2
	Automatic		6.7 sec
Maximum Speed mph			128 (electronically limited)
MPG, City/Highway	Manual	1994	NA
		1995	14/23
	Automatic	1994	16/23
		1995	17/25

M5 1991–1993

Engine Type		DOHC Inline 6,
Displacement cc/ci		3535/216
Compression Ratio		10.51
BHP @ rpm		310 @ 6900
Torque lbs-ft @ rpm		266 @ 4750
Injection Type		Bosch MH-Motronic DME
Fuel Requirement		Unleaded Premium
Transmission	Manual	Getrag 280/5, 5-Speed
	Automatic	NA
Steering		Recirculating Ball, Vehicle-Speed Sensitive Variable Power Assist
Front Suspension		MacPherson Struts, Double-Pivot Lower Arms, Coil Springs, Twin-Tube Gas Pressure Shocks, Anti-Roll Bar.
Rear Suspension		Semi-Trailing Arms, track links, CoilSprings, Anti-Roll Bar, Self-Leveling System with Single-Tube Shock Absorbers
Wheelbase (in.)		108.7
Weight (lbs.)	Manual	3804
	Automatic	NA
Wheels		2-Piece Cast Alloy 17 x 8.0J
Tires		235/45R-17 Z, Steel Belted Radial
Brake System		Vacuum Assist, Antilock Braking System
	Front	12.8-in. Vented Discs
	Rear	11.8-in. Solid Discs
0–60 mph, sec	Manual	6.1
	Automatic	NA
Maximum Speed mph		155
MPG, City/Highway	Manual	12/23
	Automatic	NA

Replacement Costs for Common Parts
525i/525i Touring, 540i/540i Sport

525i/525i Touring

Oil Filter	to 1990	$5.20
	from 1991 on	$8.50
Fuel Filter		$21.75
Fuel Pump	M20/2.5	$301
	M50/2.5	$294
Starter		$169
Alternator	to 1990	$386
	from 1991 on	$363
Clutch Kit	to 1990	$251
	from 1991 on	$239
Water Pump		$61.50
Front Bumper		$236
Hood		$477
Left Front Fender		$316
Right Rear Quarter Panel		$159
Rear Bumper		$488
Windshield		$365
Tail Light Lens		$175
Center Muffler	to 1990	$224
	1991 to 1995	$279
Rear Muffler	to 1990	$370
	1991 to 1995	$370
Oxygen Sensor	to 1990	$133.35
	1991 to 1995	$96
Catalytic Converter		$1,250
Brake Master		$319
Front Rotor (each)		$93.50
Front Pads (set)		$98.25
	+ sensor @ $6.50	
Rear Rotor (each)		$61
Rear Pads		$69
	+ sensor @ $6.50	
Front Shocks (each) w/o EDC		$132
	w/ EDC	$522.50
Rear Shocks (each)		$118
	M-Technik	$185

540i/540i Sport

Oil Filter		$10
Fuel Filter		$21
Fuel Pump		$294
Starter		$269
Alternator		$363
Clutch Kit		$446
Water Pump		$117
Front Bumper		$236
Hood		$477
Left Front Fender		$316
Right Rear Quarter Panel		$159
Rear Bumper		$488
Windshield		$365
Tail Light Lens		$175
Exhaust	Exhaust Assembly	$849
	Center Silencer	$402
	Rear Silencer	$450
	Oxygen Sensor	$133.35
Catalytic Converter	Cylinders 1–4	
	to 3/94	$1,421
	from 3/94	$1,050
	Cylinders 5–8	
	to 3/94	$1,421
	from 3/94	$1,050
Brake Master		$419
Front Rotor (each)		$93.50
Front Pads (set)		$98.25
	+ sensor @ $6.50	
Rear Rotor (each)		$81.50
Rear Pads		$107
	+ sensor @ $6.50	
2 Front Shocks (each)		$132
2 Rear Shocks (each)		$118

The 1995 BMW 525i sports a clean and functional design with heating, ventilation, air conditioning, and radio controls centered in the dash. Wood trim accents the interior color nicely.

Replacement Costs for Common Parts
535i, M5, 530i/530i Touring

535i

Oil Filter	$5.20
Fuel Filter	$21.75
Fuel Pump	$294
Starter	$245
Alternator	$386
Clutch Kit	$284
Water Pump	$71.25
Front Bumper	$236
Hood	$477
Left Front Fender	$316
Right Rear Quarter Panel	$159
Rear Bumper	$488
Windshield	$365
Tail Light Lens	$175
Center Muffler	$279
Rear Muffler	$325
Oxygen Sensor	$133.35
Catalytic Converter	$1,575
Brake Master	$319
Front Rotor (each)	$93.50
Front Pads (set)	$98.25
+ sensor	$6.50
Rear Rotor (each)	$61
Rear Pads	$69
+ sensor	$6.50
Front Shocks (each)	$132
Rear Shocks (each)	$118

M5

Oil Filter		$5.20
Fuel Filter		$21.75
Fuel Pump		$294
Starter		$245
Alternator	115A	$363
	140A	$386
Clutch Kit		$446
Water Pump		$154
Front Bumper		$236
Hood		$477
Left Front Fender		$316
Right Rear Quarter Panel		$159
Rear Bumper		$488
Windshield		$365
Tail Light Lens		$175
Exhaust Assembly		$1.430
Oxygen Sensor		$133.35
Catalytic Converter		$2,465
Brake Master		$319
Front Rotor (each)		$149
Front Pads (set)		$98.25
+ sensor		$6.50
Rear Rotor (each)		$81.50
Rear Pads		$71.25
+ sensor		$6.50
Front Shocks (each)		$132
Rear Shocks (each)		$118

530i/530i Touring

Oil Filter		$10
Fuel Filter		$21
Fuel Pump		$294
Starter		$269
Alternator		$363
Clutch Kit		$381
Water Pump		$117
Front Bumper		$236
Hood		$477
Left Front Fender		$316
Right Rear Quarter Panel		$159
Rear Bumper		$488
Windshield		$365
Tail Light Lens		$175
Exhaust Assembly		$849
Center Silencer		$402
Rear Silencer		$450
Oxygen Sensor		$133.35
Catalytic Converter	Cylinders 1–4	$1,421
	Cylinders 5–8	$1,421
Brake Master		$419
Front Rotor (each)		$93.50
Front Pads (set)		$98.25
+ sensor @ $6.50		
Rear Rotor (each)		$61
Rear Pads		$69
+ sensor		$6.50
Front Shocks (each)		$132
Rear Shocks (each)		$118

Check maintenance records. Water pumps with plastic impellers are known to fail prematurely on the 1995 BMW 525i. Service stickers in the lower right make it easy to determine when services were done.

What They Said About the . . .

525i

When the road begins to wind, it inspires a sense of confidence and man/machine rapport none of the other cars quite match. *—Popular Mechanics,* February 1992

525i Touring

Comfortable? Absolutely. Fun to drive? You bet. It just won't get you home from the day care as quickly as you might like. *—Motor Trend,* **October 1993**

530i

The taut and controlled handling that we've always loved in the 5-Series is complemented by this flexible new V-8 and a superb new gearbox that is too wonderful to accurately describe in a Western language. *—Car and Driver,* **January 1994**

535i

There's no mistaking the breed, this is a Bim 5, all right—a 4-door sedan meant for strafing apexes with the best of 'em. *—Road & Track,* **May 1988**

540i

The refined power delivery of an advanced V-8 meshes perfectly . . . making even more convincing competitors of BMW's mid-range sedans. *—Car and Driver,* **June 1993**

M5

Ahhh, but to those of us who live on the lunatic fringe of the performance envelope, the M5 is pure high-speed, tail-out perfection. *—Motor Trend,* **August 1993**

The M60/4.0-liter V-8 of a 1994 BMW 540i. BMW engineers have shrouded everything in plastic, neat and tidy. Check the radiator plastic tanks for signs of leakage and for oil leaks from valve cover gaskets.

Clean as new, the subtle front spoiler with integrated brake ducts is clearly visible from this front view of a 1993 BMW M5. Wheels are actually the same as the 1991, with differently styled wheel centers.

I Bought a . . .

1995 BMW 525i

We were attracted by the absolutely fantastic structure and build quality of this car. This car is rock solid and meticulously made and is as structurally rigid after close to 40,000 miles as the day it was built. In spite of comparatively low gearing (3,000 rpm at 70 miles per hour), the fuel economy is great—the car delivered 602.4 miles, or 31 miles per gallon, on its most recent tank.

My single dislike is the comparatively heavy and balky clutch. My worst, or perhaps most frightening experience was when a fuel line under the intake manifold came loose and sprayed a little gas around. Fortunately, no fire. In fact, the fix was quick and easy. That's the only time the car has ever been down. *—Patricia and Rex Parker, Huntington Beach, California*

1991 BMW 535i

I like the body style and the color of my 535i, Calypso (red metallic) with a beige interior. Although I do think the car could use another 100 horsepower, along with the reliability it is the performance I like the most.

Items that I don't like are the high fuel consumption—my city average is 17 miles per gallon—and the 4-speed automatic, which has a reputation of problems. Also, the passenger side windshield wiper interferes with the lip of the hood.

There have been no problems getting parts, but many are available only from a dealer. I have replaced the thrust rods, brake pads, and warped rotors once. The head gasket was also replaced, under extended warranty, because of an oil leak. *—Nurten and Phil Street, San Clemente, California*

1994 BMW 540iA and a 1995 BMW 540i 6-Speed

Handling is very good for 3,800 pounds of car, and the brakes are excellent. The 540i's engine has enough torque that it pulls strongly from any normal speed. Seating is very comfortable with plenty of legroom. The car also has all of the little extras.

Maintenance costs are relatively high. The front control arm bushings need to be replaced every 60,000 to 80,000 miles. The radiator is prone to leaking from the plastic end caps. Replacing the cabin filter requires removing the glovebox. There is the Nikasil block problem, and a breather plate on the rear of the intake manifold fails, requiring removal of the intake manifold to repair. Fluid leaks around the cam cover gaskets, the power steering lines, and the lines from the oil filter housing to the engine. The transmission is fairly sturdy but costs approximately $5,000 to rebuild. A catalytic converter costs more than $2,000 to replace. *—Gail Wisner and Dale Schaub, Anaheim Hills, California*

1991 BMW M5

In 1991 this car was considered by some press critics as the best car ever made. I think it still is one of the best. The joy of driving this car makes daily travel a much better experience.

M5s do eat belts. The belts should be changed every 18 months. The water pump should be changed every 3 years. I had the self-leveling suspension (SLS) replaced at 120,000 miles with Dinan Stage 1 suspension. Although I liked the SLS, the price of $1,000 each for the rear shocks is a shock all right. Plus, the SLS has a tendency to leak and require more maintenance than a conversion.

Would I buy another? Yes, absolutely. It is like an ultimate ownership experience. *—Michael Badger, Fountain Valley, California*

This front view of a 1995 BMW 525i Touring shows nonstandard wheels and owner-installed, painted mirrors. These larger sunroof panels can be opened independently.

E39 5-Series
1997-2001
Chapter 11

525i/525i Sport Wagon
528i/528i Sport Wagon
530i/530i Sport Wagon
540i/540i Sport Wagon
M5

The fourth-generation 5-Series does not stray too far from its predecessor in looks. It has similar visuals and the same basic mechanicals. It's hard to fault BMW; after all, why mess up a good thing?

The front suspension is an evolved version of the double-pivot MacPherson strut suspension. The 528i's front subframe is aluminum, and for the first time, rack-and-pinion steering is used in a 5-Series. The 540i uses a more traditional recirculating-ball steering.

Rear suspension is a new design and features an aluminum subframe carrying a four-link-per-side arrangement. Front brakes are also improved, with the 528i receiving aluminum calipers and ventilated front discs. The 540i retains iron calipers, while both cars have ventilated discs all around.

The 528i shares its engine with the 3-Series. For 1997 and 1998, the M52/2.8-liter inline six, and for 1999 through 2000, an aluminum block (the M52TU) with double VANOS was introduced. In 2001, BMW introduced a new design inline six, the M54. This new engine was available in two displacements, 2.5 liters and 3.0 liters. Accordingly, 5-Series powered by these engines were rebadged as the 525i and 530i, respectively.

The M62/4.4 DOHC 32-valve V-8 engine powers the 540i models. In 1996, BMW moved away from the Nikasil alloy V-8 engine blocks that had proved troublesome in the 1994 and 1995 years. For 1997, the Alusil blocks were expanded to 4.4 liters. Although power remained unchanged at 282-brake horsepower, torque increased to 310 lbs-ft at 3,900 rpm. Drivability in the low to medium speeds, where most U.S. driving is done, was improved.

Based on the 540i 6-speed, the E39 M5 builds from there. With a larger displacement V-8, larger brakes, wheels, and tires, uprated suspension settings, and distinct cosmetics, this one picks up where the previous generation M5 left off.

BMW continues to be the only manufacturer offering manual transmissions in this midsized category. The 525i, 528i, and 530i sedans are all available with a 5-speed manual, and the 540i is available with a 6-speed manual.

A variety of automatic transmissions has been used, with the 1997 to 1999 528i having an optional 4-speed automatic. A 5-speed automatic featuring Adaptive Transmission Control (ATC) and Steptronic was an option for the 2000 model year 528i. This same transmission is an option for the 525i and 530i. The optional 5-speed automatic transmission for the 540i also features ATC, a high-stall speed torque converter, as well as Steptronic.

As electronic and computer technologies improve, manufacturers are covering more and more of the scheduled maintenance items as a way of reducing the cost of ownership. A component of this is extended service intervals. Spark plugs now last for up to 100,000 miles, air filters up to 60,000 miles, and transmissions that are "lifetime" service (meaning that they will never need any routine maintenance) from the beginning. Recommended oil change intervals are up to 15,000 miles.

The E39 5-Series carries on the BMW tradition of comfortable, quiet, refined, and excellent-handling midsize sedans that offer excellent dollar value. With a variety of sedans and Sport Wagon body styles available, buyers have a great selection of models to choose from, whether it is the 525i Sport Wagon or the muscular M5.

The oldest cars of this fourth-generation 5-Series are just five years old, and there are not too many problems with the cars on record. The certified pre-owned program from BMW is available for cars that meet BMW's criteria and it may extend the original factory warranty to as much as 100,000 miles.

The 540i 6-speed offers outstanding performance and handling. The 525/528/530/540s are all available with the Sport package option, which offers slightly stiffer suspension and wider wheels. The 525/530 were new for 2001, and no data is available as yet to determine whether there are any long-term problems. Finally, the M5 is a 400-horsepower, stealthy rocket ship that is truly a stunning performance car. The manufacturer's suggested retail price is in the high-$60,000 to low-$70,000 range, and there aren't many used ones out there yet.

Ratings Chart

E39 5-Series

	525i	525i Sport Wagon	528i
Model Comfort/Amenities	***½	***½	***½
Reliability	***	***	***
Collectibility	*	*	*
Parts/Service Availability	***½	***½	***½
Est. Annual Repair Costs	**½	**½	**½

	528i Sport Wagon	530i	530i Sport Wagon
Model Comfort/Amenities	***½	***½	***½
Reliability	***	***	***
Collectibility	*	*	*
Parts/Service Availability	***½	***½	***½
Est. Annual Repair Costs	**½	**½	**½

	540i	540i Sport Wagon	M5
Model Comfort/Amenities	***½	***½	***½
Reliability	***	***	***
Collectibility	*	*	****½
Parts/Service Availability	***½	***½	***½
Est. Annual Repair Costs	**½	**½	***½

The rear view of a 1998 BMW 528i is a classic BMW look. Owners of this sedan took delivery in Europe—note the Nurburgring and Laguna Seca track outlines on the deck lid.

Manual transmission-equipped cars have experienced problems with gear selection, especially first gear, which indicates that the clutch is not properly releasing or there may be binding in the shift linkage. Dealer service technicians evaluate cars that are displaying these symptoms and working with customers to resolve any problems.

Catalytic converters on the 1997 BMW 528i models seem to be a weak point; there have been several reports of converters failing prematurely. Rattles in the exhaust system, misfiring, loss of power or a "Check Engine" warning message are indications of a failed catalytic converter.

There have been recalls on the engine auxiliary cooling fans. Fan malfunction has caused engine overheating. Reports of the wiring for the fans overheating and shorting out are common. The majority of cars affected—those built between December 2000 and September 2001—have been recalled and the necessary repairs made.

The M52/2.8-liter engines have experienced problems with the VANOS solenoids. A technical service bulletin (TSB) was issued regarding these failures.

The 525i model line offered lower base prices than the phased-out 528i models and fill the gap between the top of the 3-Series line and the more equipped 530i and 540i models.

There have been some reports of steering rack problems and electric thermostats sticking open on the 525i, as well as leaking power steering hoses on the 525i/528i/530i models.

Listen for clunking or rattling from the rear suspension when going over bumps. The rear end ball joints have shown a tendency to wear prematurely. There have also been reports of front struts leaking and failing.

The air conditioning condenser is mounted in a location that has proved susceptible to rocks and debris damage. In cars equipped with an automatic transmission, the oil cooler lines run under the radiator and can trap dirt and debris. Over time, this could actually dislodge the lines from the radiator and leak transmission fluid.

Catalytic converters on the 1997 models seem to be a weak point; there have been several reports of converters failing prematurely. Rattles in the exhaust system, misfiring, loss of power, or a "Check Engine" warning message are indications of a failed catalytic converter.

Some 540i's equipped with the 5 HP 24EH automatic transmission may experience premature wear leading to the loss of first, second, third, and reverse gears. In some instances, this has led to a warranty replacement of the automatic transmission.

There have been recalls on the engine auxiliary cooling fans. Fan malfunction has caused engine overheating. Reports of the wiring for the fans overheating and shorting out are common. The majority of cars affected—those built between December 2000 and September 2001—have been recalled and the necessary repairs made.

The revised E39 540i carries on the exemplary reputation of the previous generation's V-8–powered 5-Series.

Listen for clunking or rattling from the rear suspension when going over bumps. The rear end ball joints have shown a tendency to wear prematurely. There have also been reports of front struts leaking and failing.

Manual transmission-equipped cars have experienced problems with gear selection, especially first gear, which indicates that the clutch is not properly releasing or there may be binding in the shift linkage. Dealer service technicians evaluate cars that are

Look for indications of power steering hoses leaking. They are difficult to see and usually require putting the car on a lift to examine.

149

Manual transmission equipped cars have experienced problems with gear selection, especially first gear, which indicates that the clutch is not properly releasing or there may be binding in the shift linkage. Dealer service technicians evaluate cars that are displaying these symptoms and working with customers to resolve any problems.

Brake lamp switches may fail internally and could cause the brake lights to be always on or a no brake-lights condition.

Look for indications of power steering hoses leaking. They are difficult to see and usually require putting the car on a lift to examine.

This M5 has all of the amenities and capabilities of an already highly refined vehicle, plus the ability to sprint to 60 miles per hour in 4.8 seconds.

There have been reports of clutches slipping.

The factory tire-mounting machines may have damaged the sidewalls of some tires. This type of damage could cause sudden and unexpected tire deflation. Also, watch for rims that have suffered pothole or curb damage.

Listen for clunking or rattling from the rear suspension when going over bumps. The rear end ball joints have shown a tendency to wear prematurely. There have also been reports of front struts leaking and failing.

Specifications
525i/525i Sport Wagon 2001

Engine Type			DOHC Inline 6, 24-Valve, Double-VANOS; Steplessly Variable Valve Timing
Displacement cc/ci			2494/152
Compression Ratio			10.51
BHP @ rpm			184 @ 6000
Torque lbs-ft @ rpm			175 @ 3500
Injection Type			Siemens MS 43 with Adaptive Knock Control
Fuel Requirement			Unleaded Premium
Transmission	Manual		ZF Type C, 5-Speed
	Automatic		GM 5, 5-Speed with Adaptive Transmission Control and Steptronic
Steering			Rack and Pinion, Vehicle Speed Sensitive Power Assist
Front Suspension			MacPherson Struts, Aluminum Double-Pivot Lower Arms, Coil Springs, Twin-Tube Gas-Pressure Shocks, Anti-Roll Bar, Aluminum Subframe, with Sport Package M-Technic Sport Suspension Calibration
Rear Suspension			4-Link Integral Suspension in Aluminum, Coil Springs, Twin-Tube Gas-Pressure Shocks, Anti-Roll Bar, Aluminum Subframe, with Sport Package M-Technic Sport Suspension Calibration Touring Optional Self-Leveling Air Springs
Wheelbase (in.)			111.4
Weight (lbs.)	Manual	525i	3450
		525i Sport Wagon	3726
	Automatic	525i	3505
		525i Sport Wagon	3781
Wheels	Standard		Cast Alloy 16 x 7.0 J
	Optional		Cast Alloy 17 x 8.0J
Tires	Standard		225/55R-16 95 H, All-Season Radials
	Optional		Sport Package 235/45R-17 W
Brake System			Vacuum Assist, Antilock Braking System, Dynamic Stability Control, Dynamic Brake Control
	Front		11.7-in. Vented Discs with Aluminum
	Rear		11.7-in. Vented Discs with Aluminum Calipers
0–60 mph, sec	Manual	525i	7.3
		525i Sport Wagon	8.2
	Automatic	525i	8.0
		525i Sport Wagon	9.2
Maximum Speed mph			128 (electronically limited)
MPG, City/Highway	Manual	525i	20/29
		525i Sport Wagon	19/27
	Automatic	525i	19/27
		525i Sport Wagon	19/26

Functional and elegant, the interior of the 1998 BMW 528i is uncluttered with well-placed controls. A close look reveals the window and mirror controls on the armrest with the seat memory buttons alongside the seat.

Specifications
528i/528i Sport Wagon 1997–2000

Engine Type			DOHC Inline 6, 24-Valve, Double-VANOSI; Steplessly Variable Valve Timing
Displacement cc/ci			2793/170
Compression Ratio			10.21
BHP @ rpm			193 @ 5500
Torque lbs-ft @ rpm			206 @ 3500
Injection Type	1996–1997		Siemens MS 41.0 with Adaptive Knock Control
	1998		Siemens MS 41.1 with Adaptive Knock Control
	1999–2000		Siemens MS 42 with Adaptive Knock Control
Fuel Requirement			Unleaded Premium
Transmission	Manual		ZF Type C, 5-Speed
	Automatic	1996–1999	THM R1, 4-Speed with Adaptive Transmission Control
		2000	GM 5, 5-Speed with Adaptive Transmission Control and Steptronic
Steering			Rack and Pinion, Vehicle Speed Sensitive Power Assist
Front Suspension			MacPherson Struts, Aluminum Double-Pivot Lower Arms, Coil Springs, Twin-Tube Gas Pressure Shocks, Anti-Roll Bar Aluminum Subframe
	1999–2000 Sport Package		M-Technic Sport Suspension Calibration
Rear Suspension			4-Link Integral Suspension in Aluminum, Coil Springs, Twin-Tube Gas-Pressure Shocks, Anti-Roll Bar, Aluminum Subframe
	1999–2000 Sport Package		M-Technic Sport SuspensionCalibration
	2000	528i Sport Wagon	Optional Self-Leveling Suspension with Air Shocks
Wheelbase (in.)			111.4
Weight (lbs.)	Manual	1996	3430
		1997-1998	3450
		1999-2000	3495
		1999–2000 Sport Wagon	3726
	Automatic	1996-1998	3505
		1999-2000	3549
		1999–2000 Sport Wagon	3781
Wheels	Standard		Lightweight Forged Alloy 15x7.0J
	Optional		Cast Alloy 16 x 7.0J
	Sport Package		Forged Alloy 17 x 8.0 J
Tires	Standard		225/60R-15 96 H, All-Season Radials
	Sport Package		225/55R-16 H
Brake System			Vacuum Assist, Antilock Braking System, Dynamic Stability Control (DSC), Dynamic Brake Control(DBC)
	Front		11.7-in. Vented Discs with Aluminum Calipers
	Rear		11.7-in. Vented Discs with Aluminum Calipers
0–60 mph, sec	Manual	1996	7.4
		1997	7.7
		1998-2000	7.0
		1999–2000 Sport Wagon	7.9
	Automatic	1996	8.2
		1997	8.6
		1998-2000	7.7
		1999–2000 Sport Wagon	8.9
Maximum Speed mph			128 (electronically limited)
MPG, City/Highway	Manual		
		1996-1998	19/28
		1999	20/29
		2000	21/29
		1999–2000 Sport Wagon	18/26
	Automatic	1996-2000	18/26

Specifications
530i/530i Sport Wagon 2001

Engine Type		DOHC Inline 6, 24-Valve, Double-VANOS; Steplessly Variable Valve Timing
Displacement cc/ci		2979/182
Compression Ratio		10.21
BHP @ rpm		225 @ 5900
Torque lbs-ft @ rpm		214 @ 3500
Injection Type		Siemens MS 43 with Adaptive Knock Control
Fuel Requirement		Unleaded Premium
Transmission	Manual	ZF Type C, 5-Speed
	Automatic	GM 5, 5-Speed with Adaptive Transmission Control and Steptronic Steering Rack and Pinion, Vehicle Speed Sensitive Power Assist
Front Suspension		MacPherson Struts, Aluminum Double-Pivot Lower Arms, Coil Springs, Twin-Tube Gas Pressure Shocks, Anti-Roll Bar Aluminum Subframe; with Sport Package, M-Technic Sport Suspension Calibration.
Rear Suspension		4-Link Integral Suspension in Aluminum, Coil Springs, Twin-Tube Gas-Pressure Shocks, Anti-Roll Bar, Aluminum Subframe; with Sport Package, M-Technic Sport Suspension Calibration.
Wheelbase (in.)		111.4
Weight (lbs.)	Manual	3494
	Automatic	3549
Wheels	Standard	Cast Alloy 16 x 7.0 J,
	Optional	Cast Alloy 17 x 8.J
Tires	Standard	225/55R-16 95 H, All-Season Radials
	Sport Package	235/45R-17 W
Brake System		Vacuum Assist, Antilock Braking System, Dynamic Stability Control (DSC), Dynamic Brake Control (DBC)
Front		12.8-in. Vented Discs with Aluminum Calipers
Rear		11.7-in. Vented Discs with Aluminum Calipers
0–60 mph, sec	Manual	6.7
	Automatic	7.5
Maximum Speed mph		128 (electronically limited)
MPG, City/Highway	Manual	21/30
	Automatic	18/26

With 394 horsepower and 368 lbs-ft of torque, the 2001 BMW M5's aluminum block V-8 is potent in stock form. The engine in this car has been upgraded with Dinan cold-air intake and performance chips for even greater power. A strut tower brace has been added by the dealership.

Specifications
M5 2000–2001

Engine Type		DOHC 32-Valve (4 cam) V-8, Double-VANOS Steplessly Variable Valve Timing, 8 Individual Electronically Controlled Throttles with Normal and Sport Settings
Displacement cc/ci		4941/302
Compression Ratio		11.01
BHP @ rpm	2000	400 # 6600
	2001	394 @ 6600
Torque lbs-ft @ rpm	2000	369 @ 3800
	2001	368 @ 3800
Injection Type		Siemens MSS 52 with Adaptive Knock Control, Variable Valve Timing Electronic Throttles, g-Sensitive Lubrication System, Oil-Level/Temperature Sender, Variable Tachometer Warning Zone, Catalyst Protection and M Driving Dynamics Control Included in Control Strategy
Fuel Requirement		Unleaded Premium
Transmission	Manual	Getrag Type D, 6-Speed
	Automatic	NA
Steering		Self-Adjusting Recirculating Ball, Vehicle Speed Sensitive Power Assist with M Driving Dynamics Control (normal and sport settings)
Front Suspension		BMW M Sport Suspension in Aluminum, Struts, Double Pivot Lower Arms, Coil Springs Plus Polyurethane Auxiliary Springs, Twin-Tube Gas Pressure Shocks, Anti-Roll Bar
Rear Suspension		BMW M Sport Suspension in Aluminum, 4 Link Integral System, Coil Springs Plus Polyurethane Auxiliary Springs, Twin-Tube Gas-Pressure Shocks, Anti-Roll Bar Includes Aluminum Subframe
Wheelbase (in.)		111.4
Weight (lbs.)	Manual	4023
	Automatic	NA
Wheels		Cast Alloy 18 x 8.0 Front
		18 x 9.5 Rear
Tires		245/40ZR-18 Front
		275/35ZR-18 Rear
Brake System		Vacuum Assist, Antilock Braking System (ABS), All-Season Traction (AST), Dynamic Stability Control (DSC)
Front		13.6-in. Vented Discs
Rear		12.9-in. Vented Discs
0–60 mph, sec	Manual	4.8
	Automatic	NA
Maximum Speed mph		155 Electronically Limited)
MPG, City/Highway	Manual	13/21
	Automatic	NA

The 2001 BMW M5's trunk is fully carpeted and features concealed storage areas, luggage straps, and a cargo net. The round buttons in the rear bumper are park-distance control sensors.

Specifications
540i/540i Sport Wagon 1997–2001

Engine Type			DOHC V-8, 32-Valve, VANOS Steplessly Variable Valve Timing
Displacement cc/ci			4398/268
Compression Ratio			10.01
BHP @ rpm	1997-1998		282 @ 5700
	1999-2001		282 @ 5400
Torque lbs-ft @ rpm	1997-1998		310 @ 3900
	1999-2001		324 @ 3600
Injection Type	1997-1998		Bosch HFM-Motronic 5.2 with Adaptive Knock Control
	1999-2001		Bosch HFM Motronic 7.2 with Adaptive Knock Control
Fuel Requirement			Unleaded Premium
Transmission	Manual	540i	Getrag Type D, 6-Speed
		540i Sport Wagon	NA
	Automatic	1997	ZF 5 HP 30 EH, 5-Speed
		1998-1999	ZF 5 HP 24 EH, 5-Speed
		2000-2001	ZF 5 HP 24 EH 5-Speed with Adaptive Transmission Control (ATC and Selectable Sport Mode or Steptronic Steering
		1997-1999	Self-Adjusting Recirculating Ball, Vehicle Speed-Sensitive Power Assist
		2000-2001	Recirculating Ball, Engine-Speed Sensitive Front Suspension MacPherson Struts, Aluminum Double-Pivot Lower Arms, Coil Springs, Twin-Tube Gas Pressure Shocks, Anti-Roll Bar, Steel Subframe
		1997-2001	540i 6-Speed M-Technic Sport Suspension Calibration
Rear Suspension			4-Link Integral Suspension in Aluminum, Coil Springs, Twin-Tube Gas Pressure Shocks, Anti-Roll Bar Steel Subframe
	1997-2001	540i 6-Speed	M-Technic Sport Suspension Calibration
	1999-2001	Sport Wagon	Self-Leveling Air Springs
Wheelbase (in.)			111.4
Weight (lbs.)	Manual	540i	3748
		540i Sport Wagon	NA
	Automatic	540i	3803
		540i Sport Wagon	4056
Wheels	Standard	1997-1998	2-Piece Cast/Forged Alloy, 17x8.0J (M/T) Cast Alloy 16 x 7.0J (A/T)
		1999-2001	Cast Alloy 16 x 7.0 (A/T)
			Cast Alloy 17 x 8.0 f
			17 x 9.0 r (M/T)
	Optional	1998-2000	17 x 8.0J Front
			17 x 9.0J Rear (w/A/T & SP)
		2001	Cast Alloy 16 x 7.0 (A/T)
			Cast Alloy 17 x 8.0 f
			17 x 9.0 r (M/T)
Tires	Standard	1997-1998	235/45R-17 93W Performance Radials (MT)
			225/55R-17 95H All-Season Radials (A/T)
		1999-2001	225/55R-16 H (A/T)
			235/45R-17 93W Performance Radials (MT)
			255/40R-17 95H (Sedan w/M/T Only)
	Optional	1998-2001	235/45R-17 93W f
			255/40R-17 93W r
Brake System		1997–2000	Vacuum Assist, Antilock Braking System (ABS), Dynamic Stability Control (DSC), Dynamic BrakeControl (DBC)
		2001	All-Season Traction (AST)
	Front		12.8-in. Vented Discs with Cast Iron Calipers
	Rear		11.8-in. Vented Discs with Aluminum Calipers
0–60 mph, sec	Manual	1997	6.1
		1998-2001	5.8
		1999–2001 Sport Wagon	NA
	Automatic		
		1997	6.6
		1998	6.4
		1999-2001	6.2
		1999–2001 Sport Wagon	6.3
Maximum Speed mph			
		1997	128 (electronically limited)
		1998-2001	155 (Manual)/128 (Automatic) (electronically limited)
		1999–2001 Sport Wagon	128 (electronically limited)
MPG, City/Highway	Manual	540i	15/24
		540i Sport Wagon	NA
	Automatic	540i	18/24
		540i Sport Wagon	15/21

Replacement Costs for Common Parts
525i 2001, M5 2000–2001, 528i 1997–2000

525i 2001

Oil Filter		$8.50
Air Filter		$18
Fuel Filter		$88.75
Fuel Pump		$117
Starter		$169, Exchange
Alternator		$285–$363,
Exchange		
Clutch Kit		$221
Water Pump (remanufactured)		$79.95
Front Bumper		$311
Hood		$397
Left Front Fender		$258
Right Rear Quarter Panel		$374
Rear Bumper		$305
Windshield		$315
Tail Light Lens		$161
Header/Catalyst		$650, Exchange
Center Silencer		$299
Rear Silencer		$315
Oxygen Sensor	Regulating (2 required)	$133.35
	Monitoring (2 required)	$133.35
Brake Master		$457
Front Rotor (each)		$95.75
Front Pads (set)		$90.75
	+ sensor	$16.10
Rear Rotor (each)		$81.50
Rear Pads		$75
	+ sensor	$20
2 Front Shocks	Standard	$198
(each)	w/ Electronic Damping	
	Control	$737.50
	w/ Sport Suspension	$235
Rear Shocks (each)	Standard	$118
	w/ Sport Suspension	$165

M5 2000

Oil Filter		$10
Air Filter		$18
Fuel Filter		$135
Fuel Pump		$117
Starter		$269, Exchange
Alternator		$680
Clutch Kit		$381
Water Pump (remanufactured)		$197
Front Bumper	w/o Park Distance Control	$454
	w/ PDC	$429
Hood		$397
Left Front Fender		$258
Right Rear Quarter Panel		$374
Rear Bumper		$498.50
Windshield		$315
Tail Light Lens		$161
Header/Catalyst (each)		$2,070
Center Silencer		$607.50
Rear Silencer (each)		$620
Oxygen Sensor	Regulating (2 required)	$133.35
	Monitoring (2 required)	$133.35
Brake Master		$457
Front Rotor (each)		$249
Front Pads (set)		$132
	+ sensor	$16.10
Rear Rotor (each)		$249
Rear Pads		$86.75
	+ sensor	$20
Front Shocks (each)		$235

528i 1997–2000

Oil Filter		$8.50
Air Filter		$15
Fuel Filter		$21
Fuel Pump		$117
Starter		$169, Exchange
Alternator		$386, Exchange
Clutch Kit		$239
Water Pump (remanufactured)		$79.95
Front Bumper		$311
Hood		$397
Left Front Fender		$258
Right Rear Quarter Panel		$374
Rear Bumper		$305
Windshield		$315
Tail Light Lens		$161
Header/Catalyst		$650, Exchange
Center Silencer		$299
Rear Silencer		$450
Oxygen Sensor	Regulating	$133.35
	Monitoring	$133.35
Brake Master		$409–457
Front Rotor (each)		$95.75
Front Pads (set)		$92.50
	+ sensor	$16.10
Rear Rotor (each)		$81.50
Rear Pads		$75
	+ sensor	$20
Front Shocks (each)	Standard	$198
	w/ Electronic Damping Control	$737.50
	w/ Sport Suspension	$235
Rear Shocks (each)	Standard	$118
	w/ Sport Suspension	$165

The rear seats of the 1998 BMW 528i are split and can be folded independently to accommodate large, bulky items.

Replacement Costs for Common Parts
540i 1997–2001, 530i 2001

540i 1997–2001

Oil Filter		$10
Air Filter		$18
Fuel Filter		$21
Fuel Pump		$117
Starter		$269, Exchange
Alternator		363–680, Exchange
Clutch Kit	to 6/96	$446
	from 6/96	$381
Water Pump (remanufactured)		$117
Front Bumper		$311
Hood		$397
Left Front Fender		$258
Right Rear Quarter Panel		$374
Rear Bumper		$305
Windshield		$315
Tail Light Lens		$161
Header/Catalyst (each)		$725
Center Silencer		$299
Rear Silencer		$492
Oxygen Sensor	Regulating (2 required)	$62
	Monitoring (2 required)	$133.35
Brake Master		$409–$457
Front Rotor (each)		$113
Front Pads (set)		$96
	+ sensor	$16.10
Rear Rotor (each)		$81.50
Rear Pads		$75
	+ sensor	$20
Front Shocks (each) Standard		$198
w/ Electronic Damping Control		$737.50
w/ Sport Suspension		$235
Rear Shocks (each) Standard		$118
w/ Sport Suspension		$165

530i 2001

Oil Filter		$8.50
Air Filter		$18
Fuel Filter		$88.75
Fuel Pump		$117
Starter		$169 Exchange
Alternator		$285–363, Exchange
Clutch Kit		$344
Water Pump (remanufactured)		$79.95
Front Bumper		$311
Hood		$397
Left Front Fender		$258
Right Rear Quarter Panel		$374
Rear Bumper		$305
Windshield		$315
Tail Light Lens		$161
Header/Catalyst (each)		$650
Center Silencer		$299
Rear Silencer		$238
	w/ Aero kit	$338
Oxygen Sensor	Regulating (2 required)	$133.35
	Monitoring (2 required)	$133.35
Brake Master		$457
Front Rotor (each)		$93.50
Front Pads (set)		$96
	+ sensor	$16.10
Rear Rotor (each)		$81.50
Rear Pads		$75
	+ sensor	$20
Front Shocks (each) Standard		$198
w/ Electronic Damping Control		$737.50
w/ Sport Suspension		$235
2 Rear Shocks (each) Standard		$118
w/ Sport Suspension		$165

The optional Sport steering wheel of the 2001 BMW 525i Sport Wagon features multifunction controls at the driver's fingertips and carries the Motorsports logo.

What They Said About the . . .

525i

If you really want the added luxury and exclusiveness of a 5-Series and want to spend less for it, the 525i is a very competent car. Enthusiastic drivers should stay with the standard manual transmission and spend the money for the sport package. *—Roundel,* **February 2002**

528i Touring

BMW's 528i is a wagon that grows on you. It's unremarkable at first. At moderate speeds, its steering is thoughtlessly natural.
—Car and Driver, **June 1999**

540i

No matter what its cost, the bottom line is that the 540i with 6-speed is a true enthusiast's sedan, one that'll treat you to a taste of driving heaven.
—Road & Track, **May 1997**

M5

For people who love cars, the BMW M5 is quite simply the most desirable sedan in the world at any price. What more can we say?
—Car and Driver, **March 2000**

From the rear, the 2000 BMW 540i Sport Wagon shows that a midsize sedan can effectively be converted to a sport wagon. Single exhaust is utilized on all of the sport wagon models.

The interior of this 2000 BMW M5 shows the Luxury interior trim package with wood accents.

I Bought a . . .

2000 BMW M5

The E39 M5 generates its speed with little fuss and feedback. A downshift, a tip of the electronically controlled gas pedal, and if you're not careful, you're going over 100 miles per hour! The 6-speed makes you feel like you can leave the car in any one of the middle gears and drive anywhere from 20 miles per hour to well above the speed limit. It's a very easy car to drive.

The E39 M5 has all the luxuries: navigation system, Xenon headlights, auto dimming mirrors (inside and out), etc. No question that the M5 has grown from a race-bred car to the fastest 4-door luxury sedan around. —*Linda and Louis Goldsman, Mission Viejo, California*

1998 BMW 528i Sport

I really like the size, the balance of performance, luxury, and all-around capability of the 528i Sport. It can be comfortable and elegant when desired, yet it's also inspiring to drive on a back road or a racetrack. Gas mileage is 26 miles per gallon on average. In addition, the 528i has been a reliable and inexpensive car to own and maintain. —*Dan Tackett, San Diego, California*

2001 BMW 530i

The way our car handled that first day, as I drove through a twisting canyon, almost brought tears of joy to me. There isn't a creak, body rattle, or straining sound. The 5-speed manual transmission is the smoothest I've ever driven. Acceleration is amazing for an almost 2-ton car, and the gas mileage is in the mid-20 miles per gallon.

The only drawbacks in my mind are that the paint is soft and shows swirl marks easily, and the cup holders and stereo should be much more state-of-the-art. —*Ed Becker, Woodland Hills, California*

2001 BMW 530i

The sleek look and the handling are what we really like about the 530i. The electronics and slow NAV system are our biggest dislikes.

Our best experience was picking it up in Europe. Our worst was having to wait for the car to arrive stateside, but doing Euro-delivery and driving 130 miles per hour down the autobahn in your own car made it all worth it! —*Johnnalyn and Arnold Serrano, Corona, California*

2000 BMW 540i Touring

We have owned several BMWs and really enjoy the 540i Touring. We bought it with the idea in mind of having a versatile car that has plenty of room. It is surprisingly quick—the power is nearly as much as that of our 750iL—and it handles like an M3.

Thus far, there have been no problems with the car, just routine maintenance. —*Judy and Ray Miller, Whittier, California*

Quad exhaust tips differentiate the 2001 M5 from other models. Dinan badging on the left side of the deck lid denotes that this car features several upgrades installed at the BMW dealership.

E24 6-Series
1977-1989
Chapter 12

630CSi
633CSi
635CSi/L6
M6

Replacing the aging 2800/3.0 CS coupes, the new 6-Series coupe was introduced to the public in the spring of 1976. Designed by a team led by Paul Baracq, it is a graceful design that still looks good today. The 6-Series is based on the floor pan, suspension, and running gear of the E12 5-Series cars, and with the introduction of the E28 5-Series in 1982, the coupes inherited the E28's suspension improvements.

Even though there are four individual bucket seats, rear legroom and headroom are limited. If you are over 6 feet tall, you may also find front seat headroom limited in sunroof-equipped cars (most U.S.-specification coupes were delivered with sunroofs).

The 6-Series coupes remained visually similar throughout their production run. Even though the cars are very similar in appearance, many mechanical changes were implemented during the intervening years.

By 1980, a 3-way catalytic converter and Lambda sensor replaced the thermal reactors used in the 630CSi. Horsepower dropped slightly (from 177 brake horsepower down to 174) and torque dropped (from 196 lbs-ft to 188). However, the improvements in drivability and fuel economy more than made up for these small losses.

The 1982 model experienced the single largest number of changes. Significant changes were made to the layout of the dashboard. A trip computer was standard, and improvements were made to the HVAC system. A service interval system (SI) was introduced. In normal operation, the SI lights illuminate when the ignition switch is turned to the "ON" position and then go out as the starter is engaged.

Also in 1982, the suspension and brake systems were updated, using components brought over from the E28 5-Series sedan. In the front, two lower control arms replaced the earlier, single-arm design. The rear-most of these arms is a thrust rod that extends rearward at an angle and attaches to the frame rails with a large rubber bushing.

The manual transmissions are fairly sturdy. As the mileage increases, the second-gear syncros tend to go bad, usually noted by balkiness in selecting second gear and an occasional grinding of gears.

The 6-Series cars through 1986 offered a 3-speed ZF HP-22 automatic transmission as an option. In 1987, the ZF 4-speed automatic replaced the 3-speed automatic. This series' transmission did have some problems, particularly with regard to the California emissions testing, which required a 2,500-rpm test in neutral. The ZF 4-speed transmissions experienced a series of premature failures directly related to this emission test. Subsequently, this requirement was waived for all BMWs fitted with this transmission.

The early 3.0-liter coupes were slow, returned dismal gas mileage figures, and used the dreaded thermal reactors for emissions controls. The thermal reactors are no longer available, and it may prove difficult to pass emissions tests without them. The 1980 to 1982 3.3-liter coupe used a 3-way catalyst and Lambda sensor to meet emissions and is a much better-driving car. The 1983 to 1984 coupes received upgraded suspensions, Motronic engine controls, and improved HVAC systems.

The 635CSi and the L6 are mechanically the same; the L6 featured more luxury items during its 1987 run. The 635 features all the good stuff and makes a great driver.

The M6 is the BMW Motorsport hot rod. Sixty-thousand dollars when new, it holds its resale well. Power, luxury, glorious twin-cam 4-valve engine, and fewer than 1,800 were imported to the United States. A keeper.

Watch out for gray-market cars, especially the high-end M6 models. Federalization papers must be in order or you could find yourself with an expensive driveway ornament.

Overall, these cars offer good reliability from the big-six engines and drivetrain, and many of the parts are still available.

These cars are prone to the rear differential mount fatiguing and breaking. Have this area examined. The factory designed an improved and reinforced mount for the M6, but this area should still be inspected.

One thing to watch for is the "banjo" bolts holding the oil supply pipe in place. This pipe is located under the valve cover, right on top of the motor and supplies oil to the rocker arms. These bolts should be checked annually.

A side effect of the heat required for the thermal reactors was a high rate of cracked cylinder heads on these early cars. The cure for this was to replace the damaged head with a newer design (1980 and later) featuring improved water passages.

In 1982, the suspension systems were updated using components brought over from the E28 5-Series sedan. Over time, the thrust rod bushing deteriorates and permits unwanted movement of the front suspension. The thrust rod bushings are roughly $40 each but require the use of a hydraulic press to replace.

The same 3.0-liter 6-cylinder engine used in the E12 5-Series cars powered the 630CSi, and to counter complaints that the coupe lacked power, BMW replaced the 3.0 with a 3,210cc six-cylinder equipped with Bosch L-Jetronic fuel injection.

A ticking noise from the engine once it is at operating temperature could be an indication that a valve adjustment is needed or that the rocker shafts have excessive wear on the lobes.

If the car you are looking at has an automatic transmission, be sure to check its operation and that it shifts up and down smoothly. The transmission cooler lines have been known to chafe through. If this should happen where the lines pass near the exhaust system, a fire could develop.

Check the fuel lines and fuel injectors whenever the oil level is checked, looking for any signs of seepage or leakage. Fuel is delivered under about 40 PSI, and if the fuel lines are cracked, the fuel lines may leak and spray fuel onto the exhaust system.

Thermal reactors crack over time, and many cars have had these removed. If you live in a state that requires original emissions equipment to be installed and functioning, be aware that a new thermal reactor costs approximately $800, two reactors are required, and they are no longer available.

The brake hydraulic pressure accumulator is a frequent-failure item. The pressure accumulator carries a hefty price tag, about $170, so be sure to have this checked out beforehand.

163

Fuel tanks have been known to rust through along the horizontal seam and where the filler neck is connected. New fuel tanks are still available for under $300.

The cars are prone to the rear differential mount fatiguing and breaking. Have this area examined.

The rear suspension self-leveling hydraulic pumps are prone to failure and leaking. Be sure to have this system examined carefully for leaking or damaged components. Many coupes have had this system removed and replaced with standard rear shocks.

Drive shafts can and do fail. Sometimes it is the center bearing and sometimes it is a universal joint. Drive shafts are available through the aftermarket as rebuilt units. Expect to pay between $500 and $900 to replace a drive shaft.

A common maintenance item in the driveline is the rubber flex-disk coupling in the middle of the drive shaft. Called a "guibo," it absorbs some of the driveline stresses. Expect to spend about $300 to replace it, plus parts and labor.

The sports seats offered in the 1985 and newer cars were based on the Recaro sport seats and offered power adjustments for both driver and passenger. These can prove problematic in that the electric motors fail.

In late 1984, the 633CSi's engine was upgraded to 3,430cc, and the cars were rebadged as the 635CSi. The L6 was a one-year wonder, offered in 1987 only.

Check the fuel lines and fuel injectors whenever the oil level is checked, looking for any signs of seepage or leakage. Fuel is delivered under about 40 PSI, and if the fuel lines are cracked, the fuel lines may leak and spray fuel onto the exhaust system.

One thing to watch for is the "banjo" bolts holding the oil-supply pipe in place. This pipe is located under the valve cover, right on top of the motor and supplies oil to the rocker arms. These bolts should be checked annually.

The brake hydraulic pressure accumulator reservoir (also referred to as the brake "bomb"), is a frequent failure item. It carries a hefty price tag, about $170, so be sure to have this checked out beforehand.

BMW first introduced the M6 to the European market in April 1984. The U.S. market had to wait until the 1987 model year. With only 1,767 M6s officially imported, this exclusivity is both a blessing and a curse.

Fuel tanks have been known to rust through along the horizontal seam and where the filler neck is connected. New fuel tanks are still available for under $300.

The normal equipment wheels and tires were replaced by BBS three-piece alloy wheels that were 8.3 x 16.3 inches and used the metric Michelin TRX tires that measured 240/45mm. An expensive combination when new, the TRX tires have become difficult to find and increasingly expensive.

The early U.S. M6s had leather-covered dashboards. These dried out easily and cracked quickly. BMW eventually replaced most of these leather dashes with the same molded plastic dashboards as those used in the 635 models.

When maintained properly, the M88 motor is very reliable, with many examples covering well over 100,000 miles without needing major repairs. When abused and misused, these motors cost a small fortune to repair. A top-end rebuild can cost more than $6,000. Complete rebuilds can cost between $8,000 and $12,000.

The M88 motor began as a 3,453cc 6-cylinder and used some carryover components from the "normal" 6-cylinder. The 24-valve head, intake system, exhaust system, pistons, ignition system, and connecting rods are all different. Expect to pay a significant premium for all repair parts.

Check the fuel lines and fuel injectors whenever the oil level is checked, looking for any signs of seepage or leakage. Fuel is delivered under about 40 PSI, and if the fuel lines are cracked, they may leak and spray fuel onto the exhaust system.

Ratings Chart

E24 6-Series

	630Csi 1977–1979	633Csi 1980–1984
Model Comfort/Amenities	**½	***
Reliability	**	****
Collectibility	*	*
Parts/Service Availability	**	***
Est. Annual Repair Costs	***½	***

	635CSi/L6 1985–1989	M6 1987–1988
Model Comfort/Amenities	***½	***½
Reliability	****	***
Collectibility	**	*****
Parts/Service Availability	***	***
Est. Annual Repair Costs	***	****

Specifications
633CSi 1980–1984

Engine Type		SOHC Inline 6
Displacement cc/ci		2788/170.1
Compression Ratio		8.21
BHP @ rpm		169@5500
Torque lbs-ft @ rpm		170@4500
Injection Type		Bosch L-Jetronic
Fuel Requirement		Unleaded, 91 Octane
Emission Control		3-Way Catalyst, Lambda Sensor
Transmission	Manual	5-Speed
	Automatic	3-Speed ZF HP22
Steering		Recirculating Ball, Variable Power
Assist		
Front Suspension		MacPherson Struts, Lower Lateral
Arms, Coil Springs, Tube Shocks, Anti-Roll Bar		
Rear Suspension		Semi Trailing Arm, Coil Springs, Tube
Shocks, Anti-Roll Bar		
Wheelbase (in.)		103.4
Weight (lbs.)		3600
Wheels		14 x 6 Steel discs
Optional		14 x 6 Cast Alloy
Tires		195/70HR Steel Belted Radials
Brake System		Vacuum Assisted
	Front	11.0-in. Vented Discs
	Rear	10.7-in. Solid Discs
0–60 mph, sec		8.2
Maximum Speed mph	Manual	124
	Automatic	121
EPA Estimated mpg,		
City/Highway		19.0/23.0

Specifications
630CSi 1977–1979, 635CSi/L6 1985–1989

630CSi 1977–1979

Engine Type		SOHC Inline 6
Displacement cc/ci		2985/182
Compression Ratio		8.11
BHP @ rpm		176@5500
Torque lbs-ft @ rpm		185@4500
Injection Type		Bosch L-Jetronic
Fuel Requirement		Regular, 91 Octane
Emission Control		Thermal Reactor, Air-Injection
Transmission	Manual	4-Speed
	Automatic	3-Speed ZF 3HP20 or Borg Warner 65
Steering		Recirculating Ball, Variable Power Assist
Front Suspension		MacPherson Struts, Lower Lateral Arms, Coil Springs, Tube Shocks, Anti-Roll Bar
Rear Suspension		Tube Shocks, Coil Springs, Semi-Trailing Arms, Anti-Roll Bars
Wheelbase (in.)		103.4
Weight (lbs.)		3630
Wheels		14 x 6 Steel
Optional		14 x 6 Alloy
Tires		195/70HR Steel Belted Radials
Brake System		Vacuum Assisted 4-Wheel Discs
	Front	11.0-in. Vented Discs
	Rear	10.7-in. Vented Discs
0–60 mph, sec		9.0 (manual transmission)
Maximum Speed mph	Manual	124
	Automatic	121
MPG, City/Highway		15.0/21.0

635CSi/L6 1985–1989

Engine Type		SOHC Inline 6
Displacement cc/ci		3430/209
Compression Ratio		8.01
BHP @ rpm		182 @ 5400
Torque lbs-ft @ rpm		214 @ 4000
Injection Type		Bosch Motronic
Fuel Requirement		Premium Unleaded
Emission Control		3-Way Catalyst, Lambda Sensor
Transmission	Manual	5-Speed
	Automatic	4-Speed Automatic
Steering		Recirculating Ball, Variable Power Assist
Front Suspension		MacPherson Struts, Lower Lateral Arms, Coil Springs, Tube Shocks, Anti-Roll Bar
Rear Suspension		Semi Trailing arm, Coil Springs, Tube Shocks, Anti-Roll Bar
Wheelbase (in.)		103.4
Weight (lbs.)		3375
Wheels		Forged Aluminum, 165 x 390mm (6.5 x 15.4 inch)
Tires		Michelin TRX 220/55VR-390
Brake System		Dual-Circuit with Hydraulic Booster, Antilock Brake System
	Front	11.2-in. Vented Discs
	Rear	11.2-in. Solid Discs
0–60 mph, sec		8.2
Maximum Speed mph		132
MPG, City/Highway		19.0/23.0v

Specifications
M6 1987–1988

Engine Type		DOHC Inline 6 (S38)
Displacement cc/ci		3453/211
Compression Ratio		9.81
BHP @ rpm		256 @ 6500
Torque lbs-ft @ rpm		243 @ 4500
Injection Type		Bosch Motronic
Fuel Requirement		Unleaded, 95 Octane
Emission Control		3-Way Catalyst, Lambda Sensor
Transmission	Manual	Getrag 280/5 5-Speed
	Automatic	NA
Steering		Recirculating Ball, Variable Power Assist
Front Suspension		MacPherson Struts, Lower Lateral Arms, Coil Springs, Tube Shocks, Anti-Roll Bar
Rear Suspension		Semi Trailing Arm, Coil Springs, Tube Shocks, Anti-Roll Bar
Wheelbase (in.)		103.4
Weight (lbs.)		3570
Wheels		Forged Alloy, 415 x 210 mm
Tires		240/45VR-415 TRX
Brake System		Hydraulic Assist, ABS
	Front	11.8-in. Vented Discs
	Rear	11.2-in. Vented Discs
0–60 mph, sec		6.8
Maximum Speed mph		150 (est.)
MPG, City/Highway		12.0/20.0

This 1986 BMW 635CSi sports a factory-installed rear spoiler.

The M30/3.4-liter engine, shown here in a 1986 BMW 635CSi, uses a later-style intake manifold and Motronics engine management. Look closely at the plastic radiator tanks for signs of leaking.

Replacement Costs for Common Parts
630CSi 1977-1979, 633CSi 1980–1984

630CSi 1977-1979

Oil Filter		$5.20	
Fuel Filter		$18.60	
Fuel Pump(s)	In-Tank	$127.50	
	External	$190	
Starter		$134,	Exchange
Alternator		$192,	Exchange
Fan Clutch		$129	
Front Bumper		$379	
Hood		$865	
Left Front Fender		$682.50	
Right Rear Quarter Panel		$1,010	
Rear Bumper		$580	
Windshield		$365	
Tail Light Housing/Lens		$425	
Gas Tank		$276	
Center Silencer		$412	
Rear Muffler		$316	
Thermal Reactors	Front	$882.50 (NLA)	
	Rear	$797.50 (NLA)	
Brake Master		$240	
Front Rotor (each)		$59	
Front Pads (set)		$58.75	
	+ Sensor	$6.70	
Front Shocks		$119	
Rear Shocks		$139	

633CSi 1980–1984

Oil Filter		$5.20	
Fuel Filter		$18.60	
Fuel Pump(s)	In-Tank	$127.50	
	External	$190	
Starter		$245,	Exchange
Alternator		$180,	Exchange
Fan Clutch		$74.75	
Front Bumper		$379	
Hood		$865	
Left Front Fender		$682.50	
Right Rear Quarter Panel		$1,010	
Rear Bumper		$580	
Windshield		$365	
Tail Light Housing/Lens		$425	
Gas Tank		$276	
Catalytic Converter	9/79 to 9/81	$907	
	from 9/81	$1,355	
Center Silencer		$322	
Rear Silencer	9/79 to 9/81	$258	
	from 9/81 to 9/82	$575	
Oxygen Sensor		$45	
Brake Master		$240	
Front Rotor (each)		$59	
Front Pads (set)		$58.75	
	+ Sensor	$6.70	
Front Shocks (each)		$119	
Rear Shocks (each)		$139	
Thrust Rod Bushings (each)		$38	

The 1987 BMW M6 sports minor differences from the normal coupe, including an oil temperature gauge to keep track of engine performance. Also, the Motorsports logo is located in the tachometer face.

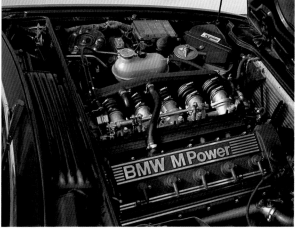

This is what it is all about. The DOHC powerplant in this 1987 BMW M6 is a tight fit. Note the heat shield on the right shock tower that serves to protect air conditioning components from exhaust system heat.

Replacement Costs for Common Parts
635CSi/L6 1985–1989, M6 1987–1988

635CSi/L6 1985–1989

Oil Filter		$5.20
Fuel Filter		$18.60
Fuel Pump(s)	In-Tank	$127.50
	External	$190
Starter	to 1987	$134, Exchange
	from 1988	$245, Exchange
Alternator	to 1986	$183, Exchange
	from 1986	$287, Exchange
Fan Clutch		$74.75
Front Bumper		$379
Hood		$865
Left Front Fender		$682.50
Right Rear Quarter Panel		
	to 11/85	$1,010
	from 11/85 to 6/87	$1,355
	after 6/87	$1,425
Rear Bumper	to 6/87	$580
	from 6/87	$309
Windshield		$365
Tail Light Housing/Lens		$425
Gas Tank		$276
Catalytic Converter	1985 to 1987	$1,421
	from 1988	$1.740
Center Silencer to 1987		$560
Rear Muffler from 1988		$797.50
Oxygen Sensor	1985 to 1987	$95
	from 1988	$133.35
Brake Master Cylinder		
	to 9/87	$240
	from 9/87	$655
Hydraulic Accumulator		$169
	Switch	$26.75
	Switch	$22.75
Front Rotor		$61
Front Pads (set)		$62.95
	+ Sensor	$6.70
Front Shocks	to 9/87	$139
	from 9/87	$196
Rear Shocks		$298
Thrust Rod Bushing (set)		$38

M6 1987–1988

Oil Filter		$5.20
Fuel Filter		$18.60
Fuel Pump(s)	In-Tank	$127.50
	External	$190
Starter		$134, Exchange
Alternator		$287, Exchange
Fan Clutch		$74.75
Front Bumper	to 6/87	$379
	from 6/87	$411
Front Spoiler	to 6/87	$438
	from 6/87	$572.50
Hood		$865
Left Front Fender		$682.50
Right Rear Quarter Panel		
	to 6/87	$1,355
	from 6/87	$1,425
Rear Bumper	to 6/87	$580
	from 6/87	$309
Windshield		$365
Tail Light Housing/Lens		$425
Gas Tank		$276
Catalytic Converter		$1,500
Rear Exhaust	to 9/87	$730
	from 9/87	$650
Oxygen Sensor		$133.35
Brake Master		$655
Hydraulic Accumulator		$169
	Switch	$26.75
	Switch	$22.75
Front Rotor (each)		$100
Front Pads (set)		$62.95
	+ Sensor	$6.50
Front Shocks		$174
Rear Shocks		$298
Thrust Rod Bushing (set)		$38

What They Said About the . . .

630CSi

As the ultimate BMW currently built for the U.S., the 630CSi answers the question: What do I buy if I want to outdo my friends who drive Jaguar XJSs and Mercedes 450SLCs? —*Road & Track,* **June 1977**

633CSi

The 633CSi is one of the world's most satisfying cars to drive. —*Road and Track,* **1980**

635CSi/L6

The 635CSi is most in its element as a high-speed tourer. —*Automobile Magazine,* **August 1987**

M6

It is a refined, selfish, egotistical snob of a thing whose gorgeous looks and capable performance make it one of the most desirable possessions you can park in a four-car garage. It is nothing less than a Bavarian Ferrari. —*The Roundel,* **December 1987**

Two versions of the E24 were offered in 1987: the L6 and the M6. Cosmetically little different from the 1986 model, the L6 offered more luxurious appointments. This L6 rides on chromed TRX wheels.

The gold-centered BBS wheels on this 1981 BMW 633CSi are nonoriginal but do not detract from the looks or value. Watch for rust in fenders and metallic paint with failing clear coat on this model.

I Bought a . . .

1983 BMW 633CSi

I liked the styling and reliability of the "big-six" engines and had looked at about 10 other 6-Series and five of the 3.0CS and CSi coupes before finally finding this car. It had a complete ownership history, is a 5-speed, and was in overall solid condition. When purchased, it had about 94,000 miles on it. I think it will run forever—it has over 175,000 miles on it now.

The rear seat room is minimal, and the cars are excessively heavy. I do as much of the routine maintenance as I can, so I don't really consider the car all that expensive to own. Probably my worst experience was removing the bell housing bolts when I replaced the clutch. I have found that parts are easy to find—the dealers stock almost all the mechanical parts.

About the only things I have replaced more often than others are brakes and pads; otherwise, I follow the owner's manual for regularly scheduled maintenance. —*Lisa Scalia and Gerry O'Connor, Manhattan Beach, California*

1986 BMW 635CSi

In the twelve years that we owned the red 635, there have been no major service problems, although even minor ones can be costly. The lower thrust arm bushings are a bit of a problem, but solvable by replacement about every 60,000 miles. The common power steering and brake booster fluid reservoir is also a constant maintenance issue. However, the engine and drivetrain are bulletproof as long as one stays on top of the maintenance. Our clutch is still original. With regular 3,000-mile oil change intervals, it uses no more oil than it did when new, which is a quart or so between changes. The compression is still good, and it should give many more trouble-free miles.

The service indicator (SI) system light in the dash can be an annoyance. The NiCad batteries die, and once that happens, it cannot be reset. With dead batteries, it also blinks and flashes. The front spoiler is very vulnerable and fairly fragile.

As far as more or less normal maintenance, the 635 is not particularly expensive to operate. However, if one lets the maintenance slide, it can be very expensive to make right. The radiators are plastic and expensive. The catalytic converter and rear muffler are very expensive to replace with BMW parts.

On the plus side, it is happy with 87 octane fuel, and it gets around 25 miles per gallon on the highway, about 20 in the city.
—*Lois and John Bergen, Fullerton, California*

1988 BMW M6

The 6-Series has always displayed classic BMW styling. People know when glancing over, there is no doubt it is a BMW! There were only about 1,400 or so examples of the limited Motorsport M6 brought into the States over three years, from 1986 through 1988, with the 1988 version being the last.

There are a few drawbacks of the M6, in particular the 15-gallon fuel tank, which allows only 200 miles per tank or so. The replacement size tires are nearly impossible to locate as Michelin has gradually discontinued the stock equipment, Michelin TRX series.

These cars are an absolute blast to drive, but one must consider the higher cost of parts associated with most BMW M cars. Most items are special order. Maintenance can be difficult, as there are extremely few competent shops that can properly service an older M car. Rubber seals, bushings, and gaskets seem to require the most attention, regardless of mileage.

Although I have put only 1,500 miles on my M6, it is a true classic that generates beautiful sounds. —*Andrew Kahn, La Canada, California*

Evolutionary changes to the interior on this 1986 BMW 635CSi: electrically adjustable sports seats, an improved HVAC and onboard computer (OBC) are located in the center dash, and the service interval system (SI) lights are visible at the 10 o'clock position behind the steering wheel.

Conceived as a direct successor to the 3.0S/Si sedans, the first-generation E23 7-Series signaled the conclusion of a reinvention of BMW's product lines. With the 733i introduction in 1978, BMW had a full range of vehicles to offer, from the 3-Series all the way to the 7-Series, and a consistent family look that was contemporary and appealing.

Sharing a strong resemblance externally with the 6-Series coupes, the interior design also shows the family ties: The instruments are large and round, situated in the driver's line of sight, the radio and heater/air conditioning controls are angled towards the driver. Wood accents in the dash and door panels lend a warm, homey atmosphere.

Benefiting from lessons learned, the 7-Series air conditioning system was fully integrated and much improved over earlier efforts. BMW's use of a General Motors air conditioning compressor meant the system was now powerful enough to cope with the higher temperatures, and the vents were well placed to provide more than adequate cooling.

Available at first with the 3.3-liter inline 6-cylinder, the 7-Series was a little longer, a little wider, and a little lower than the E3 sedans it replaced and heavier by about 400 pounds. The first-generation 7-Series had three iterations during its 9-year production run.

The L7 is a luxury version of the 735i and is the same mechanically. It differs slightly in trim levels and features a full leather interior in light gray only, including the dash. Other features include a two-stage heating for the front seats and a driver's side air bag, and the L7 was available in either Polaris Silver or Diamond Black. In addition, the L7 was available only with the 4-speed electronic automatic transmission.

Although the E23 chassis is unique to the 7-Series, many of the major mechanical components are shared with other models. Therefore, the 7-Series can be expected to experience many of the same types of mechanical problems as the E28 5-Series and the E24 6-Series. As the 7-Series evolved, more and more electrical amenities were incorporated. Check and confirm the operation of the electric windows, sunroof, mirrors, and, when equipped, the electrically adjustable seats.

The vast majority of these cars came with leather interiors. While the leather is long-lasting, look for damaged seats, and in the L7s examine the dashboards closely for leather that has weathered and dried out.

The 735i and L7 are roomy four-passenger sedans that offer a luxurious ride and comfort with traditional BMW handling. Replacements for the 3.0S/Si, these are the only vehicles in their class that offered buyers the choice of a manual or an automatic transmission.

The engine is the sturdy inline 6-cylinder that has been available since the 2500 sedans. Cars of these models built from 1978 to 1979 use thermal reactors in place of the more modern 3-way catalyst and Lambda sensors of the 1980 and newer cars. Thermal reactors are expensive—more than $800 each—and they are no longer available.

The L7 was a one-year model, from 1986 through 1987. The 5-speed manual and the ZF 4-speed manuals were used in 1985 to 1987 cars. Four-speed automatics had some problems; the automatic climate-control system is complex and expensive to repair.

A roomy sedan that offers surprisingly good handling for its size and weight, many first-generation 7-Series are high mileage and show their age. When properly maintained, they are good driving cars that still can be considered luxury cars and deliver you to your destination with a minimum of fuss while still allowing you to feel like you are driving a sports car.

Ratings Chart

E23 7-Series

	733i	735i/L7
Model Comfort/Amenities	★★★	★★★
Reliability	★★	★★½
Collectibility	★	★
Parts/Service Availability	★★★	★★★
Est. Annual Repair Costs	★★★½	★★★½

The M30/3.4-liter, shown here in a 1986 BMW 735i, can also be found in both the 5- and 6-Series. Note the notch in the radiator to clear the fan. The white relay at the right rear of the engine bay can short out by contact with the hood and cause a no-start condition. The solution is to relocate the relay to a different location.

Replacement Costs for Common Parts
733i 1978–1984, 735i/L7 1984–1987

733i 1978–1984

Oil Filter		$5.20
Fuel Filter	1978–1979	$18.60
	from 1980 on	$21.75
Fuel Pump(s)	In-Tank	$221.50
	External	$190
Starter		$134, Exchange
Alternator	1978–9/81	$169, Exchange
	9/81–9/84	$183, Exchange
Fan Clutch	1978–9/79	$129
	9/79–9/81	$74.75
	from 9/81	$129
Water Pump	1978–9/79	$75
	from 9/79	$71.52
Front Bumper		$319
Hood		$312
Left Front Fender		$219
Right Rear Quarter Panel		$639
Rear Bumper		$353
Windshield		$315
Tail Light Lens		$108
Exhaust	733i from 1978–9/79	
	Front Pipe–1	$334.02
	Front Pipe–2	$334.02
	Middle Exhaust	$402
	Rear Muffler	$201
	Thermal Reactors	
	Front	$882.50 (NLA)
	Rear	$797.50 (NLA)
	733i from 9/79 to 9/81	
	Catalyst/Front Pipe	$907.50, Exchange
	Center Muffler	$417
	Rear Muffler	$201
	Oxygen Sensor	$45
	733i from 9/81	
	Catalyst/Front pipe	$1,750, Exchange
	Muffler	$512.50
	Oxygen Sensor	$45
Brake Master	1978–9/84	$240
	9/84 on	$239
Front Rotor (each)		$59
Front Pads (set)	1978 to 8/81	$58.75
	+ Sensor	$6.70
	from 8/81 on	$96.25
	+ Sensor	$6.70
Front Shocks		$134
Rear Shocks		$116

735i/L7 1984–1987

Oil Filter		$5.20
Fuel Filter		$21.75
Fuel Pump(s)	In-Tank	$221
	External	$190
Starter		$134, Exchange
Alternator	to 1/86	$183, Exchange
	1/86 on	$287, Exchange
Fan Clutch		$129
Water Pump		$85
Front Bumper		$319
Hood		$312
Left Front Fender		$219
Right Rear Quarter Panel		$639
Rear Bumper		$353
Windshield		$315
Tail Light Lens		$108
Catalyst/Front Pipe		
	Manual Transmission	$1,695, Exchange
	Automatic Transmission	$1,306, Exchange
Muffler		$512.50
Oxygen Sensor		$138
Brake Master		$239
Front Rotor (each)	$59	
Front Pads (set)	$96.25	
	+ Sensor	$6.70
Front Shocks (each)	$165	
Rear Shocks (each)	$145	
Thrust Rod Bushings (each)		$25.75

The 1986 BMW 735i offers a traditional BMW large trunk. The spare tire is mounted upright on the right side, under the matching carpeted cover.

Powered by the M30/3.2-liter inline 6-cylinder and available with either a 4-speed manual or a 3-speed automatic, the 733i offered modern, up-to-date styling and amenities with enough interior room to accommodate four adults in comfort and, in a pinch, five adults.

The electrically adjustable seat motors have been known to fail, and the headrest adjustment mechanisms have a reputation for failing. Be sure to operate the seat adjusters to confirm functionality.

BMWs of this vintage are prone to the rear differential mount fatiguing and breaking. Have this area examined. Expect to spend in the range of $500 to $1,000 if it must be repaired.

The heating, ventilation, and air conditioning systems are complex and evolved into climate-control systems. These more advanced systems have experienced problems with the vacuum-controlled flaps and motors, and repairs are time consuming and costly. Check the system closely to verify that it functions properly.

Other common wear items in the front ends of all E23s are the steering arms, the center link, and the thrust rod bushings. Replacing the thrust rods and bushings will cost in the range of $300 to $500 for parts and labor. They tend to wear out between 60,000 and 80,000 miles.

One minor electrical problem is a relay mounted on the right side of the firewall that shorts out against the underside of the hood. The fix is to simply relocate the relay.

As the mileage increases on a 733i, the second-gear syncros tend to go bad. This is usually noted by balkiness in selecting second gear and an occasional grinding of gears. A 5-speed manual became available between 1980 and 1981.

The 1985 model year brought changes with the 735i/L7. Engine displacement was raised from 3,210cc to 3,430cc. An anti-lock braking system (ABS) became standard equipment, as did the electronically controlled ZF 4HP 22 transmissions.

Specifications
733i 1978–1984, 735i/L7 1985–1987

733i 1978–1984

Engine Type		SOHC Inline 6-Cylinder
Displacement cc/ci		3210/196
Compression Ratio		8.41
BHP @ rpm		177 @ 5500
Torque lbs-ft @ rpm		196 # 4000
Injection Type		Bosch L-Jetronic
Fuel Requirement		Regular, 91Octane
Transmission	Manual	4-Speed
	Automatic	ZF 3-Speed
Steering		Recirculating Ball, Vehicle-Speed Sensitive Variable Power Assist
Front Suspension		MacPherson Struts, Lower Lateral & Diagonal Arms, Coil Springs, Tube Shocks, Anti-Roll Bar
Rear Suspension		Semi-Trailing Arms, Coil Springs, TubeShock Absorbers, Anti-Roll Bar
Wheelbase (in.)		110.0
Weight (lbs.)	Manual	3675
	Automatic	NA
Wheels		Cast Alloy 14 x 6.5.J
Tires		205/70HR-14
Brake System		Vacuum Assist, 4-Wheel Discs
	Front	11.0-in. Vented Discs
	Rear	11.0-in. Solid Discs
0–60 mph, sec	Manual	8.6
	Automatic	NA
Maximum Speed mph		118
MPG, City/Highway		15.0/22.5 (C&D, 5/78)

735i/L7 1985–1987

Engine Type		SOHC Inline 6-Cylinder
Displacement cc/ci		3430/209
Compression Ratio		8.01
BHP @ rpm		182 @ 5400
Torque lbs-ft @ rpm		214 @ 4000
Injection Type		Bosch Motronic
Fuel Requirement		Unleaded, 87Octane
Transmission	Manual	5-Speed
	Automatic	ZF 4-Speed
Steering		Recirculating Ball, Vehicle-Speed Sensitive Variable Power Assist
Front Suspension		MacPherson Struts, Lower Lateral & Diagonal Arms, Coil Springs, Tube Shocks, Anti-Roll Bar
Rear Suspension		Semi-Trailing Arms, Coil Springs, Tube Shock Absorbers, Anti-Roll Bar
Wheelbase (in.)		110.0
Weight (lbs.)	Manual	3545
	Automatic	NA
Wheels		Cast Alloy 390 x 165TR
Tires		225/55VR390
Brake System		Vacuum Assist, Anti-Lock Braking System (ABS)
	Front	11.0-in. Vented Discs
	Rear	11.0-in. Solid Discs
0–60 mph, sec	Manual	9.1 (*Road & Track*, 9/85)
	Automatic	NA
Maximum Speed mph		119 (est.) (R&T, 9/85)
MPG, City/Highway		17.0 (R&T, 9/85)

(above) The 1986 BMW 735i offers amenities galore. The panel on the left offers a good view of the service interval system (SI) indicators in the instrument cluster. The climate controls are in the center dash, automatic transmission has selectable modes, and the electric seat controls offer memory buttons for the driver.

The rear passenger compartment of the 1986 BMW 735i seats two in luxury and three in comfort, and all passengers ride in style.

What They Said About the . . .

733i

The leather seats were just right in tension, neither too hard nor too soft, and with their 6-way adjustment and the telescoping steering wheel, the 733 can produce a comfortable driving stance for anyone under 6-foot-3. —*Motor Trend,* **October 1981**

735i/L7

Once you start the four-door moving, it gives you the impression that unless it is whooshing down the Interstate you are boring it to tears.
—*Roundel,* **July 1985**

I Bought a . . .

1986 BMW 735i

I have owned other BMWs—namely, a 1978 530i and a 1984 633CSi—and I wanted a solid, good performing four-passenger car. I didn't have to look at too many before I bought this one. I knew it was a good car when I looked at it, and the price was right.

There is little I don't like about the car, though it would be nice if there were cup holders and a map light. But of course it is a 1986, and BMW didn't believe in cup holders at that time.

Repair costs do tend to be on the high side, but so far I've never had a problem finding parts and I really wouldn't consider the car expensive to own, especially when you consider the cost to replace it (under $5,000) and the performance it offers for such a large, heavy car. The only item that I've had to replace more than once has been the electric antenna.

I would absolutely buy another BMW, but only a pre-1987. —*Gene Halloran, Santa Ana, California*

The BMW E23 7-Series sedan, like this 1986 735i, replaced the 3.0Si as top-of-the-series BMW sedan. The TRX wheels are original.

E32 7-Series
1988-1994
Chapter 14

**735i/735iL
740i/740iL
750iL**

By the mid-1980s, the first-generation 7-Series was showing its age. The competition had developed and released new models that left BMW's flagship floundering.

BMW, however, was not resting on its corporate laurels and had been busy developing the second-generation (E32 chassis) 7-Series. Tasked with instructions to develop the best car in its class, the engineering team used CAD/CAM and wind-tunnel development to design and hone the new chassis both aerodynamically as well as structurally. The improvements to torsional rigidity were nearly 50 percent above the previous-generation 7-Series. Aerodynamic improvements include flush-mounted windows with the front and rear windscreens bonded to the chassis. The floor pan had been smoothed and allowed items to be mounted up and out of the airflow. Flush panels covered the engine compartment and gas tank areas, further smoothing airflow beneath the car. The new 7-Series was also available with an additional 4.5 inches of wheelbase and was designated the 735iL.

Electronically, the E32 7-Series featured a level of sophistication that boggles the mind. An improved, multifunction onboard computer, central locking, climate-control heating and air conditioning, electrically adjustable front seats with a memory function that also adjusts the outside rearview mirrors accordingly (plus the right side mirror tilts downward for a better view of the curb when reverse gear is selected)—these are just a few of the standard amenities. Upon introduction, there were just three options: heated front seats, limited slip, and a "delete" option for the automatic transmission. A 5-speed manual transmission was available if you really wanted it.

Engine choices were initially limited to an improved version of the M30/3.4-liter inline six featuring the latest version of Motronics. By May 1988, the M70/5.0-liter V-12 had joined the stable. In 1994, the M60/4.0-liter V-8 displaced the inline six.

The E32 735i was the first of the new-generation 7-Series to reach the U.S. market. Powered by the familiar M30/3.4-liter inline six and available with either a 5-speed manual or a 4-speed automatic, the 735i offered luxurious accommodations for four adults and had enough room to carry a fifth person.

The 740i/iL's M60/4.0-liter V-8 is smooth and offers outstanding performance. The 1994 and 1995 4.0-liter M60 V-8 engines have experienced problems related to the Nikasil alloy engine block when fed with gas of a high-sulfur content, which leads to excessive cylinder bore wear. BMW offered an extended warranty (up to 100,000 miles) on affected engine blocks, and in some cases replaced engines with a later-style Alusil engine block. Look and listen for evidence of an excessively rough idle, and have the vehicle's history checked thoroughly.

The 750iLs are powered by V-12 engines. This car offers outstanding luxury and 296 brake horsepower in a large sedan that has power and smoothness of unparalleled levels. While the 750iL has a record of being expensive to own and operate, the M70 V-12 engines are generally reliable and trouble-free. The most common problems are intake manifold gasket leaks and fly-by-wire (DK) throttle motors failing. The car uses two throttle motors, each costing as much as $850. If you have the intake manifold gaskets replaced, have the fuel lines at the back of the engine replaced at the same time.

Luxurious, comfortable, classic styling—there are many positive attributes that make these second-generation 7-Series good buys. Be wary, though, of deferred maintenance and resulting high maintenance costs, and remember that so much technology is not always a good thing. With the great leaps forward also came some leading-edge problems that have plagued the E32 7-Series.

All in all, though, the E32 7-Series is made up of good cars that will run up an incredibly high number of relatively trouble-free miles when a regime of routine preventive maintenance is administered. As with all BMWs, do your research, pick the best car you can afford, budget for the repairs, and enjoy the performance, handling, and comfort these big sedans can deliver.

Ratings Chart

E32 7-Series

	735i/iL	740i/iL	750iL
Model Comfort/Amenities	★★★	★★★	★★★½
Reliability	★★½	★★½	★★
Collectibility	★	★	★
Parts/Service Availability	★★★	★★★	★★★
Est. Annual Repair Costs	★★★	★★★½	★★★½

A 1993 BMW 740i with the shorter wheelbase chassis.

Note the brake booster and fluid reservoir forward left on the engine of this 1993 BMW 740i and the VIN sticker on the fender. The power steering fluid reservoir is a dark brown bottle with a green circle on the cap.

Replacement Costs for Common Parts
735i/iL 1988–1992, 750i/iL 1988–1994, 740i/iL 1993–1994

735i/iL 1988-1992

Oil Filter		$5.20
Fuel Filter		$21
Fuel Pump(s)	In-Tank	$301.08
	External	$294
Starter		$245, Exchange
Alternator		$386
Fan Clutch		$169
Water Pump		$71.25
Front Bumper		$372
Hood		$535
Left Front Fender		$337
Right Rear Quarter Panel		$448
Rear Bumper		$398
Windshield		$404
Tail Light Lens		$248
Catalytic Converter		$1,575, Exchange
Center Silencer		$229
Rear Silencer		$335
Oxygen Sensor		$133.35
Brake Master	to 3/88	$338
	from 3/88 to 7/92	$319
Front Rotor (each)		$91
Front Pads (set)	to 6/90	$98.25
	+ Sensor	$6.50
	from 6/90	$99.25
	+ Sensor	$6.50
Front Shocks (each)	Standard	
	to 3/88	$186
	from 3/88 on	$138
	w/ Elec Damping Control	
	to 5/90	$522
	w/ M-Technik to 7/90	$159
Rear Shocks (each)	Standard	$122
	M-Technik	$249
	Self-Leveling to 7/91	$496
w/ Elec Damping Control to 5/90		$1,010
	from 5/90	$820
w/ Elec Damping Control & Self-Leveling from 5/90		$920 (each)
Thrust Rod Bushings (each)		$49

740i/iL 1993-1994

Oil Filter		$10
Fuel Filter		$18.10
Fuel Pump(s)		$294
Starter		$269, Exchange
Alternator		$363, Exchange
Fan Clutch		$134
Water Pump		$117
Front Bumper		$372
Hood		$535
Left Front Fender		$337
Right Rear Quarter Panel		$448
Rear Bumper		$398
Windshield		$404
Tail Light Lens		$248
Catalytic Converter	Cylinders 1–4	$1,421, Exchange
	Cylinders 5–8	$1,421, Exchange
Exhaust Pipe	Center Silencer	$438
	Rear Silencer	$459
	Oxygen Sensor	$133.35
Brake Master		$305
Front Rotor (each)		$91
Front Pads (set)		$99.25
	+ Sensor	$6.50
Front Shocks (each)		$159
Rear Shocks (each)		$496
Thrust Rod Bushings (each)		$49

750iL 1988-1994

Oil Filter		$10
Fuel Filter (2 required)		$18.10
Fuel Pump(s) (2 required)		$317
Starter		$429, Exchange
Alternator	to 7/90 and from 11/91	$495
	7/90 to 11/91	$425
Fan Clutch		$134
Water Pump		$194
Front Bumper	to 6/90	$361
	from 6/90	$372
Hood		$535
Left Front Fender		$337
Right Rear Quarter Panel		$448
Rear Bumper		$398
Windshield		$404
Tail Light Lens		$248
Catalytic Converter	Cylinders 1–6	$1,485, Exchange
	Cylinders 7–12	$1,485, Exchange
Exhaust Pipe	Cylinders 1–3	$276.63
	Cylinders 4–6	$191.73
	Cylinders 7–9	$406.73
	Cylinders 10–12	$261.52
Center Silencer		$399
Rear Silencer		$452
Oxygen Sensor		$133.35
Brake Master	to 3/88	$338
	from 3/88–7/92	$319
Front Rotor (each)		$91
Front Pads (set)	to 1/90	$71.25
	+ Sensor	$6.50
	from 1/90	$107
	+ Sensor	$6.50
Front Shocks (each)	to 7/90	$263
	from 7/90 on	$159
	w/ Elec Damping Control	
	to 5/90	$522.50
	w/ M-Technik to 7/90	$159
Rear Shocks (each)	Self-Leveling	$496
	w/ Self-Leveling & M-Technik	$482
	w/ EDC & Self-Leveling	
	(to 5/90)	$1,010
	w/ EDC & Self-Leveling	
	(from 5/90)	$920
Thrust Rod Bushings (each)		$44.25

A clean engine compartment indicates an owner who cares for the car. This 1989 BMW 750iL's V-12 has been treated to several Dinan upgrades to the intake system.

Check for oil leaks, coolant leaks, and listen for valve-train noise. Watch the "banjo" bolts that keep the oil-supply pipe in place. Located under the valve cover, on top of the motor, this pipe supplies oil to the rocker arms. Bolts are known to loosen up and should be checked annually.

Coolant hoses and fuel lines are subject to extreme underhood heat. The hoses should be changed every 2 to 4 years to prevent a failure from occurring.

The M30/3.4-liter engine has been around in several displacements since the Bavarias of the early 1970s. It is a robust engine that will last well over 100,000 miles when cared for in a reasonable manner.

The radiators are the aluminum core/plastic tank-type. The plastic tanks become brittle, and it is not unusual for the tanks to rupture or the hose necks to simply break off. New radiators are readily available, but expect to pay from $250 to $400 for a factory-replacement aluminum radiator.

The front suspension thrust rod bushings wear out from normal usage. Sloppiness in the front suspension and an occasional steering wheel shimmy will occur. Warped front brake rotors also are common, and the shimmy during braking place additional stress on the thrust rod bushings, wearing them out more quickly.

The engine and transmission mounts are oil-filled and when they go bad, the oil leaks out. Noticeable as a vibration when the transmission is put in gear, watch for this at the 90,000 to 120,000 mile range.

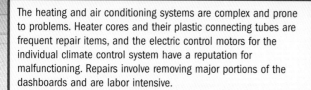

The heating and air conditioning systems are complex and prone to problems. Heater cores and their plastic connecting tubes are frequent repair items, and the electric control motors for the individual climate control system have a reputation for malfunctioning. Repairs involve removing major portions of the dashboards and are labor intensive.

The anti-lock braking system (ABS) was introduced and the self-leveling rear suspension appeared with the 735i. The self-leveling hydraulic pumps and shocks are prone to failure and leaking.

Drive shafts can and do fail. Sometimes it is the center bearing and sometimes it is a universal joint. Drive shafts are available through the aftermarket as rebuilt units; expect to pay in the range of $900 to $1,500 to replace one.

Another common maintenance item in the driveline is the rubber flex-disk coupling in the middle of the driveshaft. Called a "guibo," this rubber disk absorbs some of the driveline stresses. Expect to spend in the range of $300 parts and labor to replace it.

An engine-driven hydraulic pump provides the power assist for the brakes, steering, and self-leveling rear suspension. The brakes and steering systems share a single-pressure accumulator while the rear suspension has two accumulators. The hydraulic supply lines and rear struts are prone to leaks, noted by the rear of the car sagging, and a hard or "dead" brake pedal or sluggish steering can indicate brake system accumulator failure.

Whenever the valve covers are off, check the "banjo" bolts securing the oil-supply lines. These bolts have a reputation for loosening up over time. Be cautious when tightening these bolts; too tight, and you will crush the oil-supply line and starve the top end of the engine.

Elegant and complex, the V-12–powered 7-Series has also been a difficult and expensive car to own and maintain. Complete and through maintenance records are vital; deferred maintenance will make owning one of these cars an expensive and unpleasant experience.

Drive shafts can and do fail. Sometimes it is the center bearing, and sometimes it is a universal joint. Drive shafts are available through the aftermarket as rebuilt units; expect to pay in the range of $900 to $1,500 to replace one.

The drive-by-wire throttle motors—referred to as DK motors, one for each bank of cylinders and list at $850 each—are known to fail.

Another common maintenance item in the driveline is the rubber flex-disk coupling in the middle of the driveshaft. Called a "guibo", this rubber disk absorbs some of the driveline stresses. Expect to spend in the range of $300 parts and labor to replace.

At 4,988cc, the 750iL's M70/5.0 engine was roughly double the size of the inline sixes that powered the E30 3-Series. While these two engine designs shared their bore and stroke dimensions, there was little else they shared.

Watch for intake manifold gaskets that have deteriorated, which causes vacuum leaks that result in a poor idle. Replacement takes about 10 hours.

Coolant hoses and fuel lines are subject to extreme underhood heat. The hoses should be changed every 2 to 4 years to prevent a failure from occurring.

The radiators are the aluminum core/plastic tank-type. The plastic tanks become brittle and it is not unusual for the tanks to rupture or the hose necks to simply break off. New radiators are readily available, but expect to pay from $250 to $400 for a factory-replacement aluminum radiator.

The front-suspension thrust rod bushings wear out from normal usage. Sloppiness in the front suspension and an occasional steering wheel shimmy will occur. Warped front brake rotors also are common, and the shimmy during braking will place additional stress on the thrust rod bushings, wearing them out more quickly.

Fuel pumps fail between 100,000 and 150,000 miles. There are two, and they are just over $300 each. Water pumps fail between 60,000 and 70,000 miles.

The engine and transmission mounts are oil-filled, and when they go bad the oil leaks out. Noticeable as a vibration when the transmission is put in gear, watch for this at the 90,000 to 120,000 mile range.

Specifications
735i/iL 1988–1992, 740i/iL 1993–1994

735i/iL 1988–1992

Engine Type			SOHC Inline 6-Cylinder
Displacement cc/ci			3430/209
Compression Ratio			9.01
BHP @ rpm			208 @ 5700
Torque lbs-ft @ rpm			225 @ 4000
Injection Type			Bosch Motronic
Fuel Requirement			Unleaded, 88Octane
Emission Control			3-Way Catalyst, Oxygen Sensor
Transmission	Manual		5-Speed
	Automatic		ZF 4-Speed
Steering			Recirculating Ball, Vehicle-Speed Sensitive Variable Power Assist
Front Suspension			MacPherson Struts, Double-Pivot Lower Arms, Coil Springs, Tube Shocks, Anti-Roll Bar
Rear Suspension			Semi-Trailing Arms, Coil Springs, Tube Shock Absorbers, Anti-Roll Bar
Wheelbase (in.)		735i	111.5
		735iL	116.0
Weight (lbs.)	Manual		NA
	Automatic	735i	3880
		735iL	NA
Wheels			Cast Alloy 15 x 7.0J
Tires			225/60VR-15
Brake System			Hydraulic Assist, Anti-Lock Braking System (ABS)
Front			11.7-in. Vented Discs
Rear			11.8-in. Solid Discs
0–60 mph, sec	Manual		NA
	Automatic		9.3 (Road & Track, 7/87)
Maximum Speed mph			137 ((est.)) (Road & Track, 7/87)
MPG, City/Highway			18.0 (Road & Track, 7/87)

740i/iL 1993–1994

Engine Type			DOHC V-8
Displacement cc/ci			3982/243
Compression Ratio			10.01
BHP @ rpm			282 @ 5800
Torque lbs-ft @ rpm			295 @ 4500
Injection Type			Bosch HFM-Motronic DME with Adaptive Knock Control
Fuel Requirement			Unleaded Premium
Transmission	Manual		NA
	Automatic		ZF 5 HP 30 EH
Steering			Recirculating Ball, Vehicle-Speed Sensitive Variable Power Assist
Front Suspension			MacPherson Struts, Double-Pivot Lower Arms, Coil Springs, Twin-Tube Gas Pressure Shocks, Anti-Roll Bar, Electronic Damping Control (EDC) Optional
Rear Suspension			Semi-Trailing Arms, Track Links, Coil Springs, Anti-Roll Bar, Electronic Damping Control (EDC) Optional
		740iL	Self-leveling System with Single-Tube Shock Absorbers
Wheelbase (in.)		740i	111.5
		740iL	116.0
Weight (lbs.)	Manual		NA
	Automatic	740i	4002
		740iL	4090
Wheels			Cast Alloy 15 x 7.J
Tires			225/60R-15, Steel Belted Radial
Brake System			Vacuum Assist, Antilock Braking System
Front			11.9-in. Vented Discs
Rear			11.8-in. Vented Discs
0–60 mph, sec	Manual		NA
	Automatic		7.1
Maximum Speed mph			149 (electronically limited)
MPG, City/Highway		740i	16/23
		740iL	16/22

Specifications
750iL 1988–1994

Engine Type		SOHC V-12
Displacement cc/ci		4988/304
Compression Ratio		8.81
BHP @ rpm		296 @ 5200
Torque lbs-ft @ rpm		332 @ 4100
Injection Type		Bosch MH-Motronic Dual DME with Electronic Throttles
Fuel Requirement		Unleaded Regular
Transmission	Manual	NA
	Automatic	ZF 4 HP 24 EH
Steering		Recirculating Ball, Vehicle-Speed Sensitive Variable Power Assist
Front Suspension		MacPherson Struts, Double-Pivot Lower Arms, Coil Springs, Twin-Tube Gas Pressure Shocks, Anti-Roll Bar, Electronic Damping Control (EDC) Optional
Rear Suspension		Semi-Trailing Arms, Track Links, Coil Springs, Self-Leveling System with Single-Tube Shock Absorbers, Anti-Roll Bar, Electronic Damping Control (EDC) Optional
Wheelbase (in.)		116.0
Weight (lbs.)	Manual	NA
	Automatic	4167
Wheels		Cast Alloy 15 x 7.J
Tires		225/60R-15, Steel Belted Radial
Brake System		Hydraulic Power Assist, Antilock Braking System, All-Season Traction
	Front	11.9-in. Vented Discs
	Rear	11.8-in. Vented Discs
0–60 mph, sec	Manual	NA
	Automatic	7.1
Maximum Speed mph		155 (electronically limited)
MPG, City/Highway		12/18

The 1989 BMW 750iL sports a wheelbase chassis that is lengthened 5 inches in the rear door area. Its exhaust system is a Dinan unit.

What They Said About the . . .

735i/iL

The BMW 735i will find homes among those who seek a high quality, high performance sedan that sacrifices no comforts to achieve what performance. We don't think they'll be disappointed. —*Road & Track,* **July 1987**

740i/iL

If you ever need a reminder that the M in BMW stands for Motoren, the German word for engines, this car will bring the realization flooding back. —*Car and Driver,* **March 1993**

750iL

The wonder of all this excellence is that the car is enormous fun to drive. It's fast, it's responsive, it's comfortable, and every piece of it works with every other piece to redefine the concept of a "precision instrument". —*Car and Driver,* **November 1990**

The nappa leather seating and high-gloss burl walnut trim deliver comfort and a classy look to the 1993 BMW 740i. Sound and HVAC controls continue in center dash area.

The 1989 BMW 750iL is a big sedan with V-12 power that makes a statement. Aftermarket wheels and cross-drilled brake rotors are owner installed, as are the clear turn-signal lenses.

I Bought a . . .

1992 BMW 750iL

I fell in love with the lines on the E32 when it first came out. When BMW introduced the M70 with its state-of-the-art control system, there was no question that I would someday own one.

I don't consider the 750 an expensive car to own, but it certainly could be. Using qualified independents, an online network of other owners, and by performing some work myself, I've been able to keep my average cost of repairs and maintenance to $800 a year.

Upper control arm bushings are something I have come to classify as a wear item. Radiator end caps are made of plastic and lead to the early demise of an otherwise good radiator. The intake gaskets are a plastic compound that shrinks and expands at rates incompatible with the aluminum head and manifold. The result is leaks and the need to replace a $400 plastic gasket. I would expect more than 36,000 miles from the serpentine belt, which seems to be its life expectancy.

The worst experience was when the fuel pumps began a three-month trip to the trash barrel. They never really died but just started working half-heartedly. The car still ran, but it would stall randomly and would lose power. The dealer wanted to replace computers and sensors at a cost of $2,500. With the help of some other owners, I figured out that it was the fuel pumps, and $200 later the car was as good as new.

Yes, I would buy another, but only a preowned one. At more than $105K for a new 750 and with a resale value of less than half that at the end of the lease term, why buy a new one? —*Kevin Jorgensen, San Jose, California*

1989 BMW 735i

We purchased the vehicle to get us by for the short term. However, my wife, Lynette, insists she is perfectly happy with the this car and sees no reason to make a change. We like the good looks, overall comfort, reliability, and build quality. Our only complaint is poor fuel economy.

The thrust bushings were replaced along with the control arms and front shocks. Also replaced were the heater valve and the HVAC temperature controller, the transmission-shift cable, and a cylinder head gasket. Parts have been easy to get, and we don't really consider the car expensive to run.

We certainly would buy another; the bargain purchase price and the low operating costs will provide us with one of the least expensive cars we have ever owned. —*Lynette and Roeland Meyer, Rancho Santa Margarita, California*

1993 BMW 740i

During the time I have owned my 1993 740i, I have replaced or repaired the following items outside of routine maintenance items: rear fuel pump, engine and transmission mounts, driveshaft coupler (the flex disk), water pump, and suspension control arms. The valve cover gaskets have to be replaced more often than they should have to be. Parts seem to be readily available, so I have not experienced any problems in this regard.

Since I commute long distances, I was looking for something that was comfortable, fun to drive, and could handle any driving condition. I looked at several Mercedes as well as the 540i before deciding on this car, which is black with gray leather and has an automatic transmission. The car had 39,000 miles on it when I bought it, and currently has about 160,000 miles on it.

I really like the solid feel, the handling, and the high-end torque of the V-8. It's a fun car to drive, especially at high speeds on winding roads.
—*Frank Parth, Mission Viejo, California*

The radio and onboard computer (OBC) are nestled above the climate control system on the 1989 BMW 750iL. An electronically controlled 4-speed is specific to the V-12–powered cars.

The heater ducts for rear seat passengers of this 1989 BMW 750iL are visible below the driver's seat. The controls for rear-seat adjustments can be seen at the edge of the rear seat, below the rear seat cushion.

While BMW raised the bar for its competition with the 1988 introduction of the second-generation 7-Series, the introduction of the Mercedes-Benz S Class sedans in 1991 established a new benchmark. As good as the E32 7-Series was, BMW was certainly not resting easy. By the early 1990s, work was well underway on the third-generation 7-Series.

The results, impressive as they are, left some wondering whether this time around BMW had forsaken its legacy of sporting sedans and positioned itself closer to the competition from Japan. A spirited drive in the 740i Sport or the 750iL quickly answered this question.

In typical BMW tradition, the E38 7-Series was not a great visual departure from its predecessor. And yet, as a completely new design, it shared nothing more than the engines and transmissions with the car it replaced.

Wheelbase was lengthened to 115.4 inches for the "normal" 740i, and another 5.5 inches were added for the long wheelbase 740iL and 750iL. Overall width increased by about a half-inch and height by about an inch.

Suspension and brakes were improved versions of the now-traditional MacPherson front struts and rear semi-trailing arm suspensions. Four-wheel disc brakes completed a foundation that was complemented by All-Season Traction (AST), Adaptive Transmission Control (ATC), and antilock brakes. Electronic damping control (EDC) was optional on the V-8–powered cars and standard on the V-12–powered cars.

Interior accommodations were improved, and even greater levels of electronic amenities were incorporated. Controls for audio and phone, cruise control, and air recirculation are integrated with the steering wheel. A multi-information display provides updates from the onboard computer, audio, multifunction clock, automatic ventilation, and phone.

The third-generation 7-Series was no longer available with the inline 6-cylinder. The only engine choices were the V-8 and V-12 engines. The first year, 1995, the 740i/iL used the 4.0-liter M60 V-8 Nikasil block that was subject to premature cylinder bore wear. The 1996 V-8 models use the 4.4-liter M62 Alusil block and are not subject to this problem. The V-12–powered cars were powered by an enlarged 5.4-liter engine, designated the M73/5.4.

The M73/5.4-liter V-12 engines are generally reliable and trouble-free. The most common problems are intake manifold gasket leaks and fly-by-wire (DK) throttle motors failing. If you are having the intake manifold gaskets replaced, have the fuel lines at the back of the engine replaced at the same time. Otherwise the V-12s, like their inline 6-cylinder cousins, will run forever.

The long-wheelbase 740iL was not available during 1996 but returned for 1997. These are sophisticated, luxurious cars equipped with all the amenities. As they age, this sophistication may become a burden if the electrical components fail. Maintenance costs tend to be high, as are the costs of parts and labor to replace components. Many independent shops are unable to work on these cars, and a visit to the dealership may be the only option.

The third-generation 7-Series is fairly new, so a complete, reliable history is not available on these cars. Depending on the mileage, some may still be covered by the original factory warranty. Certified preowned cars are available, and with the release of the fourth-generation (E65 chassis) 7-Series in mid-2002, more of these will turn up on the dealer lots as lease returns and trade-ins. Luxurious, sophisticated, and a car that still is state-of-the-art, the 1995 to 2002 7-Series might be one of the best sedans ever built.

Ratings Chart

E38 7-Series

	740i/iL	750iL
Model Comfort/Amenities	★★★★	★★★★
Reliability	★★★★	★★★★
Collectibility	★★½	★★½
Parts/Service Availability	★★★★	★★★★
Est. Annual Repair Costs	★★★½	★★★★

This rear bumper incorporates park-distance control sensors (PDC), standard on the 1995 BMW 750iL. Dual exhausts are another feature of the V-12–powered cars.

The flush-mounted window glass is apparent in this view of a 1998 BMW 740i. Chrome wheels were optional and accent the metallic red color nicely.

Garage Watch 740i/iL 1995–2002

Leaking valve cover gaskets is a common problem. Look for evidence of oil leakage in this area of the engine.

Several electrical problems have occurred: in the HVAC systems, the A/C-powered "stepper" motors that divert airflow; the pixels in the dash displays for mileage and temperature tend to go bad and drop out of the display; and the taillight assemblies' contacts corrode, and the bulb holders overheat and melt.

Underhood heat is tremendous; examine the radiator and heater hoses for condition. Fuel lines are at the back of the engine and difficult to get to. These should be changed whenever the intake manifold gaskets are replaced.

Auxiliary/cooling fans have experienced failures and have on occasion overheated and melted wiring. An updated part is available, and most of the affected vehicles have been modified.

High-sulphur-content gas tends to damage the cylinder bores of the 1995 BMW 740i/iL's M60 V-8 engines, causing a loss of compression. In extreme cases, the engine will no longer have enough compression to start. In 1996, a redesigned V-8 was introduced, and it is not affected by high-sulphur-content gas.

Before purchasing a 1995 BMW 740i/iL powered by the Nikasil M60/4.0-liter V-8 engine, you may wish to take it to an authorized BMW dealer and request an idle quality check. This test will help determine if the engine has enough compression or if there is cause for further testing.

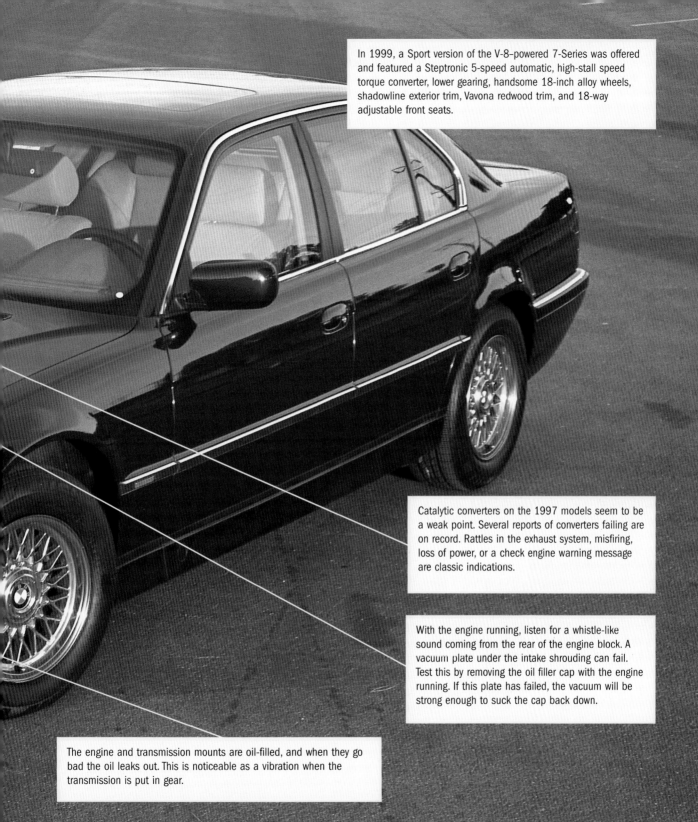

In 1999, a Sport version of the V-8–powered 7-Series was offered and featured a Steptronic 5-speed automatic, high-stall speed torque converter, lower gearing, handsome 18-inch alloy wheels, shadowline exterior trim, Vavona redwood trim, and 18-way adjustable front seats.

Catalytic converters on the 1997 models seem to be a weak point. Several reports of converters failing are on record. Rattles in the exhaust system, misfiring, loss of power, or a check engine warning message are classic indications.

With the engine running, listen for a whistle-like sound coming from the rear of the engine block. A vacuum plate under the intake shrouding can fail. Test this by removing the oil filler cap with the engine running. If this plate has failed, the vacuum will be strong enough to suck the cap back down.

The engine and transmission mounts are oil-filled, and when they go bad the oil leaks out. This is noticeable as a vibration when the transmission is put in gear.

Catalytic converters on the 1997 models seem to be a weak point. Several reports of converters failing are on record. Rattles in the exhaust system, misfiring, loss of power, or a check engine warning message are classic indications.

Occasionally, a transmission control module (TCM) develops problems, but otherwise the automatic transmissions are relatively trouble-free.

BUENA PARK
California
RAYS V12

The 5.4-liter V-12s, while improved over the previous generation's 5.0-liter 12, still require the services of top-notch mechanics to remain reliable and dependable.

The 5.4-liter V-12-powered BMW E38 750iL is a car that exudes success. From every square millimeter of leather, every perfectly uniform body seam and the finely finished trunk to the silky-smooth, impressively powerful engine, this is a car that simply says, you have arrived.

With all of the electronics included in these cars, surely the electrical subsystems are bound to malfunction.

Check for intake manifold gasket leaks, coolant and heater hoses that have deteriorated, fuel lines that have turned old and hard, and fly-by-wire throttle motors (DK motors) that have malfunctioned or failed. Remember that these engines function like two inline sixes, each with its very own fuel supply system and throttle systems.

Specifications
740i/iL/Sport 1995–2002

Engine Type	740i/iL 1995–1998			DOHC V-8
	740i/iL 1999–2001			DOHC V-8; VANOS Steplessly Variable Valve Timing
Displacement cc/ci	1995–1996			3982/243
	1997 on			4398/268
Compression Ratio				10.01
BHP @ rpm	1995			282 @ 5800
	1996–1998			282 @ 5700
	1999–2001			282 @ 5400
Torque lbs-ft @ rpm	1995			295 @ 4500
	1996–1998			310 @ 3900
	1999–2001			324 @ 3700
Injection Type	1995			Bosch HFM-Motronic M3.3 with Adaptive Knock Control
	1996–1998			Bosch HFM-Motronic M5.2 with Adaptive Knock Control
	1999–2001			Bosch JFME-Motronic M7.2 with Adaptive Knock Control
Fuel Requirement				Unleaded Premium
Transmission	Manual			NA
	Automatic	1995–1997		ZF 5 HP 30 EH
		1998–2001		ZF 5 HP 24 EH
Sport Package				Steptronic and High Stall Speed Torque Converter
Steering				Self-Adjusting Recirculating Ball, Vehicle-Speed Sensitive Power Assist
Front Suspension				MacPherson Struts, Forged Aluminum Double-Pivot Lower Arms, Variable Diameter Coil Springs, Twin-Tube Gas Pressure Shocks, Anti-Roll Bar, Optional Adaptive Ride Package Includes Electronic Damping Control and Self Leveling Rear Suspension, Sport Calibration with 740i Sport Package
Rear Suspension				4-Link Integral Suspension, Coil Springs, Anti-Roll-Bar, Twin-Tube Gas Pressure Shock Absorbers or Optional Adaptive Ride Package Includes Electronic Damping Control and Self-Leveling Rear Suspension, Sport Calibration with 740i Sport Package
Wheelbase (in.)	740i			115.4
	740iL			120.9
Weight (lbs.)	Manual			NA
	Automatic			
		1995	740i	4145
		1997–2001		4255
		1996–2001	740iL	4288
Wheels	Standard			Cast Alloy 16 x 8.0
	Optional			18 x 8.0 Front/18 x 9.5 Rear
Tires	Standard			235/60R-16 H All-Season Steel Belted Radial
	Optional			235/50ZR-18 Front/255/45ZR-18 Rear
Brake System				Vacuum Assist, Antilock Braking System (ABS)
	Front			12.8-in. Vented Discs
	Rear			12.8-in. Solid Discs
0–60 mph, sec	Manual			NA
	Automatic	1995–1998	740i	7.0
			740iL	7.2
		1999–2001		6.9
				6.8 with Sport Package
Maximum Speed mph				128 (electronically limited)
MPG, City/Highway	1995–1996			16/24
	1997–1998			17/24
	1999–2001			17/23, 15/21 with Sport Package

Specifications
740iL Protection 2000–2002

Engine Type		DOHC V-8; VANOS Steplessly Variable Valve Timing
Displacement cc/ci		4398/268
Compression Ratio		10.01
BHP @ rpm		282 @ 5400
Torque lbs-ft @ rpm		324 @ 3700
Injection Type		Bosch HFME-Motronic M7.2 with Adaptive Knock Control
Fuel Requirement		Unleaded Premium
Transmission	Manual	NA
	Automatic	ZF 5 HP 24 EH
Steering		Self-Adjusting Recirculating Ball, Vehicle-Speed Sensitive Power Assist
Front Suspension		MacPherson Struts, Forged Aluminum Double-Pivot Lower Arms, Variable Diameter Coil Springs, Twin-Tube Gas Pressure Shocks, Anti-Roll Bar, Adaptive Ride Package Includes Electronic Damping Control and Self Leveling Rear Suspension
Rear Suspension		4-Link Integral Suspension, Coil Springs, Anti-Roll Bar Adaptive Ride Package Includes Electronic Damping Control and Self-Leveling Rear Suspension
Wheelbase (in.)		120.9
Weight (lbs.)	Manual	NA
	Automatic	4630
Wheels		Cast Alloy 17 x 8.0
Tires		235/55R-17 X Run Flat
Brake System		Vacuum Assist, Antilock Braking System (ABS)
	Front	12.8-in. Vented Discs
	Rear	12.8-in. Solid Discs
0–60 mph, sec	Manual	NA
	Automatic	7.4
Maximum Speed mph		128 (electronically limited)
MPG, City/Highway		17/23

Improved dash design on this 1998 BMW 740i moved the parking brake release to the left side of the dash. Radio and telephone controls were relocated to the steering wheel.

Specifications
750iL 1995–2002, 750iL Protection 2000–2002

750iL 1995–2002

Engine Type			SOHC V-8
Displacement cc/ci			5379/328
Compression Ratio			10.01
BHP @ rpm	1995–1999		322 @ 5000
	2000–2001		326 @ 5000
Torque lbs-ft @ rpm			361 @ 3900
Injection Type	1995–1999		Bosch HFM-Motronic M5.2 Dual DME with Adaptive Knock Control
	2000–2001		Bosch HFME-Motronic M5.2.1 Dual DME with Adaptive Knock Control
Fuel Requirement			Unleaded Premium
Transmission	Manual		NA
	Automatic		ZF 5 HP 30 EH, 5-Speed Steptronic
Steering			Self-Adjusting Recirculating Ball, Vehicle-Speed Sensitive Power Assist Front Suspension MacPherson Struts, Forged Aluminum Double-Pivot Lower Arms, Variable Diameter Coil Springs, Twin-Tube Gas Pressure Shocks, Anti-Roll Bar, Adaptive Ride Package Includes Electronic Damping Control, and Self-Leveling Rear Suspension
Rear Suspension			4-Link Integral Suspension, Coil Springs, Anti-Roll Bar Adaptive Ride Package Includes Electronic Damping Control, and Self-Leveling Rear Suspension
Wheelbase (in.)			120.9
Weight (lbs.)	Manual		NA
	Automatic	1995–1996	4496
		1997–1998	4553
		1999–2001	4597
Wheels			Cast Alloy 16 x 7.5
Tires			235/60 R-16 H All-Season
Brake System			Vacuum Assist, Antilock Braking System (ABS)
	Front		13.1-in. Vented Discs
	Rear		12.9-in. Vented Discs
0–60 mph, sec	Manual		NA
	Automatic	1995	6.4
		1996–1998	6.7
		1999–2001	6.6
Maximum Speed mph			128 (electronically limited)
MPG, City/Highway	1995–1998		15/20
	1999–2001		13/20

750iL Protection 2000–2002

Engine Type		SOHC V-8
Displacement cc/ci		5379/328
Compression Ratio		10.01
BHP @ rpm		326 @ 5000
Torque lbs-ft @ rpm		361 @ 3900
Injection Type		Bosch HFME-Motronic M5.2.1 Dual DME with Adaptive Knock Control
Fuel Requirement		Unleaded Premium
Transmission	Manual	NA
	Automatic	ZF 5 HP 30 EH, 5-Speed Steptronic
Steering		Self-Adjusting Recirculating Ball, Vehicle-Speed Sensitive Power Assist
Front Suspension		MacPherson Struts, Forged Aluminum Double-Pivot Lower Arms, Variable Diameter Coil Springs, Twin-Tube Gas Pressure Shocks, Anti-Roll Bar, Adaptive Ride Package Includes Electronic Damping Control, and Self-Leveling Rear Suspension
Rear Suspension		4-Link Integral Suspension, Coil Springs, Anti-Roll Bar Adaptive Ride Package Includes Electronic Damping Control, and Self-Leveling Rear Suspension
Wheelbase (in.)		120.9
Weight (lbs.)	Manual	NA
	Automatic	4905
Wheels		Cast Alloy 17 x 8
Tires		235/55 R-17X Run Flat Protection
Brake System		Vacuum Assist, Antilock Braking System (ABS)
	Front	13.1-in. Vented Discs
	Rear	12.9-in. Vented Discs
0–60 mph, sec	Manual	NA
	Automatic	7.1
Maximum Speed mph		128 (electronically limited)
MPG, City/Highway		13/20

Replacement Costs for Common Parts
740i/iL 1995–2002, 750iL 1995–2002

740i/iL 1995–2002

Oil Filter		$10	
Fuel Filter		$21	
Fuel Pump		$230	
Starter		$269,	Exchange
Alternator	to 1995	$346,	Exchange
	from 1996	$363,	Exchange
Fan Clutch		$185	
Water Pump		$117	
Front Bumper		$346	
Hood		$695	
Left Front Fender		$330	
Right Rear Quarter Panel		$396	
Rear Bumper		$434	
Windshield		$385	
Tail Light Lens	to 6/98	$115	
	from 9/98	$187	
Catalytic Converter	to 1995	$930,	Exchange
	from 1996	$725,	Exchange
Center Silencer		$279	
Rear Silencer (each)	to 1995	$329	
	from 1996	$325	
Oxygen Sensor	to 1995	$133.35	
	from 1996 Regulating Sensor	$62	
	from 1996 Monitoring Sensor	$133.35	
Brake Master		$499	
Front Rotor (each)		$113	
Front Pads (set)		$96	
	+ Sensor	$16.10	
Front Shocks (each)	Standard	$231	
	w/ Elec Damping Control	$792	
Rear Shocks (each)	Standard	$122	
	Self-Leveling (740iL)	$482	
	w/ EDC & Self-leveling	$522	
	Thrust Rod Bushings	$29.75	

750iL 1995–2002

Oil Filter		$10	
Fuel Filter		$21	
Fuel Pump		$230	
Starter		$429,	Exchange
Alternator		$495,	Exchange
Fan Clutch		$185	
Water Pump		$187.95	
Front Bumper		$346	
Hood		$695	
Left Front Fender		$330	
Right Rear Quarter Panel		$396	
Rear Bumper		$434	
Windshield		$385	
Tail Light Lens	to 6/98	$115	
	from 9/98	$187	
Header/Catalyst		$1,300,	Exchange
Center Silencer		$279	
Rear Silencer (each)		$315	
Oxygen Sensor (2 required)		$133.35	
Monitoring Sensor (2 required)		$133.35	
Brake Master		$499	
Front Rotor (each)		$82	
Front Pads (set)		$114	
	+ Sensor	$15.50	
Front Shocks (each) w/ Elec Damping Control		$792.50	
Rear Shocks (each) w/ EDC & Self-leveling		$522.50	
Thrust Rod Bushings (each)		$29.75	

The trunk of the 1998 BMW 740i holds plenty of room for luggage, as the spare tire resides under the floor. The telephone and CD-changer are accessible behind removable side panels.

Rear seat occupants have plenty of room to relax in a 1998 BMW 740iL, which offers an additional 5.5-inches of rear leg room over the shorter 740i.

What They Said About the . . .

740i/iL

It's everything you've ever liked about a 7-Series—with performance volume cranked up."—*Motor Trend,* **June 1999**

750iL

Always at the ready, sounding like heaven and powerful as hell, the 750iL's 322-bhp 5.4-liter V-12 carries its power evenly through the rev range instead of dumping it all in a single overwhelming spike. —*Road & Track,* **April 1996**

Nikasil engine blocks in BMWs were superseded by Alusil blocks, as sported here by this 1998 BMW 740i, in 1997, which eliminated V-8 durability concerns.

I Bought a . . .

1995 BMW 750iL

We bought this 750iL when they first came out in 1995. It now has just over 120,000 miles on it and it has been basically trouble free. Early on we were having some problems in the center dash, but our dealership and BMW stepped up and took care of the problem at no cost to us.

The sedan is a great highway car, and it is hard to imagine such comfort in any other car. This car has also been to six BMW Club driving schools. You should see the look on others' faces when this big black sedan passes them! It is hard to believe a car of this stature is so composed on the track.

Our 750iL is loaded with creature comforts and power accessories, and thus far we haven't had any major problems.

—Judy and Ray Miller, Whittier, California

The high underhood heat of the V-12 results in intake manifold gasket leaks and can cause fuel lines to become brittle, something to watch for on many models, including this 1995 BMW 750iL.

The long-awaited 8-Series coupe was a technological tour-de-force and was the BMW flagship during its production. Featuring innovations like electronically controlled drive-by-wire throttle, electronic damping control (EDC), and Automatic Stability Control (ASC + T) with a traction control system, the 850 was positioned as a challenger for the V-12s from Mercedes Benz and Jaguar.

Front suspension was an evolution of BMW's traditional MacPherson strut design. In the rear, however, a new 5-link design was implemented. This new design featured bushings offering specifically engineered compliance to minimize chamber changes and to create some stabilizing toe-in of the rear tires during breaking. One subtle feature of this design was a small amount of passive rear steering when cornering. A note of caution regarding this system is that while for U.S.-specification cars this feature has been relatively trouble free, in the European-specification 850CSi there is a rear-steering control unit that is part of the overall system. While failures of this unit are rare, it does carry a list price of approximately $4,500.

In a definitive up-market move by BMW, the 8-Series was equipped with every conceivable option: automatic air conditioning, onboard computer, CD player, 4-speed automatic and later on a 5-speed automatic.

With all of these amenities, the 850 coupe did not so much replace the 6-Series coupe as supercede it. Initially, the automotive press did not give the 850i high marks. Comments that it was too heavy, underpowered, and not sporty enough abounded. Over time and with the introduction of the 850CSi and the 840Ci, the automotive media warmed up to these cars.

When looking at cars with mileage in the 70,000–80,000 range, anticipate replacing items like brake rotors, shocks, wheel bearings, batteries, hoses, belts, and so forth. These items seem to come up for replacement at about this point, so be sure to look for records of these items having been replaced.

Also note that the door windows drop slightly when the doors are opened and then raise automatically when the doors are closed. The front seats contain a complicated seatbelt harness system that adjusts to the driver, and when the transmission is put in reverse the right-side door mirror pivots slightly downward to allow the driver to better see any obstacles that might prove hazardous. There are two rear seats, but just about the only thing that will fit back there is a briefcase or gym bag. The trunk is typically BMW large and well appointed.

There are minor variations from year to year, and these are mostly cosmetic, notwithstanding the V-8 or the V-12 engines. As a rule, the V-12 cars are more expensive to maintain; they have dual systems for gas, ignition, and so forth. During the mid-1990s, BMW did incorporate revised DK throttle bodies in the V-12–powered cars. In 1995, the V-12 engine displacement was increased from 5.0 liters to 5.4 liters, and a "no-maintenance" 5-speed automatic transmission incorporating Steptronic shift control was added. If you prefer the 6-speed manual transmission, it was available only in the 850i in the 1991 to 1993 model years, or in the 850CSi.

The 8-Series coupes was the flagship of the BMW lineup. Equipped with every conceivable amenity, the driver and passenger were well taken care of. An expensive car to start with, the 8-Series is still fairly high priced, and operating and repair costs are high. Plan to budget $200 to $300 per month for routine maintenance. Parts are readily available through dealerships, but in some cases they are sinfully expensive: try $700 for a headlight. The secret to keeping your maintenance troubles to a minimum is to find a skilled and knowledgeable mechanic who knows these cars and how to correctly troubleshoot them, particularly electrical system problems.

Ratings Chart

E31 8-Series

	840Ci	850i/Ci	850CSi
Model Comfort/Amenities	****	****	****½
Reliability	****	****	****
Collectibility	****	****	*****
Parts/Service Availability	****	****	****
Est. Annual Repair Costs	***½	****	****½

Check the gaps between the body panels of all 8-Series cars for unevenness or poor fit, an indication of possible accident damage. Also, check the top of the door seal closely, where the rear window and the door window overlap. The door seal is known to chafe and tear in this area. Repair cost is approximately $600 per side.

This view details the M60/4.0-liter 32-valve engine of the 1994 BMW 840Ci. The same powerplant is used in the 5-Series and 7-Series sedans. It develops 282 brake horsepower at 5,800 rpm and features the Bosch HFM-Motronic engine management system with adaptive knock control.

High-sulphur-content gas tends to damage the cylinder bores of the 1994–1995 BMW 840's M60 V-8 engines, causing a loss of compression. In extreme cases, the engine will no longer have enough compression to start. In 1996, a redesigned V-8 was introduced, and it is not affected by high-sulphur-content gas.

The 840Ci was introduced in 1994 and powered by the M60/4.0-liter V-8 available in the 5-Series and 7-Series. In 1996, engine displacement was increased to 4.4 liters across the BMW line. This revised power plant, designated the M62/4.4, made a good thing even better.

Watch for automatic transmissions that slip and make "expensive" noises, both common in transmissions that have not been properly maintained.

With the engine running, listen for a whistle-like sound coming from the rear of the engine block. A vacuum plate under the intake shrouding can fail. Test this by removing the oil filler cap with the engine running. If this plate has failed, the vacuum will be strong enough to suck the cap back down.

Check the lower corners of the rear windshield for any sign of rust where water may have gotten in under the rubber window seal and the sunroof at the center, rear edge. Headlight adjusters are another common problem area; they work loose and the lights will actually fall out.

Watch for incomplete OBC displays (inactive pixels); twisted or distorted seats, a result of the control drive cables slipping or having broken; and torn or tearing side-window seal gaskets at the top front edge of the rear window, which are an estimated $600 per side repair cost.

Check the power steering; the power steering filter may be blocked, cutting off the fluid supply to the power steering pump, which leads to failure of the pump. Cost of a power steering pump: $360 to $625. Cost of replacing the power steering filter every year: $15.50 a year. You decide.

Be cautious of cars with damaged bodywork. While body panels are readily available, a front fender costs about $800, a headlight unit (the complete popup) is almost $700. A front bumper retails for between $850 (with the light squirters) to $870 (without the light squirters).

Common problems include deteriorated intake manifold gaskets that cause vacuum leaks and result in a poor idle, requiring 10 hours of labor to replace. Drive-by wire throttle motors (DK motors) are known to fail (one for each bank of cylinders in the M70 12-cylinder, $850 each). Fuel pumps ($300 each) and batteries (two) are also problem areas.

Between its introduction in late 1990 and the 1993 model year, the M70/5.0 V-12 engine powered the 850i. From 1995 on, the 850Ci utilized the M73/5.4-liter.

The V-12 engines use a series of "banjo" bolts on camshaft journals 1, 3, 5, and 7 to secure the oil-supply pipes that feed oil to the rocker shaft assemblies and are known to loosen and back out. Replace them with the improved-design bolts. At minimum, check these bolts whenever you have the valve covers off.

The 4-speed automatic transmissions used in the early cars have a tendency to slip as well as make noises. A factory-exchange transmission for the M70-powered cars (1991 to February 1993) lists for slightly more than $3,000. The automatic transmission for the M73-powered cars (1993-on) lists for nearly $5,000.

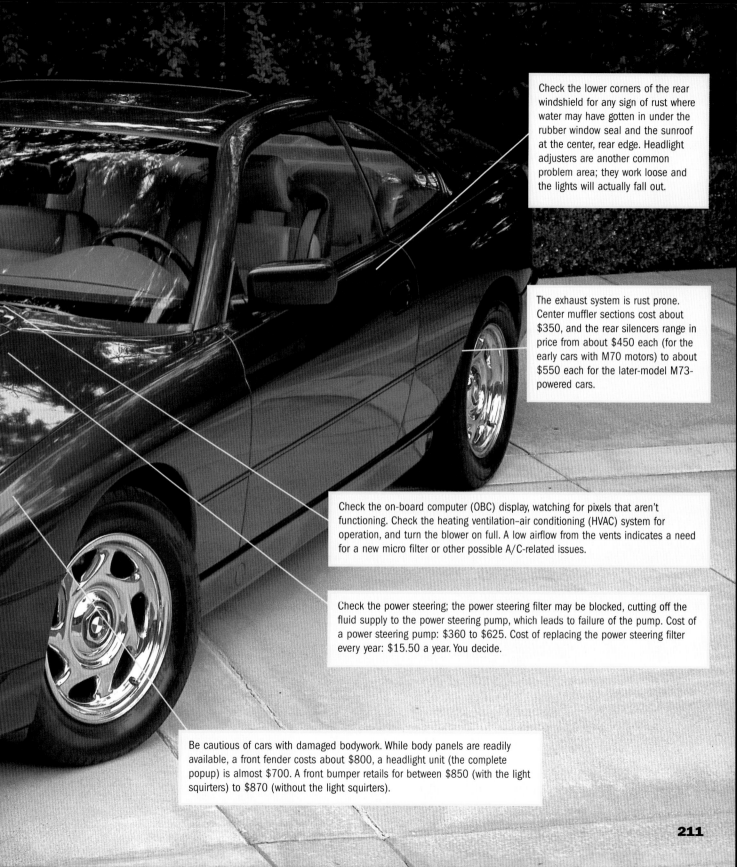

Check the lower corners of the rear windshield for any sign of rust where water may have gotten in under the rubber window seal and the sunroof at the center, rear edge. Headlight adjusters are another common problem area; they work loose and the lights will actually fall out.

The exhaust system is rust prone. Center muffler sections cost about $350, and the rear silencers range in price from about $450 each (for the early cars with M70 motors) to about $550 each for the later-model M73-powered cars.

Check the on-board computer (OBC) display, watching for pixels that aren't functioning. Check the heating ventilation–air conditioning (HVAC) system for operation, and turn the blower on full. A low airflow from the vents indicates a need for a new micro filter or other possible A/C-related issues.

Check the power steering; the power steering filter may be blocked, cutting off the fluid supply to the power steering pump, which leads to failure of the pump. Cost of a power steering pump: $360 to $625. Cost of replacing the power steering filter every year: $15.50 a year. You decide.

Be cautious of cars with damaged bodywork. While body panels are readily available, a front fender costs about $800, a headlight unit (the complete popup) is almost $700. A front bumper retails for between $850 (with the light squirters) to $870 (without the light squirters).

Parts prices for the 850CSi are, for the most part, not significantly higher than the 850i/Ci. Other than the retuned suspension and engine-management changes, many of the components are common with the 850Ci.

The M73 V-12 engine is generally reliable and trouble free. The most common problems are intake manifold gasket leaks and fly-by-wire throttle motors (DK motors) failing. If you are having the intake manifold gaskets replaced, have the fuel lines at the back of the engine replaced at the same time. Otherwise, the V-12s, like their inline 6-cylinder cousins, will run forever.

The V-12 engines use a series of "banjo" bolts on camshaft journals 1, 3, 5, and 7 to secure the oil supply pipes that feed oil to the rocker shaft assemblies and are known to loosen and back out. Replace them with the improved-design bolts. At minimum, check these bolts whenever you have the valve covers off.

Remember that only 200 or so 850CSi were imported to the United States, so service records become even more important and significant to a prospective buyer.

Check closely for any evidence of body damage, particularly the front air dam; with the lowered suspension, the chance of scraping the lower air dam is increased. Check also for the original M-style wheels on the car. If not on the car, does the owner have them?

When introduced in 1994, the 850CSi list price was just under $100,000. Powered by a 5,576cc V-12 that generated 372 brake horsepower and 402 lbs-ft of torque, this version of the E31 coupe is equipped with a 6-speed manual transmission and is capable of 0 to 60 in fewer than 6 seconds.

Check the power steering; the power steering filter may be blocked, cutting off the fluid supply to the power steering pump, which leads to failure of the pump. Cost of a power steering pump: $360 to $625. Cost of replacing the power steering filter every year: $15.50 a year. You decide.

Check the lower corners of the rear windshield for any sign of rust where water may have gotten in under the rubber window seal and the sunroof at the center, rear edge. Headlight adjusters are another common problem area; they work loose and the lights will actually fall out.

The exhaust system is rust prone. Center muffler sections cost about $350, and the rear silencers range in price from about $450 each (for the early cars with M70 motors) to about $550 each for the later-model M73-powered cars.

Be cautious of cars with damaged bodywork. While body panels are readily available, a front fender costs about $800, a headlight unit (the complete popup) is almost $700. A front bumper retails for between $850 (with the light squirters) to $870 (without the light squirters).

Specifications
840Ci 1994–1997

840Ci 1994–1995

Engine Type		DOHC 32-Valve V-8
Displacement cc/ci		3982/243
Compression Ratio		10.01
BHP @ rpm		282 @ 5800
Torque lbs-ft @ rpm		295 @ 4500
Injection Type		Bosch HFM-Motronic with Adaptive Knock Control
Fuel Requirement		Premium Unleaded
Transmission	Manual	NA
	Automatic	ZF 5 HP 30 EH 5-Speed
Steering		Recirculating Ball, Engine-Speed Sensitive Variable Power Assist
Front Suspension		Struts, Double-Pivot Lower Arms, Coil Springs, Twin-Tube Gas Pressure Shocks, Anti-Roll Bar
Rear Suspension		5 Link Integral Suspension, Coil Springs, Twin-Tube Gas-Pressure Shocks, Anti-Roll Bar
Wheelbase (in.)		105.7
Weight (lbs.)	Manual	NA
	Automatic	4123 lbs
Wheels		Cast Alloy 16 x 7.5J
		Forged Alloy 16 x 7.5J Optional
Tires		235/50HR-16 Steel Belted Radial
Brake System		Hydraulic Power Assist, Antilock Braking System
	Front	12.8-in. Vented Discs
	Rear	12.8-in. Solid Discs
0–60 mph, sec	Manual	NA
	Automatic	7.1
Maximum Speed mph		155 (electronically limited)
MPG, City/Highway		16/24

840Ci 1996–1997

Engine Type		DOHC V-8
Displacement cc/ci		4398/268
Compression Ratio		10.01
BHP @ rpm		282 @ 5700
Torque lbs-ft @ rpm		310 @ 3900
Injection Type		Bosch HFM-Motronic with Adaptive Knock Control
Fuel Requirement		Premium Unleaded
Transmission	Manual	NA
	Automatic	ZF 5 HP 30 EH with Adaptive Transmission Control and Steptronic
Steering		Recirculating Ball, Vehicle-Speed Sensitive Power Assist
Front Suspension		Struts, Double-Pivot Lower Arms, Coil Springs, Twin-Tube Gas Pressure Shocks, Anti-Roll Bar
Rear Suspension		5 Link Integral Suspension, Coil Springs, Twin-Tube Gas-Pressure Shocks, Anti-Roll Bar
Wheelbase (in.)		105.7 in.
Weight (lbs.)	Manual	NA
	Automatic	4167
Wheels		Cast Alloy 16 x 7.5J
		Forged Alloy 16 x 7.5J Optional
Tires		235/50R-16
Brake System		Hydraulic Power Assist, Antilock Braking
	Front	12.8-in. Vented Discs
	Rear	12.8-in. Solid Discs
0–60 mph, sec	Manual	NA
	Automatic	7.1
Maximum Speed mph		155 (electronically limited)
MPG, City/Highway		15/20

Specifications
850i/Ci 1990–1997

850i/Ci 1990–1994

Engine Type		SOHC V-12
Displacement cc/ci		4988/304
Compression Ratio		8.8:1
BHP @ rpm		296 @ 5200
Torque lbs-ft @ rpm		332 @ 4100
Injection Type		Bosch MH-Motronic/dual DME with Electronic Accelerator
Fuel Requirement		Unleaded Premium
Transmission	Manual	Getrag Type E, 6-Speed
	Automatic	ZF 4 HP 24 EH, 4-Speed
Steering		Recirculating Ball, Engine-Speed Sensitive Variable Power Assist
Front Suspension		Struts, Double-Pivot Lower Arms, Coil Springs, Twin-Tube Gas Pressure Shocks, Anti-Roll Bar, Electronic Damping Control (EDC) Optional
Rear Suspension		5 Link Integral Suspension, Coil Springs, Twin-Tube Gas-Pressure Shocks, Anti-Roll Bar, Electronic Damping Control (EDC) Optional.
Wheelbase (in.)		105.7 in.
Weight (lbs.)	Manual	3945
	Automatic	4123
Wheels	Standard	Cast Alloy 16 x 7.5J
	Optional	Forged Alloy 16 x 7.5J
Tires	Standard	235/50HR-16 Z
Brake System		Hydraulic Power Assist, Antilock Braking System
	Front	12.8-in. Vented Discs
	Rear	12.8-in. Solid Discs
0–60 mph, sec	Manual	6.1
	Automatic	6.9
Maximum Speed mph		155 (electronically limited)
MPG, City/Highway		12/21

850Ci 1995–1997

Engine Type		SOHC V-12
Displacement cc/ci		5379/328
Compression Ratio		10.0:1
BHP @ rpm		322 @ 5000
Torque lbs-ft @ rpm		361 @ 3900
Injection Type		Bosch HFM-Motronic Dual DME with Adaptive Knock Control
Fuel Requirement		Premium Unleaded
Transmission	Manual	NA
	Automatic	ZF 5 HP 30 EH 5-Speed with Adaptive Transmission Control and Steptronic
Steering		Recirculating Ball, Vehicle-Speed Sensitive Power Assist
Front Suspension		Struts, Double-Pivot Lower Arms, Coil Springs, Twin-Tube Gas Pressure Shocks, Anti-Roll Bar, Electronic Damping Control (EDC) Optional
Rear Suspension		5 Link Integral Suspension, Coil Springs, Twin-Tube Gas-Pressure Shocks, Anti-Roll Bar, Electronic Damping Control (EDC) Optional
Wheelbase (in.)		105.7
Weight (lbs.)	Manual	NA
	Automatic	4288
Wheels	Standard	Cast Alloy 16 x 7.5J
	Optional	Forged Alloy 16 x 7.5J
Tires		235/50R-16 Steel Belted Radials
Brake System		Hydraulic Power Assist, Antilock Brake System
	Front	12.8-in. Vented Discs, Aluminum brake Calipers
	Rear	12.8-in. Solid Discs
0–60 mph, sec	Manual	NA
	Automatic	6.1
Maximum Speed mph		155 (electronically limited)
MPG, City/Highway		12/21

Specifications
850CSi 1994–1995

Engine Type		SOHC V-12
Displacement cc/ci		5576/340
Compression Ratio		9.81
BHP @ rpm		372 @ 5300
Torque lbs-ft @ rpm		402 @ 4000
Injection Type		Bosch MH-Motronic Dual DME
Fuel Requirement		Premium Unleaded
Transmission	Manual	Getrag Type E, 6-Speed
	Automatic	NA
Steering		Recirculating Ball, Vehicle-Speed Sensitive Power Assist
Front Suspension		Struts, Double-Pivot Lower Arms, Coil Springs, Twin-Tube Gas Pressure Shocks, Anti-Roll Bar
Rear Suspension		5 Link Integral Suspension, Coil Springs, Twin-Tube Gas-Pressure Shocks, Anti-Roll Bar.
Wheelbase (in.)		105.7
Weight (lbs.)	Manual	4234
	Automatic	NA
Wheels	Front	Forged Alloy 17 x 8J
	Rear	17 x 9J
Optional	Front	Forged Alloy 18 x 8J
	Rear	18 x 9.5J
Tires	Front	235/45ZR-17
	Rear	265/40ZR-17
Optional	Front	245/40R-18 Z
	Rear	285/35R-18 Z
Brake System		Hydraulic Power Assist, Antilock Braking System
	Front	12.8-in. Vented Discs, Aluminum Brake Calipers
	Rear	12.8-in. Solid Discs
0–60 mph, sec	Manual	5.7
	Automatic	NA
Maximum Speed mph		155(electronically limited)
MPG, City/Highway		12/21

The rear bumper with lower spoiler (also called a diffuser) and the four polished round exhaust outlets mark this car as one of the 200 or so BMW 850CSi's that was sold in the United States. This low-mileage 1995 example is equipped with 18-inch aftermarket wheels and tires.

Replacement Costs for Common Parts
840Ci, 850CSi, 850i/Ci

840Ci

Oil Filter		$18
Fuel Filter	V-8 to 3/94	$18
	V-8 from 3/94	$21
Fuel Pump (2 required)		$317
Starter		$269, Exchange
Alternator		$363
Front Bumper		
	w/o Light Squirters	$870
	w/ Light Squirters	$842.50
Hood		$867.50
Left Front Fender		$780
Right Rear Quarter Panel		$1,255
Rear Bumper		$315
Windshield		$446
Tail Light Housing/Lens		$230
Center Silencer		$349
Rear Silencer (per side)		$459
Catalytic Converter	M60 (per side)	$1,421, Exchange
	M62 (per side)	$725, Exchange
Oxygen Sensor		$133.35
Power Steering Pump		$360
Power Steering Rilter		$15.50
Power Steering Resevoir		$67.50
Brake Master		$530
Front Rotor		$149
Front Pads (set)		$168
Front Shocks		$486
Rear Shocks		$132

850CSi

Oil Filter		$10
Fuel Filter (2 required)		$18.10
Fuel Pump (each, 2 required)		$510
DK Throttle Motors (each, 2 required)		$850
Starter		$429, Exchange
Alternator		$346
Plug Wires	(per bank)	$411
Clutch Kit		$585
Front Bumper	w/o Light Squirters	$870
	w/ Light Squirters	$842
Hood		$867.50
Left Front Fender		$780
Right Rear Quarter Panel		$1,255
Rear Bumper		$750
Windshield		$446
Tail Light Housing/Lens		$230
Center Silencer		$349
Rear Silencer (per bank)		$537.50
Catalytic Converter (per bank)		$1,421
Oxygen Sensor (per bank)		$133.35
Power Steering Pump		$625
Power Steering Filter		$15.50
Power Steering Reservoir		$67.50
Brake Master		$515
Front Rotor (each)		$149
Front Pads (set)		$168
Front Shocks		$132

850i/Ci

Oil Filter		$10
Fuel Filter (2 required)		$18.10
Fuel Pump (each, 2 required)	M70	$510
	M73	$342
DK Throttle Motors (each, 2 required)	M70 to 9/97	$850
	M70 from 9/97	$342
	M73	$550
Starter		$429, Exchange
Alternator	M70	$495
	M73	$346
Plug Wires	M70	$411
	M73 (per bank)	$315
Clutch kit		$585
Front Bumper	w/o Light Squirters	$870
	w/ Light Squirters	$842
Hood		$867.50
Left Front Fender		$780
Right Rear Quarter Panel		$1,255
Rear Bumper		$315
Windshield		$446
Tail Light Housing/Lens		$230
Center Silencer		$349
Rear Silencer (per bank)		$537.50
Catalytic Converter (per bank)		$1,421
Oxygen Sensor (per bank)		$133.35
Power Steering Pump		$425
Power Steering Filter		$15.50
Power Steering Reservoir		$67.50
Brake Master		$515
Front Rotor (each)	8/93	$113
	from 8/93	$149
Front Pads (set)		$168
Front Shocks (each)	w/o EDC	$486
	w/ EDC	$1,040
Rear Shocks	w/o EDC	$132
	w/ EDC	$820

The BMW 840Ci is equipped with driver and passenger airbags. The climate controls, radio, and onboard computer are visible in this 1994-model photo. Also, note that this particular 840Ci does not have a cellular telephone, although it was available as a dealer-installed option.

What They Said About the . . .

840Ci

The V-8 is terrific, the 5-speed automatic is excellent, and the styling and finish are grade-A. On any road—urban, suburban or wide-open spaces—this car rewards the serious driver. *—Road & Track,* **November 1994**

850i/Ci

The BMW 850i excels at suborbital speeds, useful on Germany's speed-limitless autobahns, with price no object. It's also a strict two-seater, overweight, and sluggish in the mid-range of U.S. highway velocities. *—Popular Science,* **January 1992**

850CSi

The 850CSi is, first and foremost, a BMW. Sporty and capable, like a Porsche. Luxurious and capable, like a Mercedes-Benz. Yet unlike either of these. *—Road & Track,* **May 1994**

At the very top of the center console, above the radio, is the onboard computer for this 1992 BMW 850i. The display pixels are a common failure item, requiring replacement of the computer display at a cost of about $1,500.

The 5.6-liter V-12 produced 372 horsepower and 402 lbs-ft of torque. The yellowish coating on the intake runners of this 1995 BMW 850CSi's engine is cosmoline and is supposed to be removed during the pre-delivery inspection. The drive-by-wire (DK) throttle motor for the right bank of the V-12 is shown in this photo as is one of the service interval system (SI) diagnostic ports.

Note the black rectangular exhaust outlets in this photo, a visual clue that this car is a BMW 850i/Ci. On all 8-Series models, including this 1992 BMW 850i, the right side rearview mirror automatically tilts downward when reverse is selected. This feature allows the driver to see the curb and obstacles more clearly.

I Bought a . . .

1994 BMW 840Ci

The 840Ci is my first BMW. I purchased it when it came off lease with about 32,000 miles on it. The car now has about 72,000 miles on it.

The particular example I found was in decent shape with low miles. Its character and solid feel are unmatched. Performance is very respectable, and its looks are timeless.

Overall, I consider the maintenance costs to be low to moderate. Like any high-priced vehicle, it requires very regular and consistent maintenance. I have repaired a minor engine oil leak, replaced the air conditioning compressor at about 55,000 miles, replaced the brakes at about 62,000 miles, and replaced the catalytic converter at about 68,000 miles.

The car has only been out of service one time, when the remote-control batteries ran down and I could not disarm the alarm.
—*Richard Yeh, Los Angeles*

1995 BMW 840Ci

I find the E31 to be one of the finest examples of form and function in an automobile. The exterior design is nothing short of a pure masterpiece, with long, sleek, lines and a wide, aggressive stance. The interior is no less impressive, with a cockpit-style layout that provides a combination of comfort, sporty styling, pleasing aesthetics, and attention to detail. To top it off, the E31 is a technological marvel whose 11-year-old design was way ahead of its time. From fly-by-wire throttle to windows and sunroof that automatically close beyond certain speeds to a sophisticated array of computer-controlled mechanics and driver's behavior pattern adjustments, the 8-Series rivals modern-day luxury and exotic cars more than a decade later
—*Mark Reid, Houston, Texas*

1991 BMW 850i

I purchased my 1991 BMW 850i early in 1997. The car had one previous owner and 16,500 miles. The Laguna Green paint and Parchment interior were immaculate, and the engine bay was clean, though the intake manifolds had the typical yellow baked-on cosmoline. BMW's 8-Series possesses timeless styling with compound curves everywhere you look, and a classic and luxuriously simple interior. The engine presents an example of industrial art.

Other than routine maintenance, my car has had zero problems, although parts and upkeep can be expensive. Keeping up with the scheduled required service is essential.

My experience with this car has been very positive. I like the heft and stance of the car. The steering is precise, although the effort to turn the wheel could be a little lower. What I like most of all is the power, torque, and smoothness of the V-12. —*Bert Smith, Incline Village, Nevada*

1994 BMW 850 CSi

My first 850CSi was a brilliant-red 1994 model. The car exceeded my expectations in all ways, from its seemingly limitless power reserves to its absolute stability at high speeds. It was clear from the outset that this was like no BMW Motorsport car I had ever owned before.

For being a supercar, the 850CSi is amazingly easy on the maintenance and upkeep costs, although it does share the common maladies of all of BMW's V-12 engines. A few of the early-production U.S.-spec models had defective software programming in the EML box, and the factory replaced these as a service campaign. Basically, though, the car is dependable, reliable, virtually bulletproof, and offers a mystique and synergy that will never be attained by lesser 8-Series or other BMW models. —*Steven Castle, Atlanta, Georgia*

The M-Steering wheel with stitching done in BMW M's colors. A 6-speed manual transmission and BMW cellular phone were standard equipment on the CSi's. Note the Yew hardwood trim and the two-tone leather seats in this photo of a 1995 BMW 850CSi.

Z3
1996-2001
Chapter 17

Since its introduction in late 1996, the Z3 has been treated to a series of upgrades and enhancements, both mechanically as well as cosmetically. The Z3 models that have been produced and their engine types include the 1.9 Roadster M44/1.9; 2.8 Roadster M52/2.8; 2.3 Roadster M52TU/2.3; 2.8 coupe M52TU/2.8; M-Roadster S52/3.2; M-Roadster S54/3.2; M-Coupe S52/3.2; M-Coupe S54/3.2; 2.5i Roadster M54/2.5; 3.0i Roadster M54/3.0; and the 3.0i M54/3.0.

Based on the E36 318ti and designated the E36/7, the Z3 shares many components with the 3-Series. The front suspension is essentially the same, MacPherson struts and arc-shaped lower control arms. The rear of the car, like the 318ti, is truncated, which necessitated use of the older-style semi-trailing arms from the E30 chassis. The Z3 benefits from firmer shocks and springs, slightly wider track (0.2 front, 0.4 rear), and slightly smaller anti-roll bars. Steering is engine-speed sensitive, variable-power assisted rack-and-pinion that is roughly 17 percent quicker than the 318i/is.

Familiar BMW kidney grills dominate the view from the front, the prominent wheel arches lead to the side vents—a styling feature of the 507—and along the sides, past the two-passenger cockpit to the truncated rear of the Z3. Something not likely to be seen for some time is a rusty fender, as the Z3's fenders feature zinc coating for corrosion protection. The Z3 is manufactured at the Spartanburg, South Carolina, facility and is the first BMW model to be completely manufactured in the United States.

In 1997, All-Season Traction (AST) became standard equipment, and the 2.8-liter six joined the lineup. Cars equipped with the larger engine also came with a heavier duty manual transmission, limited slip and strengthened rear suspension that featured revised geometry, and firmer suspensions settings. Ventilated front discs were added, the front bumper was redesigned with a larger air intake, and the rear fenders were widened. In April 1997, gas-pressure struts were added to the soft-top mechanism, making raising and lowering the top easier.

Dual roll-hoops were added in 1998. The 4-cylinder's audio system was upgraded, and an electrically powered soft-top was optional. A color-keyed hardtop also joined the option list. In 1999, the 2.3-liter 6-cylinder engine replaced the 1.9-liter 4-cylinder. The narrow body of the 4-cylinder was also phased out, and the Z3 coupe was introduced. The 2.3- and 2.8-liter engines featured the double VANOS, dual-resonance intake system, electronically controlled engine cooling, newly configured fuel injectors, and extended maintenance requirements. Ventilated front discs were standard for all models, and Adaptive Transmission Control (ATC) was added to the 4-speed automatic.

In addition to the Z3 coupe, the M-Roadster and M-Coupe, both powered by the M3s 3.2-liter engine, were introduced. The body of both the Z3 coupe and the M-Coupe is 2.6 times as twist-resistant as the roadster and is considered the most rigid body structure BMW has ever built. A result of the coupe roof design and body structure, aerodynamic drag is reduced and the interior is quieter.

The 2000 model year brought with it a minor facelift, the rear-end styling was modified with new fenders and L-shaped taillights. The soft-top gained a lining, the stereo was upgraded, cup holders were added, and two-stage airbags became standard.

The year 2001 brought with it the new-generation 2.5- and 3.0-liter, double VANOS engines. A new 5-speed automatic with Steptronic became an option; the 3.0i versions received larger, ventilated front disc brakes. Seventeen-inch wheels and tires became standard equipment. The coupe body received a new air intake grill in the front spoiler, and the center console was updated to match the roadsters.

The Z3 is a sports car, and some will have lived a pampered life. Others, particularly the M versions, may have been run hard. Buy the best one you can find, and budget for long-term items like replacing the soft-top and annual servicing. Then enjoy the driving experience these unique sports models can deliver.

Ratings Chart

Z3

	1.9	2.3	2.5i
Model Comfort/Amenities	★★★	★★★	★★★½
Reliability	★★★★	★★★★	★★★★
Collectibility	★★½	★★½	★★½
Parts/Service Availability	★★★★	★★★★	★★★★
Est. Annual Repair Costs	★★★½	★★★½	★★★½

	2.8	3.0i
Model Comfort/Amenities	★★★	★★★½
Reliability	★★★★	★★★★
Collectibility	★★½	★★½
Parts/Service Availability	★★★★	★★★★
Est. Annual Repair Costs	★★★½	★★★½

	M-Roadster	M-Coupe
Model Comfort/Amenities	★★★½	★★★½
Reliability	★★★★	★★★★
Collectibility	★★★½	★★★½
Parts/Service Availability	★★★★	★★★★
Est. Annual Repair Costs	★★★½	★★★½

The rear view of this 2001 BMW Z3 3.0i Roadster shows the dual exhaust tips, recessed third brake light, L-shaped taillights, and built-in roll hoop, all of which identify this as a newer 6-cylinder model.

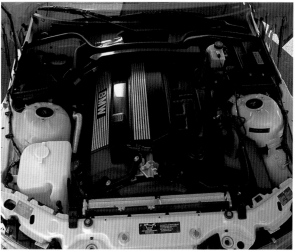

The inline-six of this 2001 BMW Z3 Roadster fills the engine compartment. Be aware that the plastic radiator tanks have a reputation for becoming brittle and cracking.

Check the service interval systems (SI) for warning lights that don't illuminate. It may indicate a burned-out bulb or bulbs that have been removed to mask a problem.

The rear upper shock mounts are a shared design with the E36 3-Series. The center of the rubber bushing has a tendency to come apart. Inexpensive to repair, the common symptom is banging from the rear suspension when going over bumps.

Convertible problems include fabric wear and fading from prolonged exposure to sunlight. The glue attaching the top to the framework can deteriorate. Watch for water leaks around the side windows. Look for evidence of mildew from the top being folded while still damp.

Watch for build-quality problems and electrical maladies on the very early cars. Check the fit and finish of the panels, and look for evidence of accident repair. Also check for rattles from the various interior storage bins.

With the soft top up, some drivers may be bothered by a blind spot when changing lanes. In addition, people over 6 feet tall may find it difficult to get into or out of the cars.

The oval-shaped interior rearview mirror design has come in for criticism and takes some getting used to.

Check for clutch judder when cold and particularly in reverse gear, a problem common to BMWs of this era and usually not an indication of a mechanical malfunction. Just be sure to have it checked by a mechanic.

Even though it was powered by only a M44/1.9-liter 4-cylinder, the 1996 introduction of the reasonably priced Z3 generated a flood of showroom traffic, and the dealers could not get enough of them.

Since the Z3 shares engines and mechanicals with the E36 3–Series, it also shares common problems with them. When evaluating a Z3, be sure to review the E36 section for specific mechanical problems.

As with any current-model BMW, check for service records and for evidence of accident damage and repairs.

Check the service interval systems (SI) for warning lights that don't illuminate. It may indicate a burned-out bulb or bulbs that have been removed to mask a problem.

Many of the mechanical items of the Z3 Coupe are shared with the E36 3-Series; therefore, problem areas regarding the engines, drivetrain, and front suspensions will overlap.

The oval-shaped interior rearview mirror design has come in for criticism and takes some getting used to.

The addition of the roof structure to the Roadster brought benefits: The Coupe body shell is 2.6 times as resistant to twisting, thus suspension engineers could develop a car that handles better; aerodynamic drag was reduced; the Coupe interior offers more luggage capacity; and noise levels inside the Coupe were lower.

Check for clutch judder when cold and particularly in reverse gear, a problem common to BMWs of this era and usually not an indication of a mechanical malfunction. Just be sure to have it checked by a mechanic.

The rear upper shock mounts are a shared design with the E36 3-Series. The center of the rubber bushing has a tendency to come apart. Inexpensive to repair, the common symptom is banging from the rear suspension when going over bumps.

225

The M-Roadster and M-Coupe versions of the Z3 are still new enough that long-term information on common problem areas is not yet available. When evaluating one for purchase, there are some areas that should be checked.

With the soft top up, some drivers may be bothered by a blind spot when changing lanes. In addition, people over 6 feet tall may find it difficult to get into or out of the cars.

Have the mounting points for the exhaust manifolds inspected carefully. There have been some reports of manifolds cracking or corroding. Also watch for engine oil leaks, and check the transmission for any signs of leaking.

These cars are high-performance sports cars and especially in the case of the Coupes, look for evidence of abuse of the brakes, tires, clutch, and other parts that could indicate the car has been used at the racetrack.

Convertible problems include fabric wear and fading from prolonged exposure to sunlight. The glue attaching the top to the framework can deteriorate. Watch for water leaks around the side windows. Look for evidence of mildew from the top being folded while still damp.

The rear upper shock mounts are a shared design with the E36 3-Series. The center of the rubber bushing has a tendency to come apart. Inexpensive to repair, the common symptom is a banging from the rear suspension when going over bumps.

Check for clutch judder when cold and particularly in reverse gear, a problem common to BMWs of this era and usually not an indication of a mechanical malfunction. Just be sure to have it checked by a mechanic.

Check for complete service records indicating the car has been maintained either by a BMW dealership or by an authorized repair station. This will also allow you to verify the mileage on the car. Although it is much more difficult to tamper with the odometer, it is not impossible.

Specifications
Z3 1.9 Roadster 1996–1998, Z3 2.3 Roadster 1999–2000

Z3 1.9 Roadster 1996–1998

Engine Type			DOHC Inline 4-Cylinder
Displacement cc/ci			1895/116
Compression Ratio			10.01
BHP @ rpm			138 @ 6000
Torque lbs-ft @ rpm			133 @ 4300
Injection Type			Bosch HFM Motronic 5.2 with Knock Control
Fuel Requirement			Unleaded Premium
Transmission	Manual		Getrag Type C, 5-Speed
	Automatic		THM R1, 4-Speed, 3 Selectable Shift Modes
Steering			Rack and Pinion, Engine Speed Sensitive Power Assist
Front Suspension			MacPherson Struts, Arc-Shaped Lower Arms, Coil Springs, Twin-Tube Gas-Pressure Shocks, Anti-Roll Bar.
Rear Suspension			Semi-Trailing Arms, Coil Springs, Twin-Tube Gas-Pressure Shocks, Anti-Roll Bar.
Wheelbase (in.)			96.3
Weight (lbs.)	Manual	1996	2690
		1997	2701
		1998	2723
	Automatic	1996	2767
		1997	2789
		1998	2811
Wheels			Cast Alloy 16 x 7.0J
Tires			225/50ZR-16 Performance Radials
Brake System			Vacuum Assist, Antilock Braking System (ABS)
	Front		11.3-in. Solid Discs
	Rear		10.7-in. Solid Discs
0–60 mph, sec	Manual	1996	9.1
		1997–1998	8.2
	Automatic	1996	9.7
		1997–1998	9.
Maximum Speed mph			116 (electronically limited)
MPG, City/Highway	Manual	1996–1997	23/31
		1998	23/32
	Automatic		22/31

Z3 2.3 Roadster 1999–2000

Engine Type		DOHC Inline 24-Valve 6-Cylinder, Double-VANOS Steplessly Variable Valve Timing
Displacement cc/ci		2494/152
Compression Ratio		10.51
BHP @ rpm		170 @ 5500
Torque lbs-ft @ rpm		181 @ 3500
Injection Type		Siemens MS 42 with Knock Control, Variable Valve Timing, Electromechanical Throttle System, Dual Resonance Intake System, Engine Cooling and Other Functions Included in Control Strategy
Fuel Requirement		Unleaded Premium
Transmission	Manual	Getrag Type B, 5-Speed
	Automatic	THM R1, 4-Speed, Adaptive Transmission Control (ATC) and 2 Selectable Shift Modes
Steering		Rack and Pinion, Engine Speed Sensitive Power Assist
Front Suspension		MacPherson Struts, Arc-Shaped Lower Arms, Coil Springs, Twin-Tube Gas-Pressure Shocks, Anti-Roll Bar
Rear Suspension		Semi-Trailing Arms, Coil Springs, Twin-TubemGas-Pressure Shocks, Anti-Roll Bar
Wheelbase (in.)		96.3
Weight (lbs.)	Manual	2899
	Automatic	2987
Wheels		Cast Alloy 16 x 7.0J
Tires		225/50R-16 92V Performance Radials
Brake System		Vacuum Assist, Antilock Braking System (ABS)
	Front	11.3-in. Vented Discs
	Rear	10.7-in. Solid Discs
0–60 mph, sec	Manual	6.8
	Automatic	7.5
Maximum Speed mph		128 (electronically limited)
MPG, City/Highway	Manual	20/27
	Automatic	19/26

Specifications
Z3 2.5i Roadster 2000–2001, Z3 2.8 Coupe 1999–2000

Z3 2.5i Roadster 2000–2001

Enginge Type		DOHC Inline 24-Valve 6-Cylinder; Double-VANOS Steplessly Variable Valve Timing
Displacement cc/ci		2494/152
Compression Ratio		10.51
BHP @ rpm		184 @ 6000
Torque lbs-ft @ rpm		175 @ 3500
Injection Type		Siemens MS 43 with Knock Control, Variable Valve Timing, Electronic Throttle System, Dual Resonance Intake System, Engine Cooling and Other Functions Included in Control Strategy
Fuel Requirement		Unleaded Premium
Transmission	Manual	Getrag Type B, 5-Speed
	Automatic	GM 5, 5-Speed steptronic with Adaptive Tansmission Control (ATC) and SelectableSport mode
Steering		Rack and Pinion, Engine Speed Sensitive Power Assist
Front Suspension		MacPherson Struts, Arc-Shaped Lower Arms, Coil Springs, Twin-Tube Gas Pressure Shocks, Anti-Roll Bar
Rear Suspension		Semi-Trailing Arms, Coil Springs, Twin-Tube Gas-Pressure Shocks, Anti-Roll Bar
Wheelbase (in.)		96.3
Weight (lbs.)	Manual	2899
	Automatic	2987
Wheels		Cast Alloy 16 x 7.0J
Tires		225/50R-16 92V Performance Radials
Brake System		Vacuum Assist, Antilock Braking System (ABS)
	Front	11.3-in. Vented Discs
	Rear	10.7-in. Solid Discs
0–60 mph, sec	Manual	7.1
	Automatic	7.2
Maximum Speed mph		128 (electronically limited)
MPG, City/Highway	Manual	20/27
	Automatic	19/26

Z3 2.8 Coupe 1999–2000

Engine Type		DOHC Inline 24-Valve 6-Cylinder, Double-VANOS Steplessly Variable Valve Timing
Displacement cc/ci		2793/170
Compression Ratio		10.21
BHP @ rpm		193 @ 5500
Torque lbs-ft @ rpm		206 @ 3500
Injection Type		Siemens MS 42 with Knock Control, Variable Valve Timing, Electromechanical Throttle System, Dual-Resonance Intake System, Engine Cooling and Other Functions Included in Control Strategy
Fuel Requirement		Unleaded Premium
Transmission	Manual	ZF Type C, 5-Speed
	Automatic	THM R1, 4-Speed, Adaptive Transmission Control (ATC), and 2 Selectable Shift Modes
Steering		Rack and Pinion, Engine Speed Sensitive Power Assist
Front Suspension		MacPherson Struts, Arc-Shaped Lower Arms, Coil Springs, Twin-Tube Gas-Pressure Shocks, Anti-Roll Bar
Rear Suspension		Semi-Trailing Arms, Coil Springs, Twin-Tube Gas-Pressure Shocks, Anti-Roll Bar
Wheelbase (in.)		96.3
Weight (lbs.)	Manual	2943
	Automatic	3031
Wheels	Standard	Cast Alloy 16 x 7
	Optional	Cast Alloy 17 x 7.5 Front
		17 x 8.5 Rear
Tires	Standard	225/50ZR-16 V Performance Radials
	Optional	225/45ZR-17 Front
		245/40ZR-17 Rear
Brake System		Vacuum Assist, Antilock Braking System (ABS)
	Front	11.3-in. Vented Discs
	Rear	10.7-in. Solid Discs
0–60 mph, sec	Manual	1999 NA
		2000 6.2
	Automatic	1999 NA
		2000 6.6
Maximum Speed mph		128 (electronically limited)
MPG, City/Highway	Manual	1999 NA
		2000 19/26
	Automatic	1999 NA
		2000 19/26

Specifications
Z3 3.0i Roadster 2000–2001, Z3 3.0i Coupe 2000–2001

Z3 3.0i Roadster 2000–2001

Engine Type		DOHC Inline 24-Valve 6-Cylinder, Double-VANOS Steplessly Variable Valve Timing
Displacement cc/ci		2979/182
Compression Ratio		10.21
BHP @ rpm		225 @ 5900
Torque lbs-ft @ rpm		214 @ 3500
Injection Type		Siemens MS 43 with Knock Control, Variable Valve Timing, Electronic Throttle System, Dual-Resonance Intake System, Engine Cooling, and Other Functions Included in Control Strategy
Fuel Requirement		Unleaded Premium
Transmission	Manual	Getrag Type B, 5-Speed
	Automatic	GM 5, 5-Speed Steptronic with Adaptive Transmission Control(ATC) and Selectable Sport Model
Steering		Rack and Pinion, Engine Speed Sensitive Power Assist
Front Suspension		MacPherson Struts, Arc-Shaped Lower Arms, Coil Springs, Twin-Tube Gas-Pressure Shocks, Anti-Roll Bar
Rear Suspension		Semi-Trailing Arms, Coil Springs, Twin-Tube Gas-Pressure Shocks, Anti-Roll Bar
Wheelbase (in.)		96.3
Weight (lbs.)	Manual	2910
	Automatic	2998
Wheels		Cast Alloy 17 x 7.5 Front
		17 x 8.5 Rear
Tires		225/50R-16 92V Performance Radials
Brake System		Vacuum Assist, Antilock Braking System (ABS)
	Front	11.8-in. Vented Discs
	Rear	10.7-in. Solid Discs
0–60 mph, sec	Manual	5.9
	Automatic	6.0
Maximum Speed mph		128 (electronically limited)
MPG, City/Highway	Manual	21/28
	Automatic	19/25

Z3 3.0i Coupe 2000–2001

Engine Type		DOHC Inline 24-Valve 6-Cylinder, Double-VANOS Steplessly Variable Valve Timing
Displacement cc/ci		2979/182
Compression Ratio		10.21
BHP @ rpm		225 @ 5900
Torque lbs-ft @ rpm		214 @ 3500
Injection Type		Siemens MS 43 with Knock Control, Variable Valve Timing, Electronic Throttle System, Dual-Resonance Intake System, Engine Cooling and Other Functions Included in Control Strategy
Fuel Requirement		Unleaded Premium
Transmission	Manual	ZF Type C, 5-Speed
	Automatic	GM 5, 5-Speed Steptronic with Adaptive Transmission Control (ATC) and Selectable Sport Mode
Steering		Rack and Pinion, Engine Speed Sensitive Power Assist
Front Suspension		MacPherson Struts, Arc-Shaped Lower Arms, Coil Springs, Twin-Tube Gas Pressure Shocks, Anti-Roll Bar
Rear Suspension		Semi-Trailing Arms, Coil Springs, Twin-Tube Gas-Pressure Shocks, Anti-Roll Bar
Wheelbase (in.)		96.3
Weight (lbs.)	Manual	2943
	Automatic	3031
Wheels		Cast Alloy 17 x 7.5 Front
		17 x 8.5 Rear
Tires		225/50R-16 92V Performance Radials
Brake System		Vacuum Assist, Antilock Braking System (ABS)
	Front	11.8-in. Vented Discs
	Rear	10.7-in. Solid Discs
0–60 mph, sec	Manual	5.9
	Automatic	6.0
Maximum Speed mph		128 (electronically limited)
EPA Estimated mpg, City/Highway		
	Manual	21/28
	Automatic	19/27

Specifications
M-Roadster 1999–2001

M-Roadster 1999–2000

Engine Type		DOHC 24-Valve Inline 6-Cylinder, VANOS Variable Valve Timing
Displacement cc/ci		3152/192
Compression Ratio		10.51
BHP @ rpm		240 @ 6000
Torque lbs-ft @ rpm		236 @ 3800
Injection Type		Siemens MS 41.2 with Knock Control (2 Sensor)
Fuel Requirement		Unleaded Premium
Transmission	Manual	ZF Type C, 5-Speed
	Automatic	NA
Steering		Rack and Pinion, Engine Speed Sensitive Power Assist
Front Suspension		MacPherson Struts, Arc-Shaped Lower Arms, Coil Springs, Twin-Tube Gas-Pressure Shocks, Anti-Roll Bar
Rear Suspension		Semi-Trailing Arms, Coil Springs, Twin-Tube Gas-Pressure Shocks, Anti-Roll Bar
Stability-Enhancement		Limited-Slip Differential, All-Season Traction (AST)
Wheelbase (in.)		96.8
Weight (lbs.)	Manual	3086
	Automatic	NA
Wheels		Cast Alloy 17 x 7.5J Front
		17 x 9.0 Rear
Tires		225/45ZR-17 Front
		245/40ZR-17 Rear
Brake System		Vacuum Assist, Antilock Braking System (ABS)
	Front	12.4-in. Vented Discs
	Rear	12.3-in. Vented Discs
0–60 mph, sec	Manual	5.2
	Automatic	NA
Maximum Speed mph		137 (electronically limited)
MPG, City/Highway	Manual	19/26
	Automatic	NA

M-Roadster 2001

Engine Type		DOHC 24-Valve Inline 6-Cylinder, Double-VANOS Steplessly Variable Valve Timing
Displacement cc/ci		3246/
Compression Ratio		10.51
BHP @ rpm		315 @ 7400
Torque lbs-ft @ rpm		251 @ 4900
Injection Type		Siemens MS 42 with Adaptive Control (2 Sensor)
Fuel Requirement		Unleaded Premium
Transmission	Manual	5-Speed
	Automatic	NA
Steering		Rack and Pinion, Engine Speed Sensitive Power Assist
Front Suspension		MacPherson Struts, Arc-Shaped Lower Arms, Coil Springs, Twin-Tube Gas-Pressure Shocks, Anti-Roll Bar, M-Calibration
Rear Suspension		Semi-Trailing Arms, Coil Springs, Twin-TubeGas-Pressure Shocks, Anti-Roll Bar, M-Calibration, Stability Enhancement, Dynamic Stability Control, (DSC), All-Season Traction (AST) with Limited-Slip Differential
Wheelbase (in.)		96.8
Weight (lbs.)	Manual	3086
	Automatic	NA
Wheels		Cast Alloy 17 x 7.5J Front
		17 x 9.0 Rear
Tires		225/45ZR-17 Front
		245/40ZR-17 Rear
Brake System		Vacuum Assist, Antilock Braking System (ABS)
	Front	12.4-in. Vented Discs
	Rear	12.3-in. Vented Discs
0–60 mph, sec	Manual	5.1
	Automatic	NA
Maximum Speed mph		137 (est.) (electronically limited)
MPG, City/Highway	Manual	19/26 (est.)
	Automatic	NA

Specifications
M-Coupe 1999–2001

M-Coupe 1999–2000

Engine Type		DOHC 24-Valve Inline 6-Cylinder, VANOS Variable Valve Timing
Displacement cc/ci		3152/192
Compression Ratio		10.51
BHP @ rpm		240 @ 6000
Torque lbs-ft @ rpm		236 @ 3800
Injection Type		Siemens MS 41.2 with Knock Control (2 Sensor)
Fuel Requirement		Unleaded Premium
Transmission	Manual	ZF Type C, 5-Speed
	Automatic	NA
Steering		Rack and Pinion, Engine Speed Sensitive Power Assist
Front Suspension		MacPherson Struts, Arc-Shaped Lower Arms, Coil Springs, Twin-Tube Gas-Pressure Shocks, Anti-Roll Bar
Rear Suspension		Semi-Trailing Arms, Coil Springs, Twin-Tube Gas-Pressure Shocks, Anti-Roll Bar
Stability-Enhancement		Limited-Slip Differential, All-Season Traction (AST)
Wheelbase (in.)		96.8
Weight (lbs.)	Manual	3131
	Automatic	NA
Wheels		Cast Alloy 17 x 7.5J Front
		17 x 9.0 Rear
Tires		225/45ZR-17 Front
		245/40ZR-17 Rear
Brake System		Vacuum Assist, Antilock Braking System (ABS)
	Front	12.4-in. Vented Discs
	Rear	12.3-in. Vented Discs
0–60 mph, sec	Manual	5.1
	Automatic	NA
Maximum Speed mph		137 (electronically limited)
MPG, City/Highway	Manual	19/26
	Automatic	NA

M-Coupe 2001

Engine Type		DOHC 24-Valve Inline 6-Cylinder, Double-VANOS Steplessly Variable Valve Timing
Displacement cc/ci		3246/
Compression Ratio		10.51
BHP @ rpm		315 @ 7400
Torque lbs-ft @ rpm		251 @ 4900
Injection Type		Siemens MS 42 with Adaptive Control (2 Sensor)
Fuel Requirement		Unleaded Premium
Transmission	Manual	5-Speed
	Automatic	NA
Steering		Rack and Pinion, Engine Speed Sensitive Power Assist
Front Suspension		MacPherson Struts, Arc-Shaped Lower Arms, Coil Springs, Twin-Tube Gas-Pressure Shocks, Anti-Roll Bar, M-Calibration
Rear Suspension Enhancement,		Semi-Trailing Arms, Coil Springs, Twin-Tube Gas-Pressure Shocks, Anti-Roll Bar, M-Calibration, Stability Dynamic Stability Control, (DSC), All-Season Traction (AST) with Limited-Slip Differential
Wheelbase (in.)		96.8
Weight (lbs.)	Manual	3131
	Automatic	NA
Wheels		Cast Alloy 17 x 7.5J Front
		17 x 9.0 Rear
Tires		225/45ZR-17 Front
		245/40ZR-17 Rear
Brake System		Vacuum Assist, Antilock Braking System (ABS)
	Front	12.4-in. Vented Discs
	Rear	12.3-in. Vented Discs
0–60 mph, sec	Manual	5.1
	Automatic	NA
Maximum Speed mph		137 ((est.)) (electronically limited)
MPG, City/Highway	Manual	19/26 (est.)
	Automatic	NA

Specifications
Z3 2.8 Roadster 1997–2000

Engine Type	1997–1998		DOHC Inline 24-valve 6-Cylinder, Variable Valve Timing
	1999–2000		DOHC Inline 24-Valve 6-Cylinder, Double-VANOS Steplessly Variable Valve Timing
Displacement cc/ci			2793/170
Compression Ratio			10.21
BHP @ rpm	1997–1998		189 @ 5300
	1999–2000		193 @ 5500
Torque lbs-ft @ rpm	1997–1998		203 @ 3950
	1999–2000		206 @ 3500
Injection Type	1997		Siemens MS 41.0 with Adaptive Knock Control
	1998		Siemens MS 41.1 with Adaptive Knock Control
	1999–2000		Siemens MS 42 with Knock Control, Variable Valve Timing, Electromechanical Throttle System, Dual-Resonance Intake System, Engine Cooling and Other Functions Included in Control Strategy
Fuel Requirement			Unleaded Premium
Transmission	Manual		ZF Type C, 5-Speed
	Automatic	1997–1998	THM R1, 4-Speed, and Economy, Sport or Manual Selectable Shift Modes
		1999–2000	THM R1, 4-Speed, Adaptive Transmission Control (ATC) and Economy or Sport Selectable Shift Modes
Steering			Rack and Pinion, Engine Speed Sensitive Power Assist
Front Suspension			MacPherson Struts, Arc-Shaped Lower Arms, Coil Springs, Twin-Tube Gas-Pressure Shocks, Anti-Roll Bar
Rear Suspension			Semi-Trailing Arms, Coil Springs, Twin-Tube Gas-Pressure Shocks, Anti-Roll Bar
Wheelbase (in.)			96.3
Weight (lbs.)	Manual	1997–1998	2844
		1999–2000	2910
	Automatic	1997–1998	2932
		1999–2000	2998
Wheels	Standard		Cast Alloy 16 x 7
Optional			Cast Alloy 17 x 7.5 Front
			17 x 8.5 Rear
Tires	Standard		225/50ZR-16 V Performance Radials
Optional			225/45ZR-17 Front
			245/40ZR-17 Rear
Brake System			Vacuum Assist, Antilock Braking System (ABS)
	Front		11.3-in. Vented Discs
	Rear		10.7-in. Solid Discs
0–60 mph, sec	Manual		6.3
	Automatic		6.7
Maximum Speed mph			128 (electronically limited)
MPG, City/Highway	Manual	1997	19/27
		1998–2000	19/26
	Automatic	1997–1998	18/24
		1999–2000	19/26

The front view of the 2001 BMW M-Roadster features a more aggressively styled front bumper, M-Double Spoke alloy wheels, and a chromed accent side grill.

Replacement Costs for Common Parts
Z3 1.9 Roadster 1996–1998, Z3 2.3 1996–1998
Z3 2.5i Roadster 2001, Z3 2.8 Roadster/Coupe 1997–2000

Z3 1.9 Roadster 1996–1998

Oil Filter		$6.25	
Fuel Filter		$21	
Fuel Pump		$112	
Starter		$166	Exchange
		+ $30	Core Chg.
Alternator		$310	Exchange
		+ $30	Core Chg.
Water Pump		$63	
Thermostat		$43.25	
Clutch Kit		$239	
Front Bumper		$311	
Hood		$677.50	
Left Front Fender		$78.50	
Right Rear Quarter Panel		$323	
Rear Bumper		$297	
Windshield		$295	
Tail Light Lens		$150	
Exhaust Pipe Catalyst (rmfg'd)		$905	Exchange
		+ $30	Core Chg.
Rear Muffler		$495	
Oxygen Sensor		$100	
Regulating Lambda Probe		$133.35	
Brake Master Cylinder		$305	
Clutch Slave Cylinder		$70.50	
Clutch Master Cylinder		$129.50	
Front Rotor (each)		$47	
Front Pads (set)		$66.50	
	Sensor	$16.10	
Front Shocks		$182	
Rear Shocks		$64	
Power Steering Pump		$307	Exchange
		+ $30	Core Chg.

Z3 2.3 1996–1998

Oil Filter		$8.50	
Fuel Filter		$21	
Fuel Pump		$112	
Starter		$166	Exchange
		+ $30	Core Chg.
Alternator	90 amp	$307	Exchange
		+ $30	Core Chg.
	120 amp	$384	Exchange
		+ $30	Core Chg.
Water Pump		$79.95	
Thermostat		$28.50	
Clutch		$229	
Front Bumper		$315	
Hood		$677.50	
Left Front Fender		$78.50	
Right Rear Quarter Panel		$258	
Rear Bumper		$297	
Windshield		$295	
Tail Light Lens		$150	
Exhaust Manifold w/Converter Cylinders 1–3		$575	Exchange
		+ $30	Core Chg.
	Cylinders 4–6	$575	Exchange
		+ $30	Core Chg.
Front Silencer		$390	
Rear Muffler		$595	
Oxygen Sensor	Regulating Probe	$133.35	
	Monitoring Probe	$133.35	
Brake Master Cylinder		$305	
Clutch Slave Cylinder		$70.50	
Clutch Master Cylinder		$129.50	
Front Rotor		$65.75	
Front Pads (set)		$61.50	
	Sensor	$16.10	
Front Shocks		$182	
Rear Shocks		$64	
Power Steering Pump		$307	Exchange
		+ $60	Core Chg.

Z3 2.5i Roadster 2001

Oil Filter		$8.50	
Fuel Filter		$55	
Fuel Pump		$112	
Starter		$190	Exchange
		+ $30	Core Chg.
Alternator	90 amp	$307	Exchange
		+ $30	Core Chg.
	120 amp	$384	Exchange
		+ $30	Core Chg.
Water Pump		$79.95	
Thermostat		$28.50	
Clutch Kit		$229	
Front Bumper		$315	
Hood		$677	
Left Front Fender		$78.50	
Right Rear Quarter Panel		$258	
Rear Bumper		$297	
Windshield		$295	
Tail Light Lens		$148	
Exhaust Manifold w/Catalyst Cylinders 1–3		$650	Exchange
		+ $30	Core Chg.
	Cylinders 4–6	$650	Exchange
		+ $30	Core Chg.
Rear Muffler		$464	
Oxygen Sensor	Regulating Probe	$133.35	
	Monitoring Probe	$135.35	
Brake Master Cylinder		$305	
Clutch Slave Cylinder		$70.50	
Clutch Master Cylinder		$129.50	
Front Rotor		$65.75	
Front Pads (set)		$61.50	
	Sensor	$16.10	
Front Shocks		$175	
Rear Shocks		$85.75	
Power Steering Pump		$307	Exchange
		+ $30	Core Chg.

Z3 2.8 Roadster/Coupe 1997–2000

Oil Filter		$8.50	
Fuel Filter		$21	
Fuel Pump		$112	
Starter		$166	Exchange
		+ $30	Core Chg.
Alternator	90 amp	$307	Exchange
		+ $30	Core Chg.
	120 amp	$384	Exchange
		+ $30	Core Chg.
Water Pump		$79.95	
Thermostat		$28.50	
Clutch Kit		$229	
Front Bumper		$315	
Hood		$677.50	
Left Front Fender		$78.50	
Right Rear Quarter Panel		$258	
Rear Bumper		$297	
Windshield		$295	
Tail Light Lens		$150	
Exhaust Pipe Catalyst		$1,290	Exchange
		+ $30	Core Chg.
Rear muffler		$595	
Oxygen Sensor (2 required)		$133.35	
Brake master Cylinder		$305	
Clutch Slave Cylinder		$70.50	
Clutch Master Cylinder		$129.50	
Front Rotor		$65.75	
Front Pads (set)		$61.50	
	Sensor	$16.10	
Front Shocks		$182	
Rear Shocks		$64	
Power Steering Pump		$307	Exchange
		+ $60	Core Chg.

Replacement Costs for Common Parts
Z3 3.0i Roadster/Coupe 2001, Z3 M-Roadster/Coupe 1999

Z3 3.0i Roadster/Coupe 2001

Oil Filter		$8.50	
Fuel Filter		$55	
Fuel Pump		$112	
Starter		$190 + $30	Exchange Core Chg.
Alternator	90 amp	$307 + $30	Exchange Core Chg.
	120 amp	$384 + $30	Exchange Core Chg.
Water Pump		$79.95	
Thermostat		$28.50	
Clutch Kit		$344	
Front Bumper		$315	
Hood		$677	
Left Front Fender		$78.50	
Right Rear Quarter Panel		$258	
Rear Bumper		$297	
Windshield		$295	
Tail Light Lens		$148	
Exhaust Manifold w/ Catalyst	Cylinders 1–3	$650 + $30	Exchange Core Chg.
	Cylinders 4–6	$650 + $30	Exchange Core Chg.
Rear Muffler		$464	
Oxygen Sensor	Regulating Probe	$133.35	
	Monitoring Probe	$135.35	
Brake Master Cylinder		$305	
Clutch Slave Cylinder		$70.50	
Clutch Master Cylinder		$129.50	
Front Rotor		$59	
Front Pads (set)		$61.50	
	Sensor	$16.10	
Front Shocks		$175	
Rear Shocks		$85.75	
Power Steering Pump		$307 + $60	Exchange Core Chg.

Z3 M-Roadster/Coupe 1999

Oil Filter		$8.50	
Fuel Filter	up to 2000	$21	
	2001 on	$30	
Fuel Pump	up to 2000	$112	
	2001 on	$785	
Starter	up to 2000	$166 + $30	Exchange Core Chg.
	2001 on	$225 + $30	Exchange Core Chg.
Alternator		$378 + $30	Exchange Core Chg.
Water Pump	up to 2000	$79.95	
	2001 on	$179	
Thermostat	up to 2000	$33.50	
	2001 on	$63.25	
Clutch Kit		$284	
Front Bumper		$391	
Hood		$697	
Left Front Fender		$78.50	
Right Rear Quarter Panel		$329	
Rear Bumper		$297	
Windshield		$295	
Tail Light Lens		$150	
Exhaust Pipe/Catalyst	up to 2000	$1,580 + $30	Exchange Core Chg.
	2001 on		
	Cylinders 1–3	$650 + $30	Exchange Core Chg.
	Cylinders 4–6	$650 + $30	Exchange Core Chg.
Rear Muffler	Left Side	$595	
	Right Side	$595	
Oxygen Sensor	up to 2000 (2 required)	$133.35	
	2001 on (4 required)	$133.35	
Brake Master Cylinder	w/o DSC	$319	
	w/ DSC	$340	
Clutch Slave Cylinder		$70.50	
Clutch Master Cylinder		$129.50	
Front Rotor (each)		$149	
Front Pads (set)		$98.25	
	Sensor	$15.50	
Front Shocks (each)		$238	
Rear Shocks (each)		$128	
Power Steering Pump	up to 2001	$307 + $60	Exchange Core Chg.
	2001 on	$321 + $60	Exchange Core Chg.

The rear view of the 2001 BMW Z3 3.0i coupe reminds many of the British MGB-GT. The coupe body allows for greater cargo-carrying capacity.

What They Said About the . . .

Z3 1.9 Roadster

It's the best-riding, most structurally robust, small open sports car in my memory. — *Road & Track,* **January 1996**

Z3 2.3 Roadster

Cornball nomenclature aside, this is an outstanding engine. Replacing the base car's 1.9-liter 4-cylinder, it forever dispels the notion that the base-model Z3 is simply a Miata clone. —*Road & Track,* **July 1999**

Z3 2.8 Roadster

With their new concoction called the Z3 2.8, BMW engineers have taken the Carroll Shelby approach to roadster design: Stuff in a high-performance powerplant, plaster on some beefy rubber, and let the action begin. —*Motor Trend,* **March 1997**

Z3 2.8 Coupe

Although the 2.8-liter engine doesn't make the power or the delightfully roarty sounds of the 3.2, it's still a very good performer.
—*Car and Driver,* **June 1999**

Z3 3.0i Roadster

If you are in the market for a sports car that handles well, offers impressive around-town grunt, gets good fuel mileage, and provides a supple yet-still-sporty ride, the Bimmer is the better choice. —*Motor Trend,* **January 2001**

Z3 3.0i Coupe

My first reaction on driving the 3.0 coupe was satisfaction. —*The Roundel,* **January 2001**

Z3 M-Roadster

It's not a Supercar, but damn close. Prospective Chevrolet Corvette convertible buyers and Porsche Boxster S intenders may want to think twice.
—*Automobile Magazine,* **March 1998**

Z3 M-Coupe

Strap a victim in the passenger seat and unleash the smooth 240-horsepower DOHC inline six, and snide comments about the off-beat styling are replaced by gasps of amazement. —*Motor Trend,* **July 1999**

Tasteful wood trim complements chrome bezels on this 2001 BMW Z3 3.0i Roadster, although complaints of rattling trim bits are common. Also, the latest-generation sport steering wheels feature a smaller airbag.

Be certain to check and see whether the auxiliary fan recall has been completed on any 2001 BMW Z3 3.0i that may be capturing your interest.

I Bought a . . .

1996 BMW Z3 1.9 Roadster

I could not be more pleased with this car. The 1.9 is very nimble and "tossible." As long as you keep the revs boiling, the car *will* get out of its own way.

This has been a problem-free car and has been very reasonable to maintain and insure. The only glitches in almost six years have been a faulty headlight switch and the endemic BMW gas gauge (both repaired under warranty). As far as buyers in the used market go, nearly all Z3s have already had the fuel level sending unit replaced.

Fortunately, the Z3 (early cars in particular) is a pretty straightforward automobile, so there are not a lot of hidden issues. —*Matthew Daub, Fleetwood, Pennsylvania*

1998 BMW Z3 2.8 Roadster

The two things I like most about my Z3 are how it drives and the speed-adjuster stereo volume.

Installing and removing the boot is a pain, and the single-layer cloth top lets a lot of noise in. The digital clock/computer is almost impossible to read with the top down, and the stereo in my 1994 Camry sounds better than the Harman-Kardon premium sound system in my Roadster.

I wouldn't consider the car expensive to own—yet. A lot of little things have gone wrong. I have replaced the passenger seatbelt, air bag sensor, driver door lock, and floor mats. I find I am making repeat trips to the dealer to get the same thing fixed. Jobs are incomplete and incorrectly done. Parts have not been difficult to find, particularly if you want to pay full price.

Would I buy another? I might. I'm not sure yet. —*Warren McElroy, Lakewood, California*

1999 BMW M-Roadster

I like the way this car looks and the way it drives, but probably what I like most about the car is the power it has. The M-Roadster is the first BMW I have owned.

I will say that for the amount of money it cost, it should have better build quality. Some trim-related items have needed repair multiple times, and dealer service has not been up to par. There really haven't been any mechanical repairs, and any parts needed have been readily available.

My best experience has been the BMW Car Club of America and driving events. I would buy another one. —*Silvy Masarian, Los Angeles*

1999 BMW M-Coupe

I have been a BMW enthusiast since the 1970s and have owned many other BMWs. I ordered my M-Coupe the instant I saw the photos. I think the design looks great, and I knew the performance would be great, too.

There haven't been any mechanical problems and the car hasn't been out of service once. Parts are easy to find; however, I would consider the M-Coupe expensive, mainly because of high insurance premiums. Other drawbacks are that the unprotected sides are vulnerable to parking lot dings, and the resale value seems to be disappointingly low.

Of course I'd buy another BMW—I love these cars! —*Leif Anderberg, Monrovia, California*

The 2001 BMW M-Roadster's M54/3.2-liter features 315 horsepower, dual VANOS, and individual throttle butterflies.

The engine of a 2001 BMW M Coupe. Be certain to check maintenance records to confirm that all services are up to date.

I Bought a . . .

2000 BMW Z3 2.3 Roadster

I was attracted by the styling of the Z. It has a classic look that is reminiscent of the old Austin Healey 3000. I like the styling, performance, and build quality of the car.

The things that I like least about the Z is how difficult it is to get out of when the top is up and the lack of trunk space. The best thing about it is the experience of a top-down ride and cruising down a country road.

Since buying my Z, I have had the seat tracks replaced, the seatbelt retractor replaced, and the rear window reglued. I have also replaced the rearview mirror to get better visibility toward the right of the car and purchased a soft-top cover to free up trunk space.

I would consider the car fairly expensive to own once the warranty is up. The higher cost of maintenance is something I wish I had known about beforehand. But would I buy another? Absolutely! —*Ken Lewellyn, Hendersonville, Tennessee*

2001 BMW Z3 3.0i Coupe

I've always had a thing for the Z3 and its unique styling. It is a well-rounded car that balances comfort with handling with safety. When the Coupe first came out, I was on the fence as far as styling goes. I quickly grew to love it, and it was in 2000 that I began my search for a Z3. I was discouraged that you basically have to order Coupes to get what you want. It's not something you see on a dealer's lot very often. I opted for the Roadster primarily because of availability. I loved it, did a lot of upgrades, and took very good care of it. But every time I'd see a Coupe drive by, I'd rubberneck and think about what I really wanted. Soon I stumbled across a 2001 Z3 Coupe outfitted much the same as my Roadster, and the price was too low to pass up. It was a factory car with about 11,000 miles and was in perfect condition. I still have very fond memories of the Roadster and will miss the drop top on those perfect spring and autumn days.

I really like the wider torque band in the 3.0. The torque comes in at lower rpm and builds quickly yet smoothly. The 2.8 was nice, but it felt a bit weak at lower rpm. Braking feels about the same, but it is hard to tell since the Coupe feels like a different car. —*Dave Regis, Folsom, California*

2001 BMW Z3 2.5i Roadster

I love this car! The styling, the color—Atlanta Blue with tan leather—and the total look. It's perfect for me.

What do I like most? Meeting fellow Z3 owners. These cars are an instant conversation starter, plus it's a guy magnet! I would never have thought that I would be totally spoiled by this car and can't even think about any other car for me in the future, so I really have to pamper this one!

So far my Z3 has not been expensive to own or maintain. Would I buy another one? In a nanosecond! —*Hope Burns, Charleston, South Carolina*

The squat look of the 2001 BMW M-Coupe is purposeful and tells followers at a glance that this is a serious performer.

The 2001 BMW M-Coupe's gauges feature aluminum-finish bezels for instruments dials. The sport steering wheel is leather covered and features Motorsports tricolor stitching.

Introduced to the world in late 1999, the Z8 traces its lineage back through the years to the 507 roadsters of the late 1950s. Worldwide production for the first year was targeted at 1,800 cars, with 400 of these intended for U.S. customers. The waiting list of buyers included many celebrities and others who did not flinch at the sticker price nor at the surcharge added on by some retailers.

With the aluminum space frame assembled, welded, and the aluminum body panels installed at the Dingolfing factory, painting and final assembly were completed at the Munich facility, about 60 miles away. Using a combination of modern-day, computer-controlled equipment and small assembly teams to complete the process, each Z8 could be considered a work of art in this modern day era of cookie-cutter, mass-production cars.

The technical specifications are impressive, and together they add up to graceful, modern-day design that takes some clues from the fabulous 507. And yet the design of the Z8 is sufficiently different that there is no mistaking the technology that went into the design and execution.

Using a front suspension that borrows heavily from the current-generation 5-Series and a rear suspension borrowing from the current 7-Series, the individual components are mounted to an aluminum space frame that is MIG-welded by hand. Additional aluminum stampings are also welded to the basic subframe, and the aluminum body panels are then attached. The finished product is claimed to be the stiffest open car currently on the market.

The 5.0-liter, DOHC 24-valve S62 V-8 is shared with the M5 sedan. Utilizing electronically actuated individual throttles—one for each cylinder—engine response is immediate and offers two settings: Normal and a more sensitive Sport setting. Throttle operation is accomplished through an innovative combination of throttle position and potentiometers that send signals to the engine control module. The control module in turn sends information to a DC servomotor. The servomotor is linked to a small gearbox that drives a shaft actuating the throttles for each bank of cylinders.

As sophisticated as this sounds, it does not stop here. Cylinders 4 and 8 have their own remote potentiometers to monitor throttle operation. If a fault is detected, this system switches to one-of-four "limp-home" modes, allowing drivers to reach their destinations, albeit at a programmed maximum speed of 62 miles per hour.

The V-8's power is transmitted through a Z8-specific clutch to a Getrag type D, 6-speed manual transmission. The transmission features shift linkage that has been modified for shorter throws. In the rear, the 4-link suspension shares some features with the 7-Series but is also unique to the Z8 in its final execution. Steering is by power-assisted, variable-ratio rack-and-pinion, again a unique feature of the Z8.

Braking is by 4-wheel ventilated discs, and, for a car as special as the Z8, special braking systems are to be expected. Dynamic Brake Control computes the speed and force of the driver's braking application to help reduce emergency stopping distances. Electronic brake proportioning also comes into play. Using the ABS wheel-speed sensors to monitor and compare wheel speeds, the system adjusts brake pressure front to rear.

The 18-inch alloy wheels are fitted with run-flat high-performance radials. Tire pressure is monitored, and an integrated visual and audible warning system tells the driver whether a tire is losing pressure. The run-flat tires are designed to permit the car to be driven for up to 300 miles at 50 miles per hour should a tire lose pressure.

This ultimate BMW is destined to be a classic and was produced in appropriate quantities: Approximately 400 were imported in 2000. This car may be the Holy Grail of present-day BMWs. If you are in the position to buy one, the line forms at your dealership's door.

The 2001 BMW Z8 is available in limited color choices. This topaz blue example shows how well the lines flow from front-to-rear.

The four-cam, 32-valve, V-8 engine of the 2001 Z8 Roadster is shared with the M5 and produces 394 horsepower at 6,600 rpm. The engine compartment is tidy and well laid out.

Replacement Costs for Common Parts
Z8 2000–2001

Oil Filter		$10
Fuel Filter		$135
Fuel Pump		$248
Starter		$270 Exchange
		+$30 Core Chg.
Alternator		$680
Water Pump		$197.25
Thermostat		$61.75
Ignition Coil (each)		$12.80
Clutch Kit		$350
Front Bumper		$420
Hood		$867.50
Left Front Fender		$440
Right Rear Quarter Panel		$725
Rear Bumper	Top	$434
	Bottom	$399
Windshield		$359
Tail Light Housing/Lens		$595
Rear Silencer (each, 2 required)		$450
Catalytic Converter		$2,070, Exchange
Oxygen Sensor (2 required)		$133.35
Clutch Slave Cylinder		$70.50
Clutch Master Cylinder		$129.50
Front Rotor (each)		$125
Front Pads (set)		$114
	Sensor (each)	$15.50
Front Shocks (each)		$290
Rear Shocks (each)		$215

The smooth simplicity of the 2001 BMW Z8 Roadster's dash and interior masks the high level of technology that is incorporated. All the amenities are there, just behind the scenes.

Ratings Chart
Z8

	1.9
Model Comfort/Amenities	★★★
Reliability	★★★★
Collectibility	★★½
Parts/Service Availability	★★★★
Est. Annual Repair Costs	★★★½

The classic lines of the 2001 BMW Z8 Roadster evoke memories of the legendary 507 Roadster. Final assembly is done at Munich, and the fit and finish are exemplary.

Some components, like the S62/5.0-liter V-8, the 6-speed manual transmission, front suspension, and brake systems are evolved from the current 5-Series and upper-level 7-Series. Each has been modified or tailored for use in the Z8.

Featuring an aluminum space frame and body shell that are built by hand at the Dingolfing factory with final assembly being done at the Munich factory, each Z8 is as special as it is significant.

There have been multiple reports of batteries draining in short periods of time. Traced to the onboard cell phone wiring, an upgraded phone wiring harness is available, and efforts are underway to replace the troublesome harnesses on an as-needed basis

Like other current-model BMWs, the Z8 has been subjected to two recalls on the auxiliary/cooling fans. This is reported to affect Z8s built between January 1, 2001 and August 31, 2001. The installation of an updated fan unit is the solution.

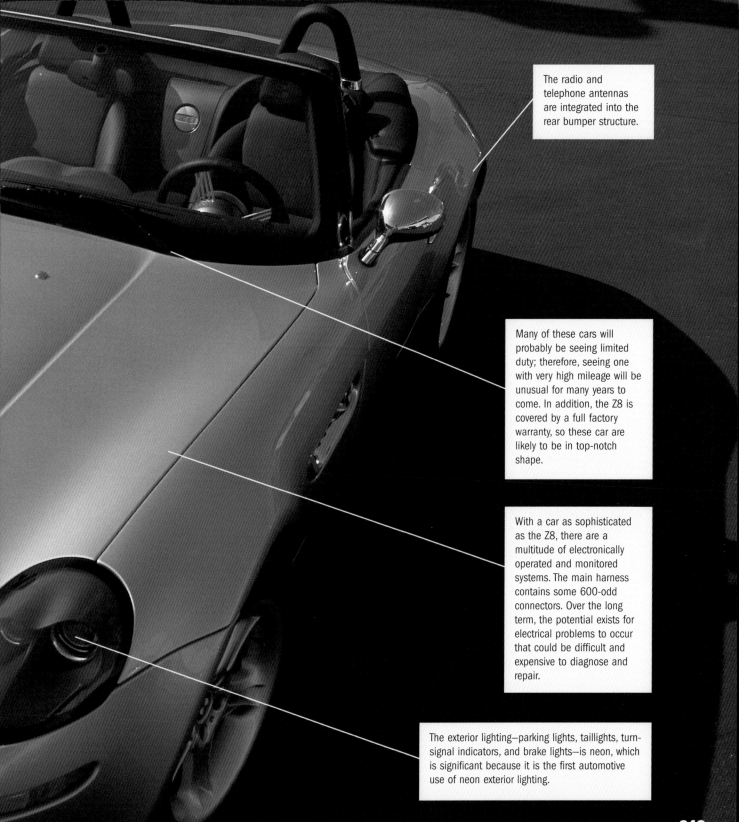

The radio and telephone antennas are integrated into the rear bumper structure.

Many of these cars will probably be seeing limited duty; therefore, seeing one with very high mileage will be unusual for many years to come. In addition, the Z8 is covered by a full factory warranty, so these car are likely to be in top-notch shape.

With a car as sophisticated as the Z8, there are a multitude of electronically operated and monitored systems. The main harness contains some 600-odd connectors. Over the long term, the potential exists for electrical problems to occur that could be difficult and expensive to diagnose and repair.

The exterior lighting—parking lights, taillights, turn-signal indicators, and brake lights—is neon, which is significant because it is the first automotive use of neon exterior lighting.

Specifications
Z8 2000–2001

Engine Type		DOHC 32-Valve (4 cam) V-8, Double-VANOS Steplessly Variable Valve Timing, 8 Individual Electronically Controlled Throttles with Normal and Sport Settings
Displacement cc/ci		4941/302
Compression Ratio		11.01
BHP @ rpm		394 @ 6600
Torque lbs-ft @ rpm		368 @ 3800
Injection Type		Siemens MSS 52 with Adaptive Knock Control, Variable Valve Timing Electronic Throttles, g-Sensitive Lubrication System, Oil-Level/Temperature Sender, Variable Tachometer Warning Zone, Catalyst Protection and M Driving Dynamics Control Included in Control Strategy
Fuel Requirement		Unleaded Premium
Transmission	Manual	Getrag Type D, 6-Speed
	Automatic	NA
Steering		Variable Ratio Rack and Pinion, Engine-Speed Sensitive Power Assist
Front Suspension		Sport Suspension in Aluminum, MacPherson Struts, Double Pivot Lower Arms with Low Friction Ball Joints at Pivot Points, Coil Springs, Twin-Tube Gas Pressure Shocks, Anti-Roll Bar, Aluminum Subframe
Rear Suspension		Sport Suspension, 4 Link Integral System with low Friction Balljoints at Pivots of Upper Lateral Arms, Lower Lateral Arm, Twin-Tube Gas-Pressure Shocks, Anti-Roll Bar.
Wheelbase (in.)		98.6
Weight (lbs.)	Manual	3494
	Automatic	NA
Wheels		Cast Alloy 18 x 8.0 Front
		18 x 9.0 Rear
Tires		Run Flat 245/45R-18 96W fr/ 275/40R-18 99 W r
Brake System		Vacuum Assist, Antilock Braking System, All-Season Traction (AST), Dynamic Stability Control(DSC)
	Front	13.1-in. Vented Discs
	Rear	12.9-in. Vented Discs
0–60 mph, sec		
	Manual	4.7
	Automatic	NA
Maximum Speed mph		155 (electronically limited)
EPA Estimated mpg, City/Highway		
	Manual	13/21
	Automatic	NA

What They Said About the . . .

BMW Z8

Suffice to say that we're all witnessing the birth of an automotive legend. *—Motor Trend,* **May 2000**

Stunning from any angle, the 2001 BMW Z8 is the first production car to use Neon exterior lighting.

I Bought a . . .

2000 BMW Z8 Roadster

I love the beautiful lines of the open Roadster. The Z8 is smooth, powerful, and unique, plus it offers BMW reliability in a supercar.

I have owned BMWs previously and currently have three. Perhaps my best experience with my Z8 thus far is the constant, positive feedback from almost everyone who sees it.

The hardtop contacts and glove compartment latch have needed repairs, although both were covered under warranty. Perhaps the only thing I don't like so far is the semi-manual soft top (a tradeoff for the low waistline of the car, which I agree with, but I still don't like the inconvenience).

Nevertheless, I will never sell this car! *—Robert P. Lacy, San Juan Capistrano, California*

2001 BMW Z8

I was attracted to the Z8 by its performance combined with an awesome cohesion of retro-style (styling cues from BMW 507, Shelby Cobra, and Jaguar E-type) and modern equipment execution. To my eyes, there is not a bad line on the car. That is a very profound statement from me. There is usually something in a car's design that falls a little short or is uninspiring. I am a professed, convicted car nut. I have owned myriad modern and classic sports and touring cars.

The only problem I have had is the battery drawing down and dying, due to the wrong cellular telephone being delivered with the car. The Z8 models through 2001 model year were equipped with a wiring setup compatible with the Motorola CPT 7000 (Startach) BMW cellular phone. During the 2001 year (early), most dealerships delivered the Motorola CPT 8000 cellular phone with the car (it was the latest model phone and provided for the 2001 cars). Unfortunately, the difference in the phones meant that the phone did not go into sleep mode when the car was off, and the phone drew down the battery. This was fixed by retrofit of a cable to the phone system in the car. This problem was quite prevalent throughout the 2001 model year.

I would say the Z8 is an expensive car to own and maintain. It is an exotic, and the parts for this car are unique to the Z8 only. That is why I purchased the additional year/14,000-miles maintenance provision from BMW. The car is covered for maintenance and warranty for 4 years or 50,000 miles. *—Greg Johnson, Irvine, California*

Phone and radio antennas are incorporated into the rear bumper of the 2001 BMW Z8.

Although it was BMW's first foray into the all-wheel drive segment, the early 1990's 325iX was not a huge seller in the United States. This time around, though, BMW's products were better known, and the SUV/SAV market was more mature and ready.

Never a company to follow exactly what others do, BMW's decision makers foresaw the market potential and scrambled to develop a vehicle that would place them in this growing segment. Based loosely on the 5-Series platform, the X5 is labeled a sports activity vehicle (SAV) rather than the more common sports utility vehicle (SUV) identifier applied to most other vehicles that fit into a similar visual frame.

Available initially with the M62/4.4-liter DOHC 32-valve V-8 and 5-speed Steptronic automatic transmission as found in the 540i and 740i sedans, by the end of the first year the X5 was also available with the M54/3.0-liter DOHC 24-valve inline 6-cylinder found in the 3-Series and 5-Series sedans.

In keeping with BMW's tradition of blazing its own trail, the inline six offered a 5-speed manual transmission as standard equipment and the 5-speed automatic as an option. The V-8–powered cars are available only with the automatic. Unlike other SUVs, the X5 features 4-wheel independent suspension and 4-wheel disc brakes with both ABS and Dynamic Brake Control (DBC). Standard equipment included all-season traction (AST), Dynamic Stability Control (DSC) and a new feature—Hill Descent Control (HDC)—which helps control downhill descent by automatically limiting speed.

As of this writing there is not much information available on the X5 4.6i, as deliveries began in December 2001.

Although there is some similarity between the X5 and the 5-Series, the X5 is structurally unique, sharing no body panels. Suspensions front and rear are mounted to tubular subframes that are in turn mounted to the X5's floor pan. Suspension is traditional BMW—MacPherson struts in front and a 4-link rear suspension with self-leveling rear air springs standard on the V-8 and optional on the 3.0i.

To maintain the handling reputation BMWs have earned, the engines in the X5 are positioned lower in the chassis than would normally be expected. Power for the front wheels comes through a center differential in a manner very similar to that used in the E30 325iX. A second driveshaft runs forward to the front differential, and the right-side halfshaft is routed through the engine oil pan, resulting in equal-length halfshafts and minimizing torque steer.

Thirty-eight percent of the torque is sent to the front wheels, and the remaining 62 percent is delivered to the rear wheels. This torque split is fixed. However, through advances in electronics, some measure of variability is provided by a combination of DSC-X, ABS, DBC, and AST. Stated in simpler terms, the electronics have the ability to reduce power or apply the brakes one wheel at a time to minimize wheel slippage. As sophisticated as this is, we still have Automatic Differential Brake (ADB). Its function is to sense which wheel is spinning and to redistribute drive to non-spinning wheels as well as to reduce engine power when wheel spin is detected. And, for descending steep hills, there is Hill Descent Control (HDC), the task of which is to maintain downhill speed between 3 and 6 miles per hour by applying the brakes at all four wheels.

The X5 is a surprisingly good-handling vehicle and offers all the expected BMW amenities plus the limited ability to explore areas you would not normally go with a BMW. The 3.0i six-cylinder is the entry-level model and is somewhat underpowered for any serious hill climbing. The V-8–powered cars offer outstanding performance and surprisingly good handling for a high-profile vehicle. Sharp looking and powerful, this vehicle makes an impressive statement and fills a niche for BMW.

The X5 is fairly new on the market, so long-term maintenance issues have yet to manifest. Without question, though, certified pre-owned vehicles offer buyers good opportunities.

Ratings Chart

X5

	X5 3.0i	X5 4.4i
Model Comfort/Amenities	★★★½	★★★½
Reliability	★★★★	★★★★
Collectibility	★★	★★
Parts/Service Availability	★★★★	★★★★
Est. Annual Repair Costs	★★★	★★★

This rear view of the 2001 BMW X5 3.0i shows that the rear hatch splits above the license plate. The top half swings up, and the rear half down. Privacy glass is an option.

The M54/3.0-liter inline-six of the 2001 BMW X5 3.0i delivers smooth power, although some may consider performance lacking.

Replacement Costs for Common Parts
X5 3.0i/4.4i 2000–2001

X5 3.0i 2000–2001

Oil Filter		$8.50
Fuel Filter		$88.75
Fuel Pump		$77.50
Starter		$225, Exchange. + $30 Core Chg.
Alternator	90 amp	$307, Exchange
	120 amp	$384, Exchange
Water Pump		$79.95
Thermostat		$28.50
Ignition Coil (each)		$12.80
Clutch Kit		$350
Front Bumper		$320
Hood		$599
Left Front Fender		$289
Right Rear Quarter Panel		$1,025
Rear Bumper		$215
Windshield		$320
	w/ Rain Sensor	$375
Tail Light Lens		$132
Exhaust Manifold w/ Catalyst		$650, Exchange
Rear Muffler		$395
Oxygen Sensor (2 required)		$133.35
Brake master Cylinder		$399
Clutch Slave Cylinder		$70.50
Clutch Master Cylinder		$129.50
Front Rotor		$85
Front Pads (set)		$96
	Sensor	$15.55
Front Shocks		$218
	w/ Front Self-Leveling	$690
Rear Shocks		$152
	w/ Rear Self-Leveling	$160

X5 4.4i 2000–2001

Oil Filter		$10
Fuel Filter		$88.75
Fuel Pump		$77.50
Starter Exchange		$270.95,
Generator (water cooled)		
	from 9/98 to 7/00	$680, Exchange
	from 7/00 on	$605, Exchange
Water Pump		$117
Thermostat		$63.25
Ignition Coil (each)		$12.80
Front Bumper		$320
Hood		$599
Left Front Fender		$289
Right Rear Quarter Panel		$1,025
Rear Bumper		$215
Windshield		$320
	w/ Rain Sensor	$375
Tail Light Lens		$132
Exhaust Manifold w/ Catalyst		$1,050, Exchange
Rear Muffler		
	Non-Sports Package (each)	$490
	Sports Package (each)	$520
Oxygen Sensor		
Regulating (each)		$133.35
Monitoring (each)		$133.35
Brake Master Cylinder		$399
Clutch Slave Cylinder		$70.50
Clutch Master Cylinder		$129.50
Front Rotor		$85
Front Pads (set)		$96
	Sensor	$15.55 (each)
Front Shocks (each)		$198
	w/ Front Self-Leveling	$690
Rear Shocks (each)		$160
	w/ Rear Self-Leveling	$160
	Sport Package	$149

This 2000 X5 4.4i has the standard 4-spoke steering wheel. The automatic climate controls and 5-speed Steptronic automatic transmission are visible in this photo.

The seatbelt-anchoring bolts for both front seats may not have been properly tightened. The nuts that secure the brake pedal assembly to the brake booster may have been cross-threaded during assembly. An attaching bolt for the left tie rod may not have been tightened properly. The bolts attaching the power steering pump pulley may not have been properly tightened.

A "Coolant Check" message is displayed on the instrument panel. This may indicate a low-coolant condition or a defective system sensor.

The M54/3.0-liter, new-generation DOHC 24-valve engine of the X5 3.0i features Double Vanos steplessly variable valve timing, plus an aluminum block and cylinder heads for increased efficiency and lighter weight.

Auxiliary/cooling fans have experienced failures and have on occasion overheated and melted wiring. An updated part is available, and most of the affected vehicles have been modified.

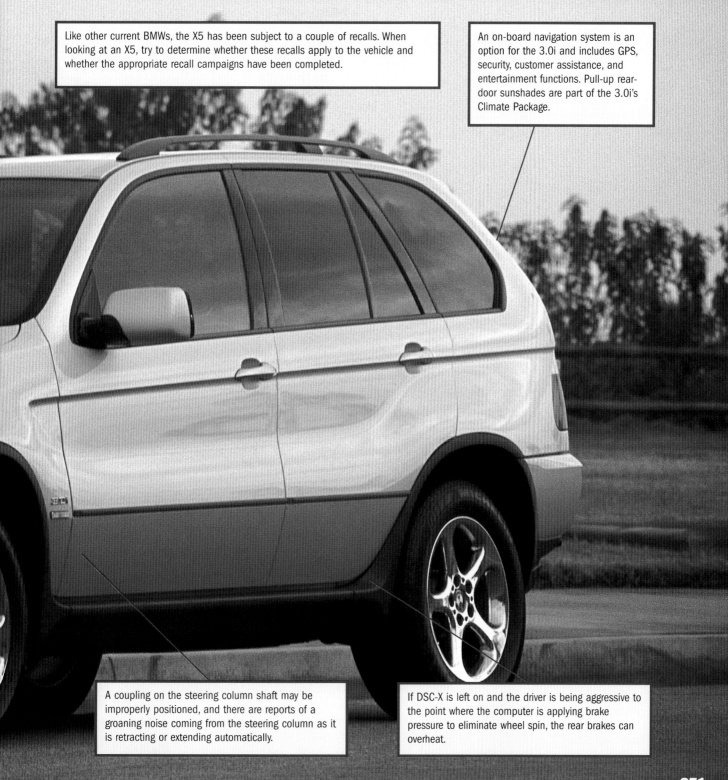

Like other current BMWs, the X5 has been subject to a couple of recalls. When looking at an X5, try to determine whether these recalls apply to the vehicle and whether the appropriate recall campaigns have been completed.

An on-board navigation system is an option for the 3.0i and includes GPS, security, customer assistance, and entertainment functions. Pull-up rear-door sunshades are part of the 3.0i's Climate Package.

A coupling on the steering column shaft may be improperly positioned, and there are reports of a groaning noise coming from the steering column as it is retracting or extending automatically.

If DSC-X is left on and the driver is being aggressive to the point where the computer is applying brake pressure to eliminate wheel spin, the rear brakes can overheat.

The X5 shares many components with the 540i sedans and also shares common problems with other current model BMWs.

The seatbelt-anchoring bolts for both front seats may not have been properly tightened. The nuts that secure the brake pedal assembly to the brake booster may have been cross-threaded during assembly. An attaching bolt for the left tie rod may not have been tightened properly. The bolts attaching the power steering pump pulley may not have been properly tightened.

A "Coolant Check" message is displayed on the instrument panel. This may indicate a low-coolant condition or a defective system sensor.

Auxiliary/cooling fans have experienced failures and have on occasion overheated and melted wiring. An updated part is available, and most of the affected vehicles have been modified. Confirm that this is the case.

A coupling on the steering column shaft may be improperly positioned, and there are reports of a groaning noise coming from the steering column as it is retracting or extending automatically.

BMW Performance Center

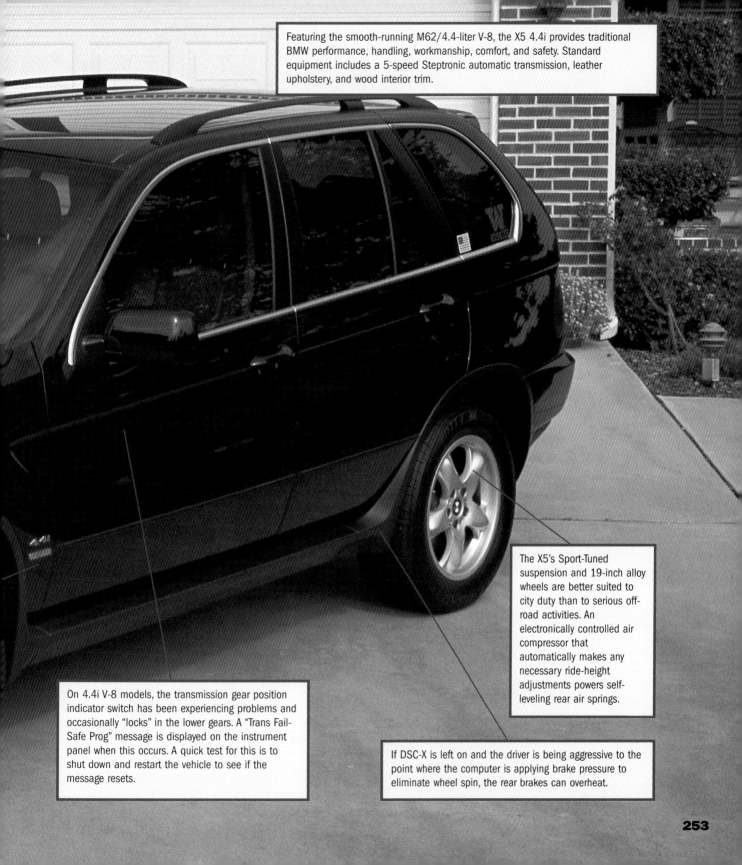

Featuring the smooth-running M62/4.4-liter V-8, the X5 4.4i provides traditional BMW performance, handling, workmanship, comfort, and safety. Standard equipment includes a 5-speed Steptronic automatic transmission, leather upholstery, and wood interior trim.

The X5's Sport-Tuned suspension and 19-inch alloy wheels are better suited to city duty than to serious off-road activities. An electronically controlled air compressor that automatically makes any necessary ride-height adjustments powers self-leveling rear air springs.

On 4.4i V-8 models, the transmission gear position indicator switch has been experiencing problems and occasionally "locks" in the lower gears. A "Trans Fail-Safe Prog" message is displayed on the instrument panel when this occurs. A quick test for this is to shut down and restart the vehicle to see if the message resets.

If DSC-X is left on and the driver is being aggressive to the point where the computer is applying brake pressure to eliminate wheel spin, the rear brakes can overheat.

Specifications
X5 3.0i 2000–2001

Engine Type		DOHC 24-Valve Inline 6-Cylinder, VANOS Steplessly Variable Intake and Exhaust Valve Timing
Displacement cc/ci		2979/182
Compression Ratio		10.21
BHP @ rpm		225 @ 5900
Torque lbs-ft @ rpm		214 @ 3500
Injection Type		Siemens MS43 with Adaptive Knock Control, Variable Valve Timing, Engine Cooling and
Other		Functions Included in Control Strategy
Fuel Requirement		Unleaded Premium
Emission Control		3-Way Catalytic Converter, Secondary Air Injection, Closed Loop Mixture Control (50 states)
Transmission	Manual	5-Speed
	Automatic	ZF 5HP 24 EH 5-Speed Steptronic with Adaptive Transmission Control (ATC) & Sport Mode
Steering		Variable Ratio Rack and Pinion, Engine-Speed Sensitive Power Assist
Front Suspension		MacPherson Struts, Double-Pivot Lower Arms, Coil Springs, Twin-Tube Gas-Pressure Shock Absorbers, Anti-Roll Bar, Sports Package Sport Suspension Calibration
Rear Suspension		4-Link Integral Suspension with Aluminum Integral Link, Forward Upper Lateral Arms and Wheel Carrier Steel Lower and Rear Upper Lateral Arms; Coil Springs; Self-Leveling (sports package sport suspension calibration)
Wheelbase (in.)		111.0
Weight (lbs.)	Manual	4519
	Automatic	4572
Wheels	Standard	Cast Alloy 17 x 7.5
	Optional	Cast Alloy 18 x 8.5
Tires	Standard	235/65R 17 All-Season
	Optional	255/55R 18 (sports package)
Brake System		Vacuum Assist, Antilock Braking System (ABS), All-Season Traction (AST), Dynamic Stability Control (DSC)
	Front	13.1-in. Vented Discs
	Rear	12.8-in. Vented Discs
0–60 mph, sec	Manual	8.1
	Automatic	8.6
Maximum Speed mph		126 (electronically limited)
MPG, City/Highway	Manual	15/20
	Automatic	15/20

The cargo floor of the 2001 BMW X5 3.0i lifts to reveal the full-size spare.

Specifications
X5 4.4i 2000–2001

Engine Type		DOHC 32-Valve (4 cam) V-8, Double-VANOS Steplessly Variable Valve Timing, 8 Individual Electronically Controlled Throttles with Normal and Sport Settings
Displacement cc/ci		4398/268
Compression Ratio		10.01
BHP @ rpm		282 @ 5400
Torque lbs-ft @ rpm		324 @ 3600
Injection Type		Motronic M 7.2, Adaptive Knock Control, Variable Valve Timing, Engine Cooling, and Other Functions Included in Control Strategy
Fuel Requirement		Unleaded Premium
Emission Control states)		3-Way Catalytic Converter, Secondary Air Injection, Closed Loop Mixture Control (50
Transmission	Manual	NA
	Automatic	5-Speed Steptronic with Adaptive Transmission Control (ATC) and Sport Mode
Steering		Variable Ratio Rack and Pinion, Engine-Speed Sensitive Power Assist
Front Suspension		MacPherson Struts, Double-Pivot Lower Arms, Coil Springs, Twin-Tube Gas-Pressure Shock Absorbers, Anti-Roll Bar, Sports Package Sport Suspension Calibration
Rear Suspension		4-Link Integral Suspension with Aluminum Integral Link, Forward Upper Lateral Arms and Wheel Carrier Steel Lower and Rear Upper Lateral Arms; Coil Springs; Self-Leveling (sport package sport suspension calibration)
Wheelbase (in.)		111.0
Weight (lbs.)	Manual	NA
	Automatic	4828
Wheels	Standard	Cast Alloy 18 x 8.5
	Optional	Cast Alloy 19 x 9.0 Front
		19 x 10.0 Rear (sports package)
Tires	Standard	255/55R 18 All-Season
	Optional	255/50R 19 Front
		285/45R 19 Rear (sports package)
Brake System		Vacuum Assist, Antilock Braking System (ABS), All-Season Traction (AST), Dynamic Stability Control (DSC)
	Front	13.1-in. Vented Discs
	Rear	12.8-in. Vented Discs
0–60 mph, sec	Manual	NA
	Automatic	6.7
Maximum Speed mph		128 (143 with sports package)
MPG, City/Highway	Manual	NA
	Automatic	13/17

The rear edge of the center console on the 2000 X5 4.4i features air vents for rear-seat occupants. Cup holders are housed in a popout panel that sits below the air vents.

What They Said About the BMW . . .

X5 3.0

If deep down inside you want an SUV but can't bear to give up the dynamic adrenaline-pumping stimulation of a great-handling sport sedan, there's no better choice than the BMW X5. —*Motor Trend,* **April 2000**

X5 4.4

In a nutshell, the optional sport-tuned suspension lacks the necessary compliance to soak up big ruts, while the ultra-sharp BMW steering that is so responsive on the road is almost too quick in the rough. —*Road & Track,* **June 2000**

The three-spoke sport steering wheel is an option on the 2001 BMW X5 4.0i. The on-board navigation system is displaying actual vehicle location.

The 4.4-liter V-8 of the 2000 X5 4.4i fills up the engine compartment. Check for oil leaks from the valve covers, and check that all safety recalls on the auxiliary fan have been performed.

The rear storage compartment of the 2000 BMW X5 4.4i is neatly finished with ample storage. A pullout cover hides the contents from view, and a spare tire is stowed below the floor.

I Bought a . . .

2001 BMW X5 3.0i

The lease price offered in an ad for this car is what attracted me. I had been looking at various cars over the past year, looking to replace a nine-year-old sedan. Until the day I saw the ad, I honestly didn't see myself driving a BMW.

I had been a passenger in a friend's SUV, and you never quite forgot that you were riding in a truck-based vehicle. The BMW X5 rides like a sedan, only with a higher line of sight for the driver. The fact that the Institute of Highway Safety rates this SUV highest in safety is just a plus. I feel safe in this car.

The climate control is difficult to adjust while driving; the plastic exterior door handles scratch easily; the plastic interior door handles look cheap; the windshield wipers squeak; there's not enough room in the center console for storage; and it has one of the smallest trunk areas of all the mid-sized SUVs.

However, the car handles beautifully. I'm not normally a person who volunteers to go driving, but I've found myself looking for excuses to drive since I bought this vehicle. You actually enjoy the time you spend in the car.

The most bizarre experience I've had to date was when I unlocked the car using my key memory, opened the door, and found the radio on. The radio had been turned off on the previous drive. There was no key was in the ignition, yet the radio was playing.

The Parking Distance Control had a malfunction, which I didn't realize until about two weeks into ownership. It turned out to be some wires that had to be adjusted. The vehicle has had no other mechanical issues to date.

I bought this car straight off the lot with the features the dealer had deemed to order, which were minimal for the most part. I would buy another, but the next time I would order the features myself and add a few options. *—Joyce Barrone, Pasadena, California*

2002 BMW X5 4.4i

I enjoyed the handling and performance of my 1985 BMW 325e that I kept for thirteen trouble-free years and 270,000 miles. My subsequent car, a 1998 Volvo S70T5M, was nice, but it didn't perform as well or handle as nicely as the BMW. So I wanted to go back to a BMW, but most of their rear-wheel drive cars are horrendous in the snow. The all-wheel-drive X5 gave me both the handling and responsiveness of a BMW with the benefit of all-wheel-drive.

The styling of the vehicle is awesome, and it's loaded with features and fun to drive. What I don't like is that I don't get to drive it enough! It's my third BMW, and I've been thrilled with all three.

Make sure you thoroughly review all features and functions of the various models, and if you custom order, as I did, request a copy of the order confirmation from BMW. My dealer gave me a copy without asking, but there have been instances in which people's cars came in missing things they thought they had ordered.

I have only had the vehicle for about three months, and thus I have had no problems. I'd buy another in a heartbeat.

—Joe Kubikowski, East Fishkill, New York

Quad exhaust tips are a visible clue to V-8 power on the 2000 X5 4.4i. This particular X5 does not have a sunroof, which adds headroom for the front seat occupants.

S everal BMW models have been imported over the years, beginning in the early 1950s and extending all the way through the New Class sedans that preceded the 1600-2 and 2002s, which are the beginning point for cars covered in this buyer's guide. With the exception of the M1, these are cars that were imported and available for sale before and during the time that BMW was struggling to survive as a car manufacturer as well as to develop distribution channels in the United States.

Sales and support infrastructures had not fully evolved, and the cars had not yet developed the solid reputation they have now. As a result, not all of the mechanical repairs were done properly, and the cars often fell into disrepair. Sometimes the cars were left in the garage, and sometimes they were traded in for newer models. Cars that survive today are usually in the hands of enthusiasts and collectors who have lovingly restored the cars to their original condition. Occasionally one of these cars becomes available and changes hands, usually at a premium price that is out of the reach of many of us and often within the community of collectors who know the cars well and are in a position to acquire the car regardless of its cost.

Less often, a previously unrestored car is discovered. The condition of these cars ranges from a basket case needing extensive work to a nearly perfect original car that needs only minor repairs.

The late 1950s and early 1960s were dark days for BMW. The early sedans were expensive, and sales were few in number. Rumor has it that BMW was losing big money on each car. At the same time, BMW was developing the 503 coupes and the 505 sedans, neither of which proved beneficial to the bottom line.

BMW persisted in producing these large sedans, coupes, and roadsters in spite of the continuing damage to the company's financial picture. At the opposite end of the spectrum, BMW was building and selling the curious "bubble cars," the Isetta, and the 600 sedans. The prices were low and the volume of production high enough to provide cash flow for

developing the 700-Series cars that, in turn, ensured BMW was able to proceed with development of the 1500 "New Class" series sedans.

Included in this section is information on cars beginning with the 501 sedans of the early 1950s, continuing through the New Class sedans of the mid-1960s, and onto the M1, which was available in Europe only between 1978 and 1981.

501 Sedans 1952–1958

These roomy sedans had graceful and sweeping lines that gave them a definite modern look. The 501 sedans are large cars, based on a wheelbase of 111.6-inches and weighing more than 2,900 pounds. To put this in perspective, the E32 7-Series wheelbase is 111.5 inches, and the car weighs just under 3,900 pounds.

Powered by a 120-ci inline six-cylinder that developed only 65-brake horsepower, the 501 sedan was not a quick car, reaching 60 miles per hour in about 30 seconds and having a top speed of barely 85 miles per hour. More power was needed, and by 1954 detail improvements to the engine resulted in peak power output of 72 brake horsepower and 5 miles per hour more top speed.

It is difficult to say how many were imported to the United States, but safe to say that obtaining replacement parts for these cars would be quite difficult.

502 Sedans 1954–1961

The 502 sedans use essentially the same chassis and body structures as the 501. The primary and significant difference is the powerplant. An aluminum-alloy, 90-degree V-8 of 2.6-liters, BMW led the way in Europe with its first postwar V-8 engine and the world's first mass-production alloy V-8.

Available in both the 501 and 502 sedans, the 2.6-liter eight delivered the power needed to propel the big sedans to a top speed of slightly more than 100 miles per hour. Not content with just one engine version, a 3.2-liter version was available in both the 502 and the upscale 502 Super.

BMW also produced a 2600 sedan that was essentially

the 501 rebadged and with the 2.6-liter V-8. A 2600 Luxus, with slightly higher trim levels, was available at the same time.

BMW offered all of these model variations at the same time, which served to confuse the buying public. In spite of this confusion, sales continued to increase, but not in sufficient quantity to support new model development.

While the 502 was a good, solid-performing sedan, BMW was struggling to survive, and very few of these cars made it to the United States. Like the 501, spare parts are difficult to find, making restoring one of these cars a difficult and expensive proposition.

503 Coupes 1956–1959

With approximately 412 produced, the 503 coupe probably deserves higher regard than it has received. Introduced and sold alongside the legendary 507 roadsters, this graceful four-seat coupe has lived in the 507's shadow.

Powered by the same 3.2-liter aluminum-alloy V-8 as the roadster and employing many of the mechanical components of the "Baroque Angel" sedans that were still in production, the 503 coupe was, and still is, a fairly large car. The all-aluminum body was hand-built in Germany by Karosserieentwurf Graf Goertz. Unlike some of the later collaborations with the Italians, the quality of the workmanship is excellent and there is little chance of rust in the body.

A rare and expensive car in the late 1950s because of the low production numbers and the scarcity of spare parts, these coupes are expensive to restore and maintain.

505 Limousine 1956–1957

Designed by Michelotti, the 505 limousine was introduced during the same period as the 503 coupe and the 507 roadster. Only two of these are believed to have been produced, so the chance of seeing one for sale is highly unlikely.

Not much is known about these cars other than that they were built on a lengthened (to 119.5-inches) chassis and were equipped at a very high level. One of the two is reported to have been used by heads of state, and these days it is on display at the BMW museum.

507 Roadsters 1956–1959

With approximately 254 built, the 507 roadster is one of the most coveted and desirable BMWs ever available. Expensive when new—nearly $9,000—today these cars can fetch prices well into the six-figure range.

Designed by Count Albrecht Goertz and debuting at the 1955 Paris Auto Show, the 507 competed with cars from Ferrari and the legendary Mercedes Benz 300SL. Powered by the aluminum-alloy 3.2-liter V-8 from the sedans, the roadsters were capable of speeds in the range of 140 miles per hour.

The aluminum-alloy bodies were virtually hand built. Options included a handsome hardtop, Rudge knockoff wheels and, toward the end of production, disc brakes.

It is hard to say how many of these were imported to the United States, but your chance of seeing one on the street is pretty rare. Even today, a 507 is a beautiful car.

Isetta 250/300 and 600 1955–1962

On one hand, BMW was selling up-market luxury cars like the 503 and 507. On the other hand, it was also struggling to survive, losing money on each of these high-end cars that was built. BMW desperately needed a low-cost car that it could sell to the masses. Not having the resources to develop and build such a car on its own, BMW, along with several other manufacturers, entered into a licensing agreement with Italian appliance manufacturer Renzo Rivolta to produce the Isetta.

It is not the first time BMW has produced a car under license; the prewar BMW Dixi was similarly licensed from Austin. BMW was known for motorcycles, and the Isetta proved to be a willing recipient of a motorcycle engine. Initially powered by a 245-cc air-cooled twin, it was not long before a 300-cc engine was in the engine bay.

Economical to buy and run, the egg-shaped Isetta, with its single-door opening from the front, room for two, and Roundels aplenty, proved to be a good seller. It laid the groundwork for the 700 series cars that followed.

Cute, funny-looking, and novel, the Isetta evolved from its egg-shape into a larger, more proper-looking car—the 600 series—which spread the rear wheels farther apart, lengthened the wheelbase, and offered a side-access door for rear-seat passengers.

Not very many of these cars are left in running order, and there is something of a cult following for them among BMW aficionados. Rust takes its toll on the bodies and the mechanical parts are difficult to obtain, but the Isetta continues to be a collectible car, and prices for restored cars are climbing.

3200CS 1962–1965

Built on the V-8 sedan chassis, the distinctive coupe body was designed by Nuccio Bertone and built in Turin. The bare steel bodies were shipped to Munich, where they were assembled and trimmed out for sale.

A heavyweight at slightly more than 4,000 pounds, the 3200CS needed all the power the V-8 could generate to reach a top speed of 124 miles per hour.

A limited-production car, approximately 603 were built. There is one styling element of these grand tourers that has continued—the counterbend in the C-column that is still seen in BMWs to this day. Rust and excessive weight are challenges.

Engine components and mechanicals are shared with the "Baroque Angel" sedans; however, body panels are nearly nonexistent. As these coupes were basically hand built, no two are exactly the same, and cosmetic repairs are labor-intensive and expensive.

700-Series 1959–1965

Presented to the public at the Frankfurt International Auto Show in early 1959, the 700 series coupes were designed by Michelotti and powered by a 30-horsepower, 700-cc, horizontally opposed 2-cylinder engine. Significantly, the car bridged the gap between the bubble car Isetta and the New Class models in development.

Absent from these cars are the traditional BMW "kidney grills." Not absent is the sporting nature BMW is known for. The chassis was adapted from the 600 sedans, the front suspension was improved, and the rear suspension was a more modern semi-trailing arm design. Bigger brakes and rack-and-pinion steering contributed to the 700's sporty feel.

The horizontally opposed 2-cylinder engine, while based on the engine from the 600 sedans, had been worked over by engine developers led by Alex von Falkenhausen, a name that was to be instrumental in BMW powerplants for many years to come. It wasn't long before the engine received raised compression, improved camshafts, and dual carburetors, resulting in an additional 10-brake horsepower.

Sales of the 700s proved brisk, with just over 27,000 being produced between 1959 and 1965. In early 1964, production of the car at the BMW factory ceased; the production capacity was needed for the New Class cars. Between 1964 and September 1965, a longer wheelbase LS version, with a revised roofline and more luxurious interior appointments, was built in a cooperative effort between Baur and BMW.

Not many 700s have survived the years. Spare parts are difficult to find, with sheet metal being nonexistent. Perhaps more important in BMW history than it is given credit for, the 700 provided needed cash and production capacity while the New Class cars were developed and introduced.

1500–2000 Sedans 1962–1972

Struggling to keep the company alive financially and warding off buyouts by its competitors, BMW desperately needed a car that could be produced in volume and sold at a price that the burgeoning middle class in postwar Germany could afford.

The 700s came close, but BMW still needed to make something happen. They needed a car that embodied the things BMWs were known for: performance, handling, and that hard-to-define special "something."

It was fourth-and-goal, two-minute-drill time for the factory.

Generally acknowledged as the car that saved the company, the New Class sedan was introduced at the Frankfurt International Auto Show in 1961. Powered by a 1.5-liter 4-cylinder Single Overhead Cam (SOHC) engine, the boxy 4-door offered comfortable seating, plenty of luggage space, front disc brakes, and independent suspension with the now-famous rear semi-trailing arms.

A factory built hot rod, the 1965 BMW 1800Ti/Sa featured stellar performance for a family sedan.

As the license plate notes, this particular 1965 BMW 1800Ti/Sa is number 184 of approximately 200 produced.

Higher compression and side-draft Webers combined to produce 130 horsepower from 1.8-liters in the 1965 BMW 1800Ti/Sa.

Although it took nearly a year for the 1500 sedan to reach production, it did deliver. In 1963, the 1800, featuring a more powerful engine and a higher level of trim, hit the streets. Followed quickly by a twin-carburetor version, the 1800Ti, these cars were as quick selling as they were good performing. The 1500 was upgraded with a 1.6-liter engine and nicer trim and continued as the entry-level New Class sedan.

All the while, the 1800 sedans were receiving performance upgrades: dual carburetors, more aggressive camshafts and tuning resulted in the 1800TI. Even more was to come in the form of the 1800TI/SA. Featuring higher compression, sidedraft Webers, and a more sporting suspension, the TI/SA engine produced 130-brake horsepower and could propel the sedan to more than 120 miles per hour.

In 1969, the sedans received a cosmetic facelift and a 2.0-liter engine. The 2000, as it was known, was available in several versions—a single carburetor model producing 114-brake horsepower (with an automatic transmission available as an option), a dual-carburetor 135-brake horsepower version, the 2000TI, and the top-of-the-line TI Luxus, often referred to as the Tilux.

By the late 1960s, the New Class sedans were due for replacement. The 2500 and 2800 sedans offered more amenities, more power, and refinement. These larger and more powerful sedans owed their existence to the engineering, performance, and reputation the New Class sedans had established.

While you will occasionally find one of the New Class sedans for sale, rust and the lack of replacement sheet metal make restoring one of these sedans difficult and expensive. The engines and transmissions are shared with the 2002s; therefore, mechanical components are easier to find.

Glas BMWs 1967–1968

As sales increased, BMW put more distance between itself and the financial struggles that were part of postwar recovery and model confusion. Along with success came the need for more production capacity—and quicker than later—to support increasing sales volume. Hans Glas Gmbh in nearby Dingolfing, a small-volume producer of Sports GT cars, was in dire financial trouble, not unlike the situation BMW had been in a few years prior.

BMW made arrangements to acquire Glas, and for one model year manufactured two of the Glas models, the 1700GT fastback coupe that utilized the 1.6-liter 4-cylinder engine from the 1600-2, and the 3000GT, a V-8 powered coupe.

With about 1,259 of the smaller fastback coupes built during their one model year, finding one on the market would be unusual indeed. The 3000GT is even more rare, with about 390 of these being produced with BMW Roundels.

If you are a serious collector, do your homework ahead of time. Little is known about these cars. Replacement sheet metal and replacement parts are virtually nonexistent. The mechanicals of the 1600GT, while shared with the 1600-2, will be difficult to find. Replacement parts for the 3000GT cars will likely be more rare than the cars themselves.

M1 1978–1981

The M1 qualifies as a supercar right alongside the exotics of the 1980s. Commissioned by BMW's Motorsports division and designed by Ital design, Marchesi of Italy built the tubular steel chassis and the cars were supposed to be assembled by Lamborghini.

Financial difficulties and production delays resulted in BMW bringing the assembly process in-house. Over the years, BMW and Baur have cooperated on several models, and the M1 was one of them. Each M1 was assembled at the Baur works and shipped to BMW Motorsport in Munich for final quality checks.

The race-derived M88/3.5-liter DOHC inline six produced 277 brake horsepower, used chain-driven cams, and was placed vertically in the chassis, requiring the use of a dry-sump oiling system. The ZF 5-speed gearbox featured a dogleg first gear and is the same unit used in the Pantera.

Total production numbers vary, but most sources agree there were between 450 and 453 produced. Approximately 49 were built as race cars, and about 400 were built as street cars. Although not officially imported to the United States, several have been imported privately through the gray market. Parts will be difficult to obtain, and mechanical repairs will be expensive.

As exotic as the M1 is, it is a street car, complete with air conditioning and electric windows. Unlike some, this is a supercar that can be driven on a regular basis.

The Giugiaro-designed BMW M1, like this 1981 model, was introduced more than 20 years ago and still turns heads today. Approximately 453 rolled off the line, both production cars and race cars.

The side view of this 1981 BMW M1 reveals some of the body's sleek features.

A pair of beauties and two of Motorsports' products, the 1981 BMW M1 and 1988 M3 both offer distinctive styling and outstanding performance.

Appendix 1
Which BMW Do I Want?
Quick and Easy Model Characteristics

Model	Years Mfg'd	Body	A/T	Man	Cyl
Type 114					
1600-2	66-71	2dr	3sp	4sp	4
2002	68-76	2dr	3sp	4sp	4
2002tii	72-74	2dr	NA	4sp	4
E3 Sedans					
2500	69-71	4dr	3sp	4sp	6
2800	69-71	4dr	3sp	4sp	6
Bavaria	72-75	4dr	3sp	4sp	6
3.0S/Si	73-77	4dr	3sp	4sp	6
E9 Coupes					
2000C/CS	65-69	2dr	3sp	4sp	4
2800CS	69-72	2dr	3sp	4sp	6
3.0CS	73-75	2dr	3sp	4sp	6
3-Series					
E21					
320i	76-79	2dr	3sp	4sp	4
320i	80-83	2dr	3sp	5sp	4
E30					
318i	84-85	2/4dr	3sp	5sp	4
318i/is/iC	91-92	2/4/C	NA	5sp	4
325e/es	84-87	2/4dr	4sp	5sp	6
325i/is/iX	87-91	2/4dr	4sp	5sp	6
325iC	87-92	2dr	4sp	5sp	6
325iX	87-91	2/4dr	4sp	5sp	6
M3	87-91	2dr	NA	5sp	4
E36					
318i/is/iC	92-95	2/4/C	4sp	5sp	4
318ti	92-95	HB	4sp	5sp	4
318i/is/iC	96-99	2/4/C	4sp	5sp	4
318ti	96-99	HB	4sp	5sp	4
323i/is/iC	96-99	2/4/C	4sp	5sp	6
325i/is/iC	92-93	2/4/C	4sp	5sp	6
325i/is/iC	94-95	2/4/C	4sp	5sp	6
328i/is/iC	96-99	2/4/C	4sp	5sp	6
M3	1995	2dr	5sp	5sp	6
M3	96-99	2/4/C	5sp	5sp	6
E46					
323i/Ci	99-00	2/4dr	5sp	5sp	6
325i/Ci/Xi	2001-on	2/4/C/H	5sp	5sp	6
328i/Ci	99-00	2/4dr	5sp	5sp	6
330i/Ci/Xi	2001-on	2/4/C	5sp	5sp	6
M3	2001-on	2dr	6SMG	6sp	6
5-Series					
E12					
530i	75-78	4dr	3sp	4sp	6
528i	79-81	4dr	3sp	4&5sp	6
E28					
524td	84-86	4dr	4sp	5sp	6
528e	84-88	4dr	4sp	5sp	6
533i	83-85	4dr	4sp	5sp	6
535i/is	85-89	4dr	4sp	5sp	6
M5	87-88	4dr	NA	5sp	6
E34					
525i	89-90	4dr	4sp	5sp	6
525i	91-95	4/Wgn	4sp	5sp	6
530i	94-95	4/Wgn	4sp	5sp	8
535i	89-93	4dr	4sp	5sp	6
540i	1994	4/Wgn	5sp	NA	8
540i	95-96	4/Wgn	5sp	6sp	8
M5	91-93	4dr	NA	5sp	6
E39					
525i	2001-on	4/Wgn	5sp	5sp	6
528i	96-99	4/Wgn	4sp	5sp	6
528i	2000	4/Wgn	5sp	5sp	6
530i	2001-on		5sp	5sp	6
540i	1997-on	4/Wgn	5sp	6sp	8
M5	2000-on	4/Wgn	NA	6sp	8
6-Series					
E24					
630CSi	76-79	2dr	3sp	4sp	6
633CSi	80-84	2dr	3sp	5sp	6
635CSi/L6	85-89	2dr	4sp	5sp	6
M6	87-88	2dr	NA	5sp	6
7-Series					
E23 Sedans					
733i	78-81	4dr	3sp	4sp	6
733i	81-84	4dr	3sp	5sp	6
735i	84-87	4dr	4sp	5sp	6
L7	86-87	4dr	4sp	NA	6
E32 Sedans					
735i	88-92	4dr	4sp	5sp	6
735iL	88-92	4dr	4sp	5sp	6
740i	93-94	4dr	5sp	NA	8
740iL	93-94	4dr	5sp	NA	8
750iL	88-94	4dr	4sp	NA	12
E38 Sedans					
740i/iL	1995	4dr	5sp	NA	8
740i/iL	96-02	4dr	5sp	NA	8
750iL	95-02	4dr	5sp	NA	12
8-Series					
E31					
840Ci	94-95	2dr	5sp	NA	8
840Ci	96-97	2dr	5sp	NA	8
850i/Ci	91-94	2dr	4sp	6sp	12
850Ci	95-97	2dr	5sp	NA	12
850CSi	94-95	2dr	NA	6sp	12
Z3					
1.9 Rdstr	96-98	2dr	4sp	5sp	4
2.3 Rdstr	99-00	2dr	4sp	5sp	6
2.5i Rdstr	2001-on	2dr	5sp	5sp	6
2.8 Rdstr	97-00	2dr	4sp	5sp	6
2.8 Coupe	99-00	2dr	4sp	5sp	6
3.0i Rdstr	2001-on	2dr	5sp	5sp	6
3.0i Coupe	2001-on	2dr	5sp	5sp	6
M-Roadster	99-00	2dr	NA	5sp	6
M-Roadster	2001-on	2dr	NA	5sp	6
M-Coupe	99-00	2dr	NA	5sp	6
M-Coupe	2001-on	2dr	NA	5sp	6
Z8					
	2000-on	2dr	NA	6sp	8
X5					
3.0i	2001-on	4dr	5sp	5sp	6
4.0i	2000-on	4dr	5sp	NA	8

Legend
2dr = 2 door
4dr = 4dr sedan

Appendix 2
BMW Performance at a Glance

Model	Years	WB	HP/RPM	Torque/RPM	Est 0-60	Est MPG
Type 114						
1600-2	67-71	98.4	96/5800	105.6/3000	11.4	22/28
2002	68-71	98.4	113/5800	116/3000	11.3	22/27
2002	72-73	98.4	113/5800	116/3000	10.3	24.5
2002	74-76	98.4	98/5800	106/3500	10.3	24.5
2002tii	72-73	98.4	140/5800	145/4500	9.8	22.7
2002tii	1974	98.4	125/5500	127/4000	9.5	23.5
E3 Sedans						
2500	69-71	106.0	170/6000	176/3700	10.0	20.9
2800	69-71	106.0	192/6000	174/3700	10.0	18.0
Bavaria	1972	106.0	192/6000	174/3700	9.3	18.0
Bavaria	73-75	106.0	190/5800	213/3500	10.7	17.0
3.0S/Si	73-77	106.0	176/5500	185/4500	11.4	17.2
E9 Coupes						
2000C/CS	65-69	100.4	135/5800	123/3600	11.3	18.7
2800CS	69-72	103.3	192/6000	174/3700	9.3	19.0
3.0CS	73-75	103.3	170/5800	185/3500	10.0	17.0
3-Series						
E21						
320i	76-79	100.9	110/5800	112/3750	12.0	21.5
320i	80-83	100.9	101/5800	100/4500	11.1	25.0
E30						
318i M	84-85	101.2	101/5800	103/4500	11.4	27/38
318i A	84-85	101.2	101/5800	103/4500	N/A	27/34
318i/is/iC	91-92	101.2	134/6000	127/4600	10.0	27/38
325e/es M	84-87	101.2	134/6000	127/4600	11.4	27/38
325e/es A	84-87	101.2	121/4250	170/3250	N/A	27/34
325i/is M	87-91	101.2	168/5800	164/4300	8.5	18/23
325i/is A	87-91	101.2	168/5800	164/4300	10.3	18/23
325iC M	87-92	101.2	168/5800	164/4300	8.6	18/23
325iC A	87-92	101.2	168/5800	164/4300	10.5	18/23
325iX	87-91	101.2	168/5800	164/4300	8.5	18/23
M3	87-91	101.2	192/6750	170/4750	7.6	17/29
E36						
318i/is/iC M	92-94	106.3	138/6000	129/4500	9.9	22/30
318i/is/iC A	92-94	106.3	138/6000	129/4500	11.4	22/30
318i/iC M	1995	106.3	138/6000	129/4500	10.6	22/32
318i/iC A	1995	106.3	138/6000	129/4500	10.8	21/29
318ti M	92-95	106.3	138/6000	129/4500	9.3	22/32
318ti A	92-95	106.3	138/6000	129/4500	10.3	21/29
318i/iC M	96-98	106.3	138/6000	133/4300	9.9/10.6	23/32
318i/iC A	96-98	106.3	138/6000	133/4300	10.8/11.6	22/31
318ti M	96-99	106.3	138/6000	133/4300	9.3	23/32
318ti A	96-99	106.3	138/6000	133/4300	10.3	22/31
323i/is/iC M	96-99	106.3	168/5500	181/3950	7.7	20/30
323i/is/iC A	96-99	106.3	168/5500	181/3950	8.8	19/27
325i/is/iC A	92-93	106.3	189/5900	181/4200	7.8	19/28
325i/is/iC M	94-95	106.3	189/5900	181/4200	8.8	20/28
328i/is M	1996	106.3	190/5300	206/3950	7.0	20/29
328i/is A	1996	106.3	190/5300	206/3950	7.7	20/27
328iC M	96-97	106.3	190/5300	206/3950	7.3	20/29
328iC A	96-97	106.3	190/5300	206/3950	8.2	19/27
328i/is M	97-99	106.3	190/5300	206/3950	6.6	20/29
328i/is A	96-99	106.3	190/5300	206/3950	7.2	18/26
328iC M	98-99	106.3	190/5300	206/3950	6.9	20/29
328iC A	98-99	106.3	190/5300	206/3950	7.5	20/27
M3 M	1995	106.3	240/6000	225/4250	6.1	19/27
M3 A	1995	106.3	240/6000	225/4250	6.9	19/28
M3 M	1996	106.3	240/6000	240/4000	5.9	19/27
M3 M	97-99	106.3	240/6000	236/3800	5.7	20/28
M3 A	97-99	106.3	240/6000	225/3800	6.4	19/28
M3 Conv M	1999	106.3	240/6000	236/3800	5.8	19/26
M3 Conv A	1999	106.3	240/6000	236/3800	6.6	17/25
E46						
323i M	99-00	107.3	170/5500	181/3500	7.1	20/29
323i A	99-00	107.3	170/5500	181/3500	8.2	19/27
323Ci M	99-00	107.3	170/5500	181/3500	7.1	20/29
323Ci A	99-00	107.3	170/5500	181/3500	8.2	19/27
325i Sedan M	01-on	107.3	184/6000	175/3500	7.1	20/29
325i Sedan A	01-on	107.3	184/6000	175/3500	8.1	19/27
325Xi Sedan M	01-on	107.3	184/6000	175/3500	7.6	19/27
325Xi Sedan A	01-on	107.3	184/6000	175/3500	8.8	19/26
325i SptWgn M	01-on	107.3	184/6000	175/3500	7.4	20/29
325i SptWgn A	01-on	107.3	184/6000	175/3500	8.5	19/27
325XiSptWgn M	01-on	107.3	184/6000	175/3500	7.8	19/26
325XiSptWgn A	01-on	107.3	184/6000	175/3500	9.0	19/26
325Ci Cpe M	01-on	107.3	184/6000	175/3500	7.1	20/29
325Ci Cpe A	01-on	107.3	184/6000	175/3500	8.1	19/27
325Ci Conv M	01-on	107.3	184/6000	175/3500	7.7	19/27
325Ci Conv A	01-on	107.3	184/6000	175/3500	8.9	29/26
328i M	99-00	107.3	193/5500	206/3500	6.6	21/29
328i A	99-00	107.3	193/5500	206/3500	7.2	18/27
328Ci M	99-00	107.3	193/5500	206/3500	6.6	21/29
328Ci A	99-00	107.3	193/5500	206/3500	7.2	18/27
330i Sedan M	01-on	107.3	225/5900	214/3500	6.4	21/30
330i Sedan A	01-on	107.3	225/5900	214/3500	7.0	19/27
330Ci Cpe M	01-on	107.3	225/5900	214/3500	6.4	21/30
330Ci Cpe A	01-on	107.3	225/5900	214/3500	7.0	19/27
330Ci Conv M	01-on	107.3	225/5900	214/3500	6.9	20/28
330Ci Conv A	01-on	107.3	225/5900	214/3500	7.5	18/26
330Xi M	01-on	107.3	225/5900	214/3500	6.9	20/27
330Xi A	01-on	107.3	225/5900	214/3500	7.5	17/25
M3 Coupe	01-on	107.5	333/7900	262/4900	4.5	16/24
M3 Conv	01-on	107.5	333/7900	262/4900	5.4	16/23
5-Series						
E12						
530i	75-78	103.8	176/5500	185/4500	9.0	19.0
528i	79-81	103.8	169/5500	170/4500	8.2	22.0
E28						
524td	84-86	103.3	115/4800	155/2400	11.7	24/30
528e M	84-88	103.3	121/4250	170/3250	10.3	22/32
528e A	84-88	103.3	121/4250	170/3250		
533i M	83-85	103.3	181/6000	195/4000	7.7	19/29
533i A	83-85	103.3	181/6000	195/4000	9.4	
535i/is M	85-89	103.3	182/5400	214/4000	7.7	17/28
535i/is A	85-89	103.3	182/5400	214/4000	9.4	
M5	87-88	103.3	256/6500	243/4500	6.7	10/19
E34						
525i M	89-95	108.7	189/5900	184/4200	8.6	19/28
525i A	89-95	108.7	189/5900	184/4200	9.1	18/25
525iT M	93-95	108.7	189/5900	184/4200	9.7	18/25
530i M	94-95	108.7	215/5800	214/4500	7.5	16/23
530i A	94-95	108.7	215/5800	214/4500	8.8	16/25
530iT A	94-95	108.7	215/5800	214/4500	9.1	16/25
535i M	89-93	108.7	208/5700	225/4000	7.6	15/23
535i A	89-93	108.7	208/5700	225/4000	8.7	16/22
540i M	1996	108.7	282/5800	295/4500	6.2	14/23
540i A	94-96	108.7	282/5800	295/4500	6.7	16/23
M5	91-93	108.7	310/6900	266/4750	6.1	12/23
E39						
525i M	01-on	111.4	184/6000	175/3500	7.3	20/29
525i A	01-on	111.4	184/6000	175/3500	8.0	19/27
525i SptWgn M	01-on	111.4	184/6000	175/3500	8.2	19/27
525i SptWgn A	01-on	111.4	184/6000	175/3500	9.2	19/26
528i M	1996	111.4	193/5500	206/3500	7.4	19/28
528i M	97-98	111.4	193/5500	206/3500	7.7	19/28
528i M	99-00	111.4	193/5500	206/3500	7.0	20/29
528i SptWgn M	99-00	111.4	193/5500	206/3500	7.9	18/26
528i A	96-98	111.4	193/5500	206/3500	8.6	18/26
528i A	99-00	111.4	193/5500	206/3500	7.7	18/26
528i SptWgn A	99-00	111.4	193/5500	206/3500	8.9	18/26
530i M	01-on	111.4	225/5900	214/3500	6.7	21/30
530i A	01-on	111.4	225/5900	214/3500	7.5	18/26
540i M	1997	111.4	282/5700	310/3900	6.1	15/24
540i M	1998	111.4	282/5700	310/3900	5.8	15/24
540i M	99-on	111.4	282/5700	324/3600	5.8	15/24
540i A	1997	111.4	282/5700	310/3900	6.6	18/24
540i A	1998	111.4	282/5700	310/3900	6.6	18/24
540i A	99-on	111.4	282/5400	324/3600	6.2	18/24
540i SptWgn A	99-on	111.4	282/5400	324/3600	6.3	15/21
M5	2000	111.4	400/6600	369/3800	4.8	13/21
M5	01-on	111.4	394/6600	368/3900	4.8	13/21
6-Series						
E24						
630CSi M	76-79	103.4	175/5500	185/4500	9.0	15/21
630CSi A	76-79	103.4	175/5500	185/4500		
633CSi M	80-84	103.4	169/5500	170/4500	8.2	19/23
633CSi A	80-84	103.4	169/5500	170/4500		
635CSi M	85-89	103.4	185/5400	214/4000	8.2	19/23
635CSi A	85-89	103.4	185/5400	214/4000		
L6	1987	103.4	185/5400	214/4000		
M6	87-88	103.4	256/6500	243/4500	6.8	12/20

266

Model	Years	WB	HP/RPM	Torque/RPM	Est 0-60	Est MPG
7-Series						
E23 Sedans						
733i	78-81	110.0	177/5500	196/4000	8.6	15/22
735i	84-87	110.0	182/5400	214/4000	9.1	17.0
L7	86-87	110.0	182/5400	214/4000	9.1	17.0
E32 Sedans						
735i	88-92	111.5	208/5700	225/4000	9.3	18.0
735iL	88-92	116.0	208/5700	225/4000	9.3	18.0
740i	93-94	111.5	282/5800	295/4500	7.1	16/23
740iL	93-94	116.0	282/5800	295/4500	7.1	16/22
750iL	88-94	116.0	296/5200	332/4100	7.1	12/18
E38 Sedans						
740i	1995	115.4	282/5800	295/4500	7.0	16/24
740iL	1995	120.9	282/5800	295/4500	7.2	16/24
740i	96-98	115.4	282/5700	310/3900	7.0	17/24
740i	99-01	115.4	282/5700	310/3900	6.9	17/24
740iL	96-98	120.9	282/5700	310/3900	7.2	17/23
740iL	99-01	120.9	282/5700	310/3900	6.9	17/23
750iL	95-96	120.9	322/5000	361/3900	6.4	15/20
750iL	97-98	120.9	322/5000	361/3900	6.7	15/20
750iL	99-01	120.9	326/5000	361/3900	6.6	13/20
8-Series						
E31						
840Ci	94-95	105.7	282/5800	295/4500	7.1	16/24
840Ci	96-97	105.7	282/5700	310/3900	7.1	15/20
850i/Ci M	91-94	105.7	296/5200	332/4100	6.1	12/21
850i/Ci A	91-94	105.7	296/5200	332/4100	6.9	12/21
850Ci	95-97	105.7	322/5000	361/3900	6.1	12/21
850CSi	94-95	105.7	372/5300	402/4000	5.7	12/21
Z3						
1.9 M	1996	96.3	138/6000	133/4300	9.1	23/31
1.9 A	1996	96.3	138/6000	133/4300	9.7	22/31
1.9 M	1997	96.3	138/6000	133/4300	8.2	23/31
1.9 A	1997	96.3	138/6000	133/4300	9.4	22/31
1.9 M	1998	96.3	138/6000	133/4300	8.2	23/32
1.9 A	1998	96.3	138/6000	133/4300	9.4	22/31
2.3 M	99-00	96.3	170/5500	181/3500	6.8	20/27
2.3 A	99-00	96.3	170/5500	181/3500	7.5	19/26
2.5 Rdstr M	01-on	96.3	184/6000	175/3500	7.1	20/27
2.5 Rdstr A	01-on	96.3	184/6000	175/3500	7.2	19/26
2.8 Rdstr M	97-98	96.3	189/5300	203/3950	6.3	19/27
2.8 Rdstr A	97-98	96.3	189/5300	203/3950	6.7	18/24
2.8 Rdstr M	99-00	96.3	193/5500	206/3500	6.3	19/26
2.8 Rdstr A	99-00	96.3	193/5500	206/3500	6.7	19/26
2.8 Cpe M	99-00	96.3	193/5500	206/3500	6.2	19/26
2.8 Cpe A	99-00	96.3	193/5500	206/3500	6.6	19/26
3.0 Rdstr M	01-on	96.6	225/5900	214/3500	5.9	21/28
3.0 Rdstr A	01-on	96.3	225/5900	214/3500	6.0	19/25
3.0 Cpe M	01-on	96.3	225/5900	214/3500	5.9	21/28
3.0 Cpe A	01-on	96.3	225/5900	214/3500	6.0	19/27
M-Roadster	99-00	96.8	240/6000	236/3800	5.2	19/26
M-Roadster	01-on	96.8	315/7400	251/4900	5.1	19/26
M-Coupe	99-00	96.8	240/6000	236/3800	5.1	19/26
M-Coupe	01-on	96.8	315/7400	251/4900	5.1	19/26
Z8	00-on	98.6	394/6600	368/3800	5.0	13/21
X5						
3.0i M	01-on	111.0	225/5900	214/3500	8.1	15/20
3.0i A	01-on	111.0	225/5900	214/3500	8.6	15/20
4.4i	00-on	111.0	282/5400	324/3600	6.7	13/17
4.4i SprtPkg	00-on	110.0	282/5400	324/3600	6.7	13/17

Legend

1. An "A" or "M" following model designation indicates "Automatic" or "Manual" transmission performance figures.
2. "Est MPG" is presented as city/highway mpg. These are estimates and actual mileage averages may vary.

Appendix 3
BMW Resources

There are countless resources available to research any BMW that you may be interested in purchasing or simply learning more about. Listed here are some of the ones I most frequently use in my search for additional knowledge about BMWs.

Autobytel.com
www.autobytel.com

Bimmers.Com
www.bimmers.com

BMW Automobile Club of America
www.bmwacaportland.com

BMW-Related Message Boards
www.roadfly.org/bmw
www.bimmer.org

BMW of North America, LLC
1-800-334-4BMW
www.bmwusa.com

BMW Car Club of America
(864) 250-0022
www.bmwcca.org

Carfax Inc.
www.carfax.com

Consumer Reports
www.consumerreports.org

Edmunds
www.edmunds.com

Kelly Blue Book
www.kbb.com

Koala Motorsports
www.koalamotorsport.com

Appendix 4
BMW Engine Designations

Similar to the E-number chassis designations, BMW also assigned designations to their engines. Throughout this buyer's guide are references to various engines, usually by their capacity—both in cc's or liters—and also by the M engine family designation. If you hang around with BMW enthusiasts long enough, you will hear them refer to the engine type as well as the chassis type.

The following table is a list of the engines by their M and S designation and a brief description of the various engines.

Engine Family	Description
M10	SOHC inline 4-cylinder, chain-driven camshaft, 1.8- and 2.0-liter commonly found in the 1600-2/2002/320i and 1984–1985 318i.
M20	SOHC inline 6-cylinder, timing belt, 2.0-, 2.3-, 2.5- or 2.7-liter as found in the 325e/325i/325is and 528e.
M21	SOHC inline 6-cylinder diesel, timing belt. As used in the 524td.
M30	SOHC inline 6-cylinder, chain-driven camshaft. The "big six" as found in the CS coupes, 5-Series, 6-Series and 7-Series.
M42	DOHC inline 4-cylinder, 1.8-liter.
M44	DOHC inline 4-cylinder, 1.9-liter.
M50	DOHC inline 6-cylinder, 2.0-, 2.3-, or 2.5-liter.
M50TU	DOHC inline 6-cylinder, VANOS, 2.0-, 2.3-, or 2.5-liter.
M52	DOHC inline 6-cylinder, VANOS, 2.0-, 2.3-, 2.5-, 2.8-liter.
M52TU	DOHC inline 6-cylinder, dual VANOS, 2.5- and 3.0-liter
M54	DOHC inline 6-cylinder, dual VANOS, 2.5- and 3.0-liter as used in the 325/330 and 525/530.
M60	V-8, 3.0- or 4.0-liter as used in the 530i, 540i, 740i, and 840Ci.
M62	V-8, 3.5- or 4.4-liter as used in the 540i, 740i, and 840Ci.
M70	V-12, 5.0-liter as used in the 750iL and 850i/Ci
M73	V-12, 5.4-liter as used in the 750iL and 850Ci
M88/3	DOHC inline 6-cylinder, 3.5-liter as used in the M5 and M6.
S14	DOHC inline 4-cylinder 2.3-liter as used in the E30 M3.
S38	DOHC inline 6-cylinder, 3.6- and 3.8-liters, Used in the E34 M5.
S50	DOHC inline 6-cylinder, VANOS, 3.0-liter as used in the E36 M3s.
S50US	DOHC inline 6-cylinder, VANOS, 3.0-liter used in the E36 M3's.
S52	DOHC inline 6-cylinder, 3.2-liter, dual VANOS, multiple throttles. Used in E36 M3s.
S52US	DOHC inline 6-cylinder, 3.2-liter, dual VANOS. Used in E36 M3s, Z3 M-Roadster and M-Coupe.
S62	DOHC, V-8, quad VANOS, 5.0-liter used in M5s.
S70	V-12, 5.6-liter as used in the 850CSi.

VANOS (VAriable NOckenwellen Steuerung) is variable camshaft control that allows the valve timing to be varied, enhancing low-to-medium speed torque, emissions control, and (depending on model) fuel economy. BMW uses three types of VANOS systems:
- Single VANOS, two-stage–Operates on the intake camshaft only and provides two stages of valve timing.
- Single VANOS, steplessly variable–Used most commonly on the V-8 engines and also operates only on the intake camshaft. Varies the intake/valve timing between two settings based on operating conditions.
- Double VANOS, steplessly variable–Operates on both intake and exhaust camshafts based on engine operating conditions.

M and S alpha designations are what BMW identifies their engines with. M signifies a standard engine and S signifies a Motorsport-developed engine.
- A good example of this is the M62/S62 engine. The M62 is the standard production engine as used in the 540, 740, and 840 models. The S62 is the Motorsports-modified engine used in the M5 and Z8 models.

Appendix 5
BMW Chassis E Designations

Starting with the 1968 BMW 2500 sedans, BMW began using internal E designations to number their chassis designs. BMW also used a Type designation for the 1600-2/2002s and the Nu Klasse sedans.

The E (for engineering) designation is something that you will see used throughout this book. Chapters are broken down by New Class or E designations and include the models that fall under that designation. A further designation is the generation. For example, over its lifespan the 3-Series has gone through four chassis designations, or generations. In 1992 both the 3-Series' second and third generations were produced—the second-generation E30 325iC was being sold alongside the third-generation E36 325 sedans and the development of the E36 3-Series convertibles was completed.

The following reference table identifies the Type or E designation, the model BMW, and the years each particular car was generally available in the United States. Absent from this list are those models that were not officially imported to the United States.

Designation	Model	Years
Type 114	1600-2/2002	1967-1976
Type 118	1500/1600/1800	1962-1970
Type 121	2000/2000ti/2000 Tilux	1966-1970
E3	2500/2800/Bavaria/3.0S/3.0Si	1968-1977
E9	2000C/2800CS/2800CA/2800CS/3.0CS	1968-1974
E12	530i/528i	1975-1981
E21	320i/320is	1976-1983
E23	733i/735i/L7	1978-1987
E24	630CSi/633CSi/635CSi/L6/M6	1977-1989
E28	524td/528e/533i/535i/535is/M5	1982-1988
E30	318i/318is/325e/325i/325is/325iC/325iX, M3	1984-1992
E31	840Ci, 850i/Ci/CSi	1991-1997
E32	735i/iL, 740i/iL, 750iL	1988-1994
E34	525i/530i/535i/540i/M5	1989-1995
E36	318i/318is/318iC/318ti/325i/325is/325iC/ 328i/328is/328iC/323i/323is/323iC/M3/Z3	1992-1999
E38	740i/740iL/750iL	1995-2001
E39	525i/528i/530i/540i/M5	1996-2001
E46	323i/323Ci/325i/325Ci/325Xi 328i/328Ci/330i/Ci/Xi/M3	1999-2001
E52	Z8	2000-2001
E53	X5/3.0i/4.4i/4.6i	1999-2001

Acknowledgments

Thanks to James McDowell, Larry Koch, Rob Mitchell, Thomas Salkowsky of BMW NA; Charles Berthon, Rudy Chavez, Ron Haskill, Ted Kennedy, Andrew McIntyre, Long Beach BMW, Long Beach, California; Kevin Hite of Crevier BMW, Santa Ana, California; Rug Cunningham, Glenn Guriell of Cunningham BMW, El Cajon, California; Michael Chandler of Shelly BMW, Buena Park, California; Wynne Smith, Executive Director, BMW Car Club of America, National Office; BMW Car Club of America, Los Angeles Chapter.

Additional thanks to the independent repair shops and owners who took the time from their busy days to answer my questions and incessant requests for "just one more" piece of information: Nelson Jones of 2002ad, Sun Valley, California; Brett Anderson of Koala Motorsports; Vera and George Kratochwill of Bimmers Clinic, Reseda, California; John Norris of GT International, West Los Angeles, California; Jim Sanders of Anaheim Hills Car Care, Anaheim Hills, California; Richard Michelangelo of Michelangelo Motorwerkes, Lake Forrest, California; Jim, Spence, and Stan Stansfield of Mesa Performance, Costa Mesa, California; Chris Welch and Mickey Miller of Bullet Performance, Costa Mesa, California; B.T. Fields of B.T. Fields BMW, Signal Hill, California; and Don Fields, New Jersey.

Thanks, as well, to those individuals who graciously gave their time, their energy, archival information, and friendship: George Aguilar, Leif Anderberg, David Boen, Jo Carle, Paul DaCruz, Stephen Donnell, Eddy Funahashi, William Gau, Gordon Haines, Jay Jones, Carl McGinn, Amanda McLaren, Gordon Medencia, Mike Miller, Fillipo Morelli, Polly and Sam Nakawatase, Art Simonds, Dan Tackett, Tom Van Gunten.

To the following BMW owners who offered their cars and their time enthusiastically for use in this book, I thank you, too: Lori and Robbie Adelson, Craig Alviso, Michael Badger, Trish and Mark Bailey, Joyce Barrone, Morgan Bateman, Ed Becker, Lois and John Bergen, Sandra Bergen, Kitty, Nina and Peter Birk, Shelia and Henry Botkin, Jerry Boydston, Juan Bruce, Hope Burns, Steven Castle, Dan Covill, Lisa and Alan Clark, Gina and Rug Cunningham, Matthew Daub, Pat and Clint DeWitt, Alex and Kristin Domingo, Crystal and Marc Edwards, Jennifer Faneuff, Brian T. Fields, Jeff Fleischer, Stacey and Brian Foster, Steve and Corinne Gellman, Linda and Louis Goldsman, Ray Grunch, Rani and Randy Guitar, Gene Halloran, Michele and Michael Harley, James Heise, Brad Herrin, James Hineline, Brandon Ho, Paul Jackson, Donna Jimenez, Greg Johnson, Andrew Kahn, Leigh and Thomas Kelley, Darren Keene, Josey and Frank Kunowski, Bob Lacy, Dot and Bob Lanham, Ken Lewellyn, Lynette and Roeland Meyer, Ann and David Maier, Randy Luenebrink, Warren McElroy, Robyn and Blaine McNutt, Julie and Malcom Morgan, David Outwater, Patricia and Rex Parker, Frank Parth and Joy Gumz, Mark Pyeatte, Eric Quon, Dave Regis, Mark Reid, Lisa Scalia and Gerry O'Connor, Johnnalyn and Arnold Serrano, Bert Smith, Nurten and Phil Street, Gustave Stroes, Jim Stansfield, Handini and Darmo Tandjung, Bridgette and Hani Thomas, Eric Townsend, Jim Tulk, Mehrdad Vahid, Randy Walters, Gail Wisner and Dale Schaub, Lori Woodell, Lisa and Shannon Yauchzee, Richard Yeh, Andre Yurovsky.

Special thanks to my editors, Chad Caruthers and Darwin Holmstrom.

Thanks to my mentor, Randy Leffingwell, for your help with the "Buying a Used BMW" section and a special thank you for making time in your overwhelming schedule to coach and encourage me throughout this project. Your words of wisdom continue to guide me.

One final thanks to my wife, Pamela Welty, for your understanding, patience, and assistance throughout this project.

Index

Corvette Buyer's Guide
ISBN 0-7603-1009-2

Porsche 911 Buyer's Guide
ISBN 0-7603-0947-7

Original BMW M-Series
ISBN 0-7603-0898-5

BMW Cars
ISBN 0-7603-0921-3

BMW Motorcycles
ISBN 0-7603-1098-X

How to Draw Cars Like a Pro
ISBN 0-7603-0010-0

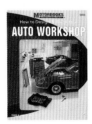

**How to Design and Build Your
Auto Workshop**
ISBN 0-7603-0553-6

BMW
ISBN 1-8612-6250-7

**Cannonball Run:
The Great American Outlaw
Road Race**
ISBN 0-7603-1090-4